"Michele Wucker provides an updated assessment of the challenges that confront society, that need to be addressed, yet we ignore. Public officials would serve us well by getting busy addressing the Gray Rhinos that are out there, rather than waiting for the next predictable surprise."

—Max Bazerman,
Straus Professor Harvard Business School,
Co-Director of Center for Public Leadership,
and author of *The Power of Noticing*

"As Michele Wucker warns us: It's not if; it's when. This is a book for our time, when we face multiple, evident existential threats. . . . This book reminds us that denial will not save us, and provides strategies for navigating a way forward to survival by ferreting out the opportunities born of crisis."

—Mira Kamdar, author of *Planet India*

"In a lucid and accessible style, Michele Wucker forces us to see the knowns we have been treating as unknowns, and teaches us to see opportunities in crisis. This book is a useful primer for rethinking how we manage everything from our personal life to the global economy."

—Parag Khanna,
author of *Connectography* and
How to Run the World

"*The Gray Rhino* offers strategies for dealing with the biggest and most dangerous weak spot for organizations, companies, and nations: the willful failure of business and policy leaders to perceive warning signals. . . . This important, insightful, and original book will be a must-read for global decision makers and thought leaders."

—William Saito,
CEO of Intecur and author of *The Team*

Also by Michele Wucker

Why the Cocks Fight:
Dominicans, Haitians, and the Struggle for Hispaniola

Lockout:
Why America Keeps Getting Immigration Wrong
When Our Prosperity Depends on Getting It Right

THE
GRAY
RHINO

HOW TO RECOGNIZE
AND ACT ON THE OBVIOUS
DANGERS WE IGNORE

MICHELE
WUCKER

St. Martin's Press ☵ New York

www.stmartins.com

Design by Meryl Sussman Levavi

The Library of Congress Cataloging-in-Publication Data is available upon request.

ISBN 978-1-250-05382-4 (hardcover)
ISBN 978-1-250-11560-7 (international edition)
ISBN 978-1-4668-8700-8 (e-book)

Our books may be purchased in bulk for promotional, educational, or business use. Please contact your local bookseller or the Macmillan Corporate and Premium Sales Department at 1-800-221-7945, extension 5442, or by e-mail at MacmillanSpecialMarkets@macmillan .com.

First Edition: April 2016

10 9 8 7 6 5 4 3 2 1

CONTENTS

PREFACE

Visiting Buenos Aires in March 2001, it was hard not to see the approaching economic catastrophe.

"Closed" signs hung on many shop doors; taxi drivers carried on and on about the dire straits of the country in terms that were dramatic, even allowing for the Argentine penchant for embellishment; the cover of the leading newsmagazine featured a picture of the controversial finance minister wearing a Hannibal Lecter mask, referencing the horror movie *The Silence of the Lambs*, and the question "Did he have to cannibalize the country to save it?"

I had just come from the annual meeting of the Inter-American Development Bank in neighboring Chile, where bankers, ministers, and journalists furrowed their brows over Argentina's financial problems, the Chileans no doubt feeling somewhat smug given their long-standing national rivalry with Argentina.

If you'd seen the numbers—foreign debt rising, dollars leaving the country, reserves plummeting, expensive restructurings that padded bankers' pockets but didn't do much to help Argentina dig out of its hole—you had to know that there was no way Argentina could keep up. With its peso pegged to the dollar, it couldn't easily devalue the currency to jump-start the economy. Investors were selling Argentine bonds en masse; prices had fallen to what in retrospect was a still generous eighty cents on the dollar. But you didn't have to see the numbers to come to this conclusion.

As a financial journalist specializing in Latin America, a few weeks later I wrote about a proposal, floated by a group of respected academics and Wall Streeters, for Argentina and its creditors to reduce its debt by 30 percent in order to avoid a bigger, chaotic "haircut" later. After I published the article, several Wall Street bankers called me to say that this was what needed to happen, but they couldn't say so in public or they'd be fired. Even though traders spoke about Argentina's pending default as a matter of "when" rather than "if," no bank dared tell its shareholders that it would be the first to voluntarily part with a single penny of what it was owed. Nine months later, the worst came true. Argentina's currency collapsed, and the banks that didn't want to give up 30 percent ended up losing roughly 70 percent of their money.

Fast-forward a decade to Greece. Like Argentina, Greece was trying to paper over its debt problem with a series of bailouts that only postponed the day of reckoning. Other European economies, though not so bad off as Greece, were struggling as well. In spring 2011, I published a paper for the New America Foundation arguing that Greece needed to learn from Argentina's failure to recognize and respond to a highly probable financial catastrophe by restructuring its debt sooner—before it was too late.

The reaction to the Greek problem was very different from the reaction to what happened in 2001: this time investors spoke openly, in public, about what needed to happen in Greece—that is, what Argentina should have done in 2001. It came down to the wire, but early in 2012 Greece's government and its private-sector creditors came to an agreement that kept the country from defaulting on its private debt and bringing Europe and the global economy down with it. The country's government creditors were a different story, which would bring Greece and all of Europe to a new crisis in 2015.

In 2011, the organizers of the Global HR Forum, a Korean organization focused on human-resources challenges, asked me to attend their November conference in Seoul and speak about whether the world faced a new economic crisis. Well, I told them, we hadn't yet climbed out of the one we were in. We were still dealing with the same mess we'd been in for the past few years. It wasn't just Greece; huge fiscal and trade imbalances in other countries across Europe also threatened to pull the euro apart and drag the global economy along with it. To American eyes, European leaders seemed to be doing no more than muddling through the crisis. They were not making the politically difficult choices that could get them out of trouble. So I spoke about the choices between kicking the can down the road and making tough decisions on some of the biggest issues facing the global economy: growth and austerity, short and long term, fiscal and monetary policy, consumption and investment, cheap labor and human capital, producing goods or knowledge.

When the Greek private-sector deal came through a few months later, the contrast between the story lines of Argentina and Greece got me wondering: What made the difference? How were Greece and its private-sector creditors able to make the proverbial "stitch in time" that prevented a catastrophe for its own economy and threatened to bring down the rest of Europe with it? Those are the questions that planted the seed for writing *The Gray Rhino*. They also would come into play again for Greece, because, despite the breathing room the country won when it cut a deal with banks and hedge funds, it still owed a lot more to the International Monetary Fund and the European Union. These "official" creditors, funded by national governments, ultimately depended on taxpayers—particularly German ones—who balked at doing what the private creditors had done.

Since the release of Nassim Nicholas Taleb's *The Black Swan: The Impact of the Highly Improbable* and its extraordinary timing just ahead of the 2008 financial crisis, many people in financial markets and policy circles have obsessed over Black Swan or Fat Tail crises—that is, events that individually may be highly improbable but which as a group occur far more often than most people realize. Yet those analysts and planners didn't have a similar way to focus their energies on things that were dangerous, obvious, and highly probable. To me, it seemed that behind many Black Swans was a converging set of highly *likely* crises.

As I began to look for examples of Gray Rhinos, it became clear that so many of the big crises of the past had started as highly obvious but ignored threats, and that the biggest challenges today are also obvious but ignored. I began seeing evidence everywhere of clear dangers that were recognized but weren't being addressed, from climate change and financial crisis at the global-policy level to disruptive technologies that reshaped entire industries (as digital technologies did to media, destroying jobs and companies but creating new multibillion-dollar fortunes for founders of new firms) and highly personal problems that may not qualify as high-impact on a global scale but certainly had a profound effect on the individuals facing them. There were so many times when we should have done better at responding to obvious threats: Hurricane Katrina, the 2008 financial crisis, the 2007 Minnesota bridge collapse, cyber attacks, wildfires, water shortages, and other disasters that you'll read about in this book.

As Hurricane Sandy roared up the East Coast in October 2012, I reflected on the storm-warning systems that gave New York several days to prepare. In the aftermath of the storm, it became clear that although emergency-response officials had learned some lessons from the government's disastrous handling of Katrina, there were many examples of people, companies, organizations, and government agencies that had not prepared for the storm. And after Sandy it wasn't at all clear whether the people who had the power to make necessary changes to protect New York in the future would do so.

At about that time, the organizers of the annual meeting of the World Economic Forum in Davos invited me to speak on the theme of "dynamic resilience"—specifically, "weak signals" leading up to crisis situations. It was a perfect chance to reflect further on why we are so bad at responding to evidence of impending disaster. I launched the Gray Rhino concept in January of 2013 with a presentation at Davos, along with the Japanese author and crisis expert William Saito, who was talking about neon swans, events whose fate was sealed by willful collective failure to perceive signals that, in hindsight, become blindingly obvious. Our presentations had a common theme. The problem, ultimately, was not weak signals but weak responses to signals. It was a reluctance to see and act on warning signs that were apparent to not insignificant numbers of people.

When my agent first circulated the proposal for *The Gray Rhino* to editors, several of them responded that it wasn't counterintuitive enough to say that we needed to pay attention to highly obvious crises, because people already know they are there and are dealing with them. That made me realize that I was onto something even more important and frightening than I had realized. In fact, my idea was so counterintuitive that I had to point out, emphatically, that, no, most people and organizations were not handling the biggest threats effectively.

As I researched the book, I also discovered that the flip side of many highly obvious dangers was opportunity. Often, awareness of a threat and a strategy for responding benefited the cynics: in finance, certainly, many investors thrive on the gyrations of markets, making money hand over fist from rubes who throw money into market bubbles, and, again, when market panic sets in. Many times, as with disruptive technologies, threats arose because someone else identified a new opportunity. In other instances, reimagining how to address a risk opens the imagination. In 2014, the Global Commission on the Economy and Climate calculated that the world likely will spend $90 trillion over the next fifteen years just to replace, maintain, and expand the aging infrastructure of its cities in order to meet the demands of growing urban populations. With that in mind, the commission proposed that, instead of just following business as usual, cities use those funds to deploy new technologies to improve growth, create jobs, boost company profits, spur economic development, and save some of the nearly $400 billion in economic output lost annually to the stresses caused by urban sprawl in the United States alone.

Under the Knife

Solutions to 30,000-foot-high financial, geopolitical, and giant corporate crises are susceptible to the same human tendency toward procrastination as the most common of everyday challenges. In fact, they are the combined, magnified effect of the many humans whose collective actions produce those shared problems.

On the most personal level, I couldn't help but connect having to undergo two gum surgeries to the Gray Rhino framework. Yes, I realize that periodontal woes are mundane next to hurricanes and high finance. But our ability to respond to potentially catastrophic risks is vulnerable to the same quirks of human nature that make us ignore those lectures from our dentists to do a better job of flossing and get a cleaning every six months. After you get back from a cleaning and your teeth feel all squeaky and nice to run your tongue over, it's easy to be extra diligent about flossing—for a few days. Then the reality of everyday routine sets in and you skip those molars way back that are so hard to reach around . . . and maybe you skip a few days, or—be honest—more than a few days. We all do it, and don't think much of the consequences until it's too late.

I learned the hard way, as do so many people, when my dentist told me that I needed a gum graft. Though going under the knife is no fun, there are few better ways for remembering to be diligent. I now keep a whole set of gum-cleaning tools, including some I didn't know existed before my surgery, and I use them. Gingivitis is very minor in the scheme of highly obvious problems. It's one of the simplest examples, though, of how it sometimes takes a major blow to get us to pay attention to what could have been prevented with much less pain and inconvenience.

Failure to Yield

The same was true in my neighborhood in New York City, when it took a triple tragedy to get the city to pay attention to a glaringly obvious problem that had already taken lives and been ignored for far too long.

On a rainy Saturday night in January 2014, I was at my computer taking a Twitter break from working on this manuscript when tweets started coming fast and furious about police activity a few blocks from my apartment. Streets were cut off, and police cars and ambulances were screaming toward the scene. When the full story came out, it was horrifying. A nine-year-old boy, Cooper Stock, had been crossing the street with his father in the crosswalk in front of his home, with a walk signal and the right of way, when a taxi "failed to yield," as the clinical police term has it. The cab ran over Cooper and injured his father, who had to watch his son's life slip away right in front of him.

Just two blocks away and less than an hour earlier, a tour-bus driver failed to see Alex Shear, a seventy-four-year-old father and a famed collector of Americana whose friends called him "the Pied Piper of the American Dream." Shear reportedly was crossing against the light when the bus—whose driver didn't see him because the design of the bus created a blind spot—dragged him to his death as passengers screamed at the driver to stop.

The following week, I joined my neighbors and friends, many of whom had children who went to school with Cooper, and others who knew Alex Shear, for a candlelight vigil in front of Cooper Stock's home. The crowd overflowed from the sidewalk onto the street on which the cab had hit Cooper until police blocked off Ninety-seventh Street so that people could get close to the neighbors, family friends, and local elected officials who were calling for a stop to preventable traffic deaths. As I tried to find a place from which to watch and listen, carefully staying as close as I could to the parked cars on West End Avenue to keep from going out into the street, it was hard not to be aware of the danger.

Days later, Samantha Lee, a twenty-six-year-old medical student, was killed crossing Ninety-sixth Street when an ambulance hit her and threw her body into the path of an oncoming car. Though news reports initially indicated that she had been crossing mid-block, video showed her in the crosswalk.

Pedestrian traffic accidents may not have the wide impact of many of the threats discussed in this book, but for the families affected the results were devastating. Looking at a Gray Rhino dynamic on a personal scale can help us to understand the flaws in human nature and in government that lead to dire consequences when larger issues are at hand.

The triple traffic deaths highlighted several instances of problems that had long been known but had been all but ignored: poorly designed, high-traffic streets with a highway entrance and an exit in front of a middle school; and traffic laws that generally let drivers who hit pedestrians off the hook with little more than a slap on the wrist, if that. (The cabbie who hit Cooper Stock got a summons for "failure to yield.") The lead-up to the tragedies had many of the hallmarks of a Gray Rhino, just as the aftermath had much in common with dangers that municipal leaders don't address until the damage is done. In this case, New York had failed to act on long-standing evidence that it needed to change its policies.

I always pause and look both ways a few extra times before I cross West End Avenue, because I knew someone who had been killed there several years earlier. In 2005, a sport-utility vehicle hit the *Newsweek* editor Tom Masland at the corner of Ninety-fifth Street and West End Avenue. I had met him briefly through a mutual friend, who had given me a copy of her book to take to him after I visited her in the Dominican Republic. Though I didn't know Masland well, it was a shock to hear the news about him and to have to call our friend to tell her what had happened. It should not have been a surprise to anyone that the West Nineties were a death trap. Right where the SUV hit Masland, cars stream off the West Side Highway on Ninety-fifth and Ninety-sixth Streets. West End Avenue between Ninety-fifth and Ninety-seventh has always been congested with cars turning to get onto the highway.

A 2008 traffic study recommended ways to make New York's streets safer, but nothing was done, a point that was not lost on Cooper Stock's family and friends. In November 2013, just weeks before the tragedies, the local Community Board had issued yet another study and set of recommendations for making things safer. That same month, advocates warned that pedestrian deaths were rising across the city, up by more than 15 percent since 2011. In 2011, seven children died after being hit by vehicles; the death toll rose to 12 in 2012 and to 13 in 2013. Total pedestrian deaths in New York rose from 150 in 2012 to 173 in 2013.

Cooper Stock's death was the tipping point. The family of the nine-year-old boy spoke up and said that things had to change; voices rallied around them and joined together with those of the family and friends of so many other children, men, and women who died when they didn't have to. In this case, the lever was a human story: an important lesson for how to get a highly obvious threat on the agenda.

Crises help to push through changes, but too often the changes are a dollar short on top of being a day late. The most obvious problems often get the most dramatic, though hardly the most effective, solutions.

The city's initial response to the triple tragedies in my neighborhood was shocking: it cracked down on jaywalking, with cops beating up and bloodying the face of an eighty-four-year-old Chinese man who didn't understand them. From January to mid-February, the number of tickets to pedestrians across the city increased eightfold, while the number of tickets issued to drivers fell.

The local Community Board unanimously passed a resolution demanding that the city change the penalty for drivers who kill or severely injure pedestrians while violating traffic regulations, so that, at a minimum, they would have their licenses permanently revoked. It was shocking that such a seemingly sensible recommendation had not been adopted decades earlier.

In February 2014, Mayor Bill de Blasio issued a forty-two-page set of proposals, based on Sweden's Vision Zero model, intended to help the city reach a stated (if not entirely realistic) goal of eliminating traffic deaths. He pledged to place stronger emphasis on enforcing laws against traffic violations by drivers.

And yet . . . Two days after he announced the traffic plan, news cameras caught Mayor De Blasio's caravan speeding. A few days later, a *New York Post* photographer snapped a shot of the mayor jaywalking. The incidents showed just how hard it is to change behaviors that we know are dangerous, and that even after a crisis strikes we're terrible at acting to prevent the next one.

If we're so bad at recognizing and responding to threats, what can we do about it? What's the point if we can't change who we are? While we may not be able to change who we are, we can be more aware of why we do what we do. Recognizing the quirks of human nature that shape our decisions has the power to change our actions. Recent work in behavioral economics and examples from businesses, organizations, communities, and governments show many ways in which we can do a better job of recognizing obvious threats and responding to them.

Our trouble responding in a timely and effective way also has to do with the systems we've set up that make it harder to act. Our political and financial systems are based on powerful financial and social incentives to act with the short term in mind. As a result, we don't make enough of the long-term investments of time and resources that we need to head off problems before they become bigger and harder to solve.

The Gray Rhino is a road map for recognizing and learning from the times we've failed to get out of the way of a clear and present danger, and applying those lessons to the decisions we make when we have a chance not only to prevent a crisis, reducing human and financial costs, but also to create opportunities.

Getting out of the way of a Gray Rhino can mean many things. It can mean embracing a threat and turning it into an opportunity. Yet it also can mean avoiding damage or, at least, minimizing it. Acting in time can make a situation dramatically better. It can also merely keep a crisis from deteriorating, like the stimulus plans that followed the 2008 financial crash. Often enough, so much damage is done that things can never get back to normal, but if the damage done is the least of many worse outcomes it's still a significant improvement. Avoiding being trampled rarely, if ever, means keeping the status quo.

THE
GRAY
RHINO

1

MEET THE GRAY RHINO

In the autumn of 2001, Glenn Labhart was chief risk officer at Dynegy. The energy company was considering buying an energy trading company whose stock had fallen by 80 percent in recent weeks, sending shock waves through the energy markets. Dynegy's chairman and CEO, Charles Watson, knew the company well—or thought he did—and had a plan to buy its energy marketing capabilities for a song, stabilize the energy markets, combine the two companies' trading capabilities, and protect itself from the exposure it already had in case the company failed. It was a chance to be a white knight, and to make some money in the process.

Labhart, a plainspoken, no-nonsense Texan, was a seventeen-year veteran oil-and-gas trader and a former risk consultant who now had a $42 billion portfolio of trading, power generation, and energy assets, along with the associated insurance and credit risk, under his oversight. He already had helped steer Dynegy through the recent California energy crisis and the aftermath of the 9/11 terrorist attacks. He had developed a dynamic tool to provide real-time risk-management information. Now he was tasked with assessing the risks associated with the $25 billion deal and advising the board.

He did a value-at-risk analysis of the company to generate a set of metrics not unlike the dashboard of a car, with its speedometer and gas gauge. It had already become obvious that Dynegy would have to put more capital into the company it was considering buying and assume a significant amount of its debt. The more Labhart looked at the company's financials, though, the more concerned he became. "I extrapolated out to one year for risk-adjusted return on capital, and the results were sobering," he told me in a conversation over coffee. He just couldn't figure out how the company had calculated the profitability and cash flow of its trading operations. When he tried to envision standing in front of a ratings agency and justifying the deal, he simply couldn't picture it.

Nearly fifteen years later, Labhart vividly recalled a 7:30 AM due diligence meeting, at the venerable Houston law firm Baker Botts, with Dynegy executives and their lawyers about their risk assessment. He told them bluntly, "If we're going to do this kind of deal, we need to ask them how they value risk on non-liquid assets." He presented his report to the board, warning members that the numbers didn't seem to add up and that they needed to do more due diligence or hold off on the deal. "The report said we didn't need to do this," Labhart recalled. "I said we needed to ask more questions, but the train had left the station. I wish I'd had more lead time."

The company to be acquired was, of course, Enron, the corporation that went down in the annals of business history as an example of the colossal failure of auditors, analysts, and investors to recognize that a firm valued at $90 billion was merely a house of cards. It has become a classic example of greed and willful ignorance of warning signals.

Recounting the story, Labhart quickly sketched a daunting organizational chart, outlining the short-term and long-term assets and liabilities and flows within the company. He drew an arrow and a circle around the thing that had set off alarm bells for him: the way the company marked its assets to market—an accounting practice commonly used for securities trading but which this company used to value its turbines. "How do you mark-to-market a turbine?" he asked. Unlike frequently traded stocks and bonds, turbines are large, unwieldy machines that simply don't lend themselves to easy exchange—and for which, therefore, prices are hard to determine.

While Labhart wished his report had gotten the board's attention soon enough to prevent the deal earlier, his warning wasn't completely in vain. The report did convince board members to be sure to include protections in the deal, just in case he turned out to be right. "When you're chief risk officer, you're being second-guessed a lot because you're taking a negative look," Labhart said in hindsight. But even when you're second-guessed there may still be room to make a difference.

As the date of the proposed merger neared, Labhart worked with management on a contingency clause that would reduce Dynegy's credit risk by giving it ownership of the Northern Natural Gas Company, the only pipeline Enron owned and its most profitable physical asset. Enron put the 16,500-mile pipeline up as collateral.

On November 19, 2001, Enron filed with the SEC notifying it of $690 million in new debts, leaving Dynegy in a very difficult position. It had already channeled $1.5 billion in financing to Enron and assumed responsibility for nearly another billion dollars of debt. Rating agencies downgraded Enron's debt to junk status. On November 28, as Enron's stock price approached zero, Dynegy withdrew its offer. Early the next year, as its own stock price wobbled because of the debacle, it took possession of the pipeline, which, at least temporarily, stabilized Dynegy. The following year, the Global Association of Risk Professionals named Labhart Financial Risk Manager of the Year.

Dynegy's experience and Enron's collapse may be a particularly dramatic case, but the episode has much in common with events that unfold every single day for people faced with evidence of danger: we simply don't want to see it. We avoid asking the questions for which we don't want to know the answers, because we don't want to deal with the consequences of knowing, especially when inconvenient truths get in the way of the stories we tell ourselves about how wonderful things will be if they go the way we've told ourselves they would. We view risks through rose-colored glasses, downplaying the possibility that our bets may go wrong—even as we overreact to less likely yet more emotionally resonant threats.

Even when we do recognize the existence of a clear and present danger, perverse incentives embedded in our political and financial systems—a heavy emphasis on short-term thinking, poorly allocated resources, and mispriced risks—are often arrayed against doing the right thing to get out of the way. As a result, we can't count on the best designed warning systems in the world to sound the alarm loud enough to persuade our leaders to do what they need to do. Even when we acknowledge evidence of danger, all too often we don't act until the threat is fully upon us—and, sometimes, when it's too late.

But the consequences of the grim unfolding of human nature and perverse incentives—the Enrons, WorldComs, Long-Term Capitals, collapsed buildings and bridges, and disasters of all kind that litter our history, from the geopolitical to the humanitarian and the personal—are not inevitable.

In recent years, behavioral economists have identified many of the cognitive biases that keep us from acting in our best interests, and helped draw much needed attention to the ways in which warped perceptions and emotional and irrational motivations shape the decisions we make. In Chapters 2 and 3, we'll explore some of these biases, along with strategies for countering them. An equally difficult challenge, to be addressed in Chapter 4, is the set of perverse incentives, structural obstacles, and crass calculations of self-interest—the tragedy of the commons—that prevent individuals, businesses, and governments from acting in time even when we recognize the many problems in front of us.

There are examples among the wreckage of people who see the danger, are willing to say something, and sometimes can prevent at least part of the worst-case scenario from unfolding. Their success is a combination of leadership and character, awareness of the ways in which we humans trip ourselves up and how we can avoid those mistakes, and sometimes sheer luck in having the right set of circumstances—for example, sufficient resources and a critical mass of others who recognize a challenge and are motivated to respond.

Breaking the Rules

Imagine that you're on safari in Africa, where you've traveled far for a chance to see a rhinoceros alive before it's too late. The Western black rhino was declared extinct in 2011, after five years without a sighting, and the number of all remaining black rhinos is in the low thousands. You know time is running out. You've seen the grisly photos of dead rhinos, with their horns brutally hacked off of their faces by poachers to be traded in Asia at a dearer price than that for cocaine or heroin.

It's been three days, and you and your two best friends are anxious to see what you came for, to shoot a prize trophy not with a gun but with your top-of-the-line camera. The sun is so fierce that you can see the heat shimmering in the air. But you and your friends are determined, so focused on your mission that you ignore your guide's instructions and drift away while he's not looking.

You're nearly ready to give up and return to the group. But, suddenly, there they are: a rhino cow and her calf. The massive mother flicks away flies with her tail and her long ears. You realize that you've forgotten to breathe: the very definition of a breathtaking sight.

The calf is several yards away from the mother, who is looking in the other direction. You creep closer, trying to get just the right angle. Getting a picture with your telephoto lens is one thing, but a close-up would be worth the risk. You forget everything the guide has told you about avoiding startling the rhinos by keeping out of their immediate territory, staying downwind, and being quiet. They're more afraid of you than you are of them, he'd said.

Your friends are also too excited to remember the admonition to be quiet. "Try to get him to look at you so we can get a picture of his face," one whispers. Without thinking about the consequences, the other friend whistles. The calf looks your way, but, unfortunately, so does the mother. That's when you realize your mistake. You've disturbed a rhino cow. Worse yet, you've managed to get closer to her calf than she is. The baby rhino quickly scampers back to her side, but she's still angry. She shifts her weight from one side to the other as she decides what to do.

That's the least of your problems, though, because a bull rhino has appeared nearby, and he has noticed you, too. He's easily half again as big as the cow. He lowers his head and paws the ground with his left hoof, preparing to charge. The tip of his horn is pointed right at you as he gathers all two tons of his weight and prepares to launch himself in your direction.

You've already ignored the advice the guide gave you—that the best way to avoid being charged by a rhino is not to provoke the animal in the first place. Once the rhino charges, it's nearly impossible to stop him. But it's too late now. The rhino has taken his first steps, and starts accelerating to his top speed of close to forty miles an hour.

As he bears down on you, you freeze. What to do? You could climb a tree, but there is none high or strong enough. Throw something in his path? Can you make enough noise to scare him? You could run in a zigzag pattern or in the opposite direction, but the heat has sapped your energy. If you were close enough to the safari vehicle, you could get the driver to put the pedal to the metal, but you've wandered too far from the group for that. You look at your friends for ideas, but they're paralyzed, too. Your final option is to wait for the rhino to get close and then jump out of the way, counting on his inability to turn quickly to save you from being trampled. If there is one thing you must remember about what to do when a rhino charges, your guide has told you, it is this: Do not stand still. Freezing is not an option. But, so far, by (seemingly) making no choice that's what you've chosen to do.

Problematic Pachyderms

Thinking about what to do when facing a rhino's charge is very much the way many leaders approach an impending threat, whether it's a tectonic geopolitical shift with implications for the future of the world as we know it; a market disruption or a management challenge that affects the future of a company, organization, country, or region; or a personal decision with consequences for us or our families. When crisis looms, leaders need to make decisions quickly. Each choice depends on what happened beforehand; every error compounds the stakes. Good decisions ahead of time—like staying away from potentially angry rhinos—make all the difference. Once mistakes have been made, the stakes rise and the options narrow to the point where the choices are not between good and bad but among bad, worse, and almost unthinkable.

A Gray Rhino is a highly probable, high-impact threat: something we ought to see coming, like a two-ton rhinoceros aiming its horn in our direction and preparing to charge. Like its cousin, the Elephant in the Room, a Gray Rhino is something we ought to be able to see clearly by virtue of its size. You would think that something so enormous would get the attention it deserves. To the contrary, the very obviousness of these problematic pachyderms is part of what makes us so bad at responding to them. We consistently fail to recognize the obvious, and so prevent highly probable, high-impact crises: the ones that we have the power to do something about. Heads of state, CEOs of businesses and organizations, like all of us, are often worse at handling Gray Rhinos than they are at acting swiftly when an unexpected crisis arises seemingly out of the blue. This has huge and dangerous implications for leaders, who are particularly vulnerable to threats they ought to see coming but nevertheless fail to recognize and react to in time.

When facing a rhinoceros that's about to charge, doing nothing is seldom the best option. Yet all too often that's exactly what happens. Danger rarely comes as a complete surprise; instead, it follows many missed opportunities for taking precautions, reading and responding to warning signals. The impulse to freeze is hard to overcome. Sometimes the grip of denial is so strong that we do nothing at all; or, even worse, as in many market booms leading to bust, we do more of what was dangerous in the first place. Think of the family who wouldn't evacuate ahead of a hurricane. The smoker who just wouldn't quit. The president who wouldn't give up his cheeseburgers until he had a heart attack. The gambler who kept digging himself deeper into a hole in the false hope of climbing out.

Perverse incentives and calculated self-interest can turbocharge our natural impulse for denial. Think of the bankers who were warned of the dangers of subprime loans but wouldn't get out of these risky investments, and the policy-makers who wouldn't step in. ("This time" is rarely, if ever, different.) The officials who knew how badly bridges had deteriorated but kept putting off needed repairs. The foremen of a factory building with cracks in the walls who insisted on business as usual until the whole thing collapsed. The supervisors and executives, warned of suspicious accounting, who refused to listen to the whistle-blowers. The engineers who knew how dangerous a flawed fifty-seven-cent ignition switch could be but did nothing to change it. The CEO of a market-leading company that failed to respond to the disruptive new technologies that took away its head start seemingly overnight and left it struggling to stay alive. The aging patriarch who knows the clock is ticking and it's time to let the new generation take over but prefers to drive his company or country into the ground rather than relinquish control.

Many of the biggest problems the world faces are Gray Rhinos. Look at climate change, for which scientists have presented a clear case that more than 350 parts per million (ppm) of carbon dioxide is dangerous for the planet. Yet we are at 400 ppm and rising, as efforts taken so far seem to make only a dent. Rising sea levels are causing one catastrophic weather event after another: in New York City, hundred-year storms Irene and Sandy two years in a row; in the Philippines, Typhoon Haiyan, the most powerful storm ever measured. In 2013, forty-one weather-related disasters each left more than $1 billion in damages, a record.

Unsustainable national debt levels, anemic economic growth, and profound changes in labor-market dynamics have left many countries vulnerable to a new round of financial crises. Widening income disparities will intensify social unrest and political turmoil, sparking riots, toppling governments, and destroying economies. Water shortages around the world are already threatening populations, stability, and supply chains, and will only get worse: by 2030, the United Nations predicts, half of the world will face water shortages as demand outpaces supply by 40 percent. This will dry up crops and cause people to go hungry, force tens of millions of people to move from their homes, and could even spark wars over water sources that cross national boundaries.

Across the globe, in both developing and developed nations, youth unemployment is a huge problem contributing to desperation, unrest, and outright violence, along with a huge loss of human potential. By 2045, Africa will be home to 400 million people between the ages of fifteen and twenty-four who will need livelihoods, without which they will direct their considerable energies to protesting and worse. Africa's youth already make up 60 percent of its jobless, and the problem will only intensify. How will Africa provide enough jobs for the rising number of youths and prepare the new generation for whatever the jobs of the future end up being—or risk the kind of unrest that makes the aftermath of the Arab Spring look like a child's playground?

Disruptive technologies like 3-D printing will decimate some industries and launch new ones, just as the Internet has done over the past two decades to media companies that did not respond to change. Crumbling infrastructure will cost lives and bring cities and economies to their knees. More than a million people are moving to cities each week, feeding projections that by 2050 two-thirds of the world's population will live in cities. Yet overburdened transportation systems, creaky power grids and sewage systems, outdated economic-growth models, and disengaged citizens mean that these rapidly growing metropolises cannot respond quickly enough to provide needed services, create jobs, and weave a new social fabric. Adding to the urban threat is the fact that most major cities lie along coastlines, where rising sea levels and increasingly violent weather—the result of the climate-change Gray Rhino—threaten the people who live in them. The frequency of pandemics warns of a much bigger global-health threat to come: it's not a matter of *if* but *when*.

Ask any cyber security expert how likely it is that any given company or organization will suffer a major attack and he won't hesitate to tell you that the odds are more than 100 percent; these incursions go on constantly. "There are two types of companies: those who have been hacked, and those who don't yet know they have been hacked," Cisco's CEO, John Chambers, told the leaders assembled in Davos, Switzerland, for the 2015 annual meeting of the World Economic Forum. Cases like Target and Neiman Marcus are small potatoes compared with what is coming. The hackers who attacked Sony did serious damage to the company's reputation and ignited a geopolitical confrontation. These are just the beginning.

All of these challenges, like rhinos grazing on the distant horizon, began as distant threats. The closer they get, the higher the cost of heading them off; yet the further off they are (or we convince ourselves they are) the less likely we are to do anything about them. Persistent threats can exhaust us, making it seem that we'll never win, or making us complacent as the threatened disaster inches toward us too slowly to make us jump out of the way.

In some cases, these Gray Rhinos have the potential to become herds: rising sea levels, coinciding with the move to coastal cities, increasing the number of people at the risk of typhoons and hurricanes. Water and food shortages go hand in hand. So do water and energy, since it takes water to produce energy, and energy to produce water. Interconnections among global markets mean that a bank failure in one country has the potential to send financial systems around the world reeling and, in turn, throw people out of work and spark riots in the street.

In the zoological world, a rhinoceros herd is called a "crash"; I cannot think of a better choice of words. Any one of the threats described here can be overwhelming in and of itself. Combined, they are daunting. Prioritizing them is anything but easy. The pressures of daily life make it hard enough to cope with simple challenges, much less things that are so complex and overwhelming that they seem hard to grasp.

An Ounce of Prevention

But, you may say, these are all highly obvious crises. Global leaders recognize that they exist and are doing something about them, aren't they? Unfortunately, it's just not so. Our track record on many of the most obvious crises is dismal. One high-profile summit after another, from the G20 on the economy to the United Nations on climate to you name it, ends with little to show for all the hype and money spent on fancy hotels, catering, travel, and security details for global leaders who, despite the best of intentions, end up doing little more than hand-wringing.

Each year, the World Economic Forum surveys a thousand CEOs, government, media, and NGO leaders, asking them to rank which threats they believe are most likely to affect them in the coming year and how big an impact those threats will have. In 2007, the second edition of the Global Risks report identified a global asset-price collapse as the top risk in terms of potential severity and the sixth most likely to happen. By 2008, the report cited "mispricing of financial risk" as a central theme. Just months before Lehman Brothers collapsed, it noted that the predicted housing recession, liquidity crunch, and high oil prices were all happening, heightening the risk of a major collapse. Though the report based its assessment on the opinions of business leaders themselves, when it was released in time for the Forum's annual meeting in January 2008, the business leaders gathered in Davos, Switzerland, pushed back, not wanting to recognize what they themselves had predicted.

In 2013, major systemic failure of the financial system was at the top of the list, followed by rising greenhouse-gas emissions and failure to adapt to climate change. Those surveyed also saw as both highly probable and high-impact a set of challenges: wealth gaps, unsustainable government debt, pandemics, and cyber threats, mismanaged urbanization, water-supply crises, food shortages, risks associated with an aging population, rising religious fanaticism. The 2013 survey asked leaders to assign their own countries a score on a scale of 1 to 5, from least to most able to deal with economic and environmental risks. The ten countries with a critical mass of respondents scored under 3.5, and four of them were under 3. In other words, all of them were mediocre at best in how much they had done to prepare for highly likely threats. Switzerland, Germany, and the United Kingdom scored highest on preparedness, with the United States and China close behind; Russia and Japan had the lowest scores; and India, Brazil, and Italy were in the middle.

Other surveys report similar results. When the United Nations

Global Compact and Accenture surveyed a thousand CEOs in 2013, only 32 percent of those CEOs believed the economy was on track to meet the demands of a growing population within environmental and resource constraints, and just 33 percent believed that business was doing enough to meet those challenges.

Child death rates are dropping dramatically, yet every day 18,000 children die of preventable diseases, according to UNICEF. Pneumonia (17 percent of deaths), diarrhea (9 percent), and malaria (7 percent) are the biggest killers. They don't have to be: we know the causes of these diseases; the amounts of money required to prevent them are well within reach; and there's no disagreement that these are terrible ailments that need to be addressed.

Even at times when we think we're dealing with a problem, we can be sorely wrong. Initial headlines about Typhoon Haiyan suggested that preparations for the storm had headed off a major disaster. As the typhoon approached in November 2013, an Associated Press article cited efforts by the Philippines to become more serious about preparations to reduce deaths from violent storms. "Public service announcements are frequent, as are warnings by the president and high-ranking officials that are regularly carried on radio and TV and social networking sites," the article said. "President Benigno Aquino III assured the public of war-like preparations, with three C-130 air force cargo planes and 32 military helicopters and planes on standby, along with 20 navy ships." Yet twenty-four hours later the headlines were very different: as many as 10,000 dead and more than 600,000 displaced. Sometimes no amount of preparation is enough.

Haiyan was not the only storm in which people died because of the overconfidence or complacency of leaders. In New Orleans, the Federal Emergency Management Agency shared a detailed, 113-page disaster plan with Louisiana state officials in January 2005, presenting an analysis of what would happen in a Category 3 hurricane, based on a simulation dubbed Hurricane Pam: "thousands of fatalities," "floating coffins," and "large quantities of hazardous waste . . . [that] would result in airborne and waterborne contamination." Yet as Hurricane Katrina, a near-exact replica of the fictional Pam storm, approached that August—just months after officials had reviewed a clear plan for what to do, and right after follow-up workshops the month before and *the same month*—the city delayed its response and ignored nearly all the recommendations. The threat was as obvious as could be. The response plan was there. Yet it was almost as if the storm and the thoughts that went into preparation for it did not exist. The small element of uncertainty—when a storm would strike and how big it would be—was just enough to put officials into denial.

We all know that the sooner you deal with a problem the easier and the less costly it is to fix: a stitch in time saves nine. This principle goes all the way back to Hippocrates: *Morbum evitare quam curare facilius est.* An ounce of prevention is worth a pound of cure—or, as the French say, *Mieux vaut prévenir que guérir.* In German, *Vorsorge ist besser als Nachsorge.* In Spanish, *Mas vale prevenir que lamentar!* Or, in Swedish, *Bättre stämma i bäcken än i ån."* (Better to dam the brook than the river.)

Alas, these maxims remain nice in theory but aren't put into action nearly often enough. Of all the tricks that human nature plays on us, inertia is one of the most powerful forces preventing us from getting out of the way of a known challenge. How many students wait until the last minute to do that term paper, or pull all-nighters just before the final exam when studying earlier would have given them a much better chance of getting a good grade? How long have you waited past the recommended oil-change date for your car (and how much more would an engine rebuild cost than that simple oil change)? How many warnings might we ignore when a printer is running out of ink, and how inconvenient is it when the printer runs out before we've ordered a refill? Think of the impact of such everyday procrastinations magnified by the billions of people in companies, governments, even leaders making important decisions that affect millions, even billions, of other people.

The Little Dutch Boy of the Hans Brinker story walked by a trickling leak in a dike that prevented canal water from inundating fields and villages. But if he hadn't known that a trickle could become a flood he wouldn't have had the presence of mind to save his village. Alas, this legend turns out not to be Dutch; it is the product of the imagination of an American novelist. Nor could it even have happened, since dikes are giant piles of earth that would not have cracked the way the story depicts; it would have been impossible to save a compromised dike with a mere thumb. But the lesson in the story rings true all the same, and echoes the message that goes back in time to Hippocrates: decisive action can make all the difference if it comes in time.

No matter how good our intentions, all too often the only time we can act in the face of a threat is when it's on top of us and when the cost is highest. This creates a vicious circle: we expend so much energy and capital in dealing with crises that could have been better handled early on that we believe we don't have the resources to invest in heading off other threats early enough. It's like claiming that we can't afford to change the oil in our car because all our money goes to replacing an engine that would not have blown up if we had had the simple foresight to change the oil in the first place. This is the central paradox of Gray Rhino threats: rise to the threat too soon, while the threat is on the horizon, and your hands are tied; rise to the threat when you can access the resources you need, and the cost is astronomical, whether it's a matter of softening the blow or picking up the pieces.

Not If but When

In *The Black Swan: The Impact of the Highly Improbable*, Nassim Nicholas Taleb writes about catastrophes with outsized consequences that are so rare and unthinkable that people weren't prepared to face them because they couldn't even conceive of their existence. At one point, Europeans knew only about white swans and could not picture such a thing as a black swan, hence the title: something so far out of the range of preconceived notions that most of us cannot imagine its existence. Black Swans are rare, create extreme impacts, and are not predictable, even though, in retrospect, the factors leading up to them may become clear. Taleb is talking about the descent of Europe into the Great War; the 1987 stock-market crash; the invention of the Internet; the rise of Islamic fundamentalism, and other such outlier events. The book was published in 2007, just as the credit bubble and risky mortgage lending and the derivatives industries of the early 2000s were leading to the failure of Lehman Brothers and the subsequent financial turmoil and deep recession that would come to be known as the Second Great Contraction. Its timing thus turned out to be opportune for providing a powerful metaphor for understanding the crisis that unfolded.

In a section of the book attacking humans' overestimation of our ability to predict the future, Taleb jokingly speculated that someone might write an attack on his work under the name "The White Swan." The Gray Rhino is not a rebuttal but a complement to the Black Swan. Taleb himself would argue that his readers who obsess about predicting the next Black Swan completely missed his point. It's enticing to believe that we can predict the improbable, but we can't. We just have to realize that unpredictable events will throw many of our assumptions out of whack.

Black Swans lurk outside of our ability to predict. Gray Rhinos are threats that we ought to see but often don't see, or that we see but willfully ignore. Most Gray Rhinos are not the case of signals that were too weak but of listeners determined to ignore them and systems that encourage and accept as normal our failure to respond. There will always be people who are stubborn enough to ignore even the most obvious threat. But, as a rule, if a threat is obvious enough that a reasonable person can see it coming, it is a Gray Rhino, not a Black Swan.

Despite Taleb's railing against our perception of our ability to accurately see into the future, most of the crises in the world are very likely occurrences. The biggest threats facing leaders are not highly *improbable* Black Swans but highly *probable* Gray Rhinos. We may not be able to foresee the details or the timing, but the outlines of the biggest threats facing us are hard to ignore.

Why worry about an odd bird when you're facing a two-ton beast that is snorting, pawing the ground, and looking straight at you as it prepares to run you down? Gray Rhino crises are obvious and easy to picture. You can't argue that a rhino doesn't exist because it's the wrong color: white, black, Sumatran, Javan, and Indian rhinos are all gray. Their potential impact is massive, whether political, economic, environmental, military, or humanitarian. Often, you've seen a Gray Rhino before because it may have happened to you or to others: a market crash, a war, a heart attack, a hurricane. It generally warns you before charging. The question is not *if* but *when* a Gray Rhino will happen.

The financial crisis that spun out of control in 2007–08 was a Black Swan for some, but plenty of people weren't surprised: the crisis in the making was a crash of Gray Rhinos converging. There were many warning signals that the financial bubble that grew between 2001 and 2007 was well on its way to bursting. Plenty of people saw them and acted on their instincts. To students of financial volatility and the work of Charles Kindleberger, it was obvious that big problems were on the way. The International Monetary Fund and the Bank for International Settlements issued repeated warnings in the years leading up to the crisis. In 2004, an FBI report warned of widespread mortgage fraud. By 2008, foreclosures were at record levels. Christine Lagarde, then the French finance minister, warned at the 2008 G7 summit that a financial tsunami was on the way. William Poole, the former president of the Federal Reserve Bank of St. Louis, and Richard Baker, Representative of Louisiana, predicted Fannie Mae and Freddie Mac's problems. Plenty of investors, both individuals and institutions, saw the problems. Some of them acted early enough to get out of trouble unscathed; others made fortunes on the collapse. Goldman Sachs, as we now know, bet against mortgages through derivatives contracts it bought from AIG. It even took out insurance against the collapse of AIG, because it saw that coming, too. The lawsuits that followed the financial crisis showed in excruciating detail how many firms knew that a collapse was on the way and bet against the securities they were selling to their own clients.

The 2008 financial crisis was far from a case of a lack of evidence in advance of the problem. The early signs were there. Many people read them. Others may not have acted quickly enough but were moving in the right direction, as shown by the Gallup Investor Optimism Index, which peaked at 178 in January 2000 but fell steeply from 95 in mid-2007 to 15 in the summer of 2008, not long before Lehman Brothers' collapse. The index would plunge to a low of negative 64 that winter.

Yet the people in government and in leadership positions in business and finance who could have done something to prevent the crisis didn't take this evidence seriously enough. Some may have chosen not to listen because they didn't want to hear it. Others listened, then did a cold, hard cost-benefit analysis and calculated that the risks of staying in the game were worth it. The system was gamed to encourage behavior that was complacent at best, and irresponsible at the extremes.

Some people still insist, "Nobody saw 2008 coming." Even former U.S. Federal Reserve Chairman Alan Greenspan has continued to claim that he didn't see it. In 2013, he wrote in *Foreign Affairs* magazine that "virtually every economist and policymaker of note" was blind to the coming calamity. That's not the case at all, but the failure to respond to the warning signs, even in hindsight, is typical. With many Gray Rhinos, like the 2008 disaster, not everyone will own up to the signals having been there.

The very refusal to recognize what ought to be an obvious threat is part of the Gray Rhino phenomenon. For a Gray Rhino to exist, enough has to have gone wrong that a threat is looming and a crisis becomes highly probable. At least some credible experts will have sounded the alarm. People know that something bad is going to happen. Or, at least, they should.

When George Soros saw the writing on the wall for the pound sterling, he bet $10 billion and earned, along with $2 billion in profits, the nickname "the man who broke the Bank of England." In 1992, he realized that the relationship among the countries of Europe's Exchange Rate Mechanism was at the breaking point. He borrowed British pounds and invested in German marks, triggering a run on the pound, which drove the value down by 15 percent against the Deutschemark and 25 percent against the dollar. Britain soon left the Exchange Rate Mechanism and floated the pound. Soros saw a highly probable event coming and made it into an opportunity for himself. In fact, one of the key lessons of Gray Rhino thinking is to see opportunity in responding to an imminent crisis.

Gray Rhinos may seem to appear most often as threats, but frequently they are value neutral: a combination of good and bad, depending on your perspective and how good you are at identifying ways to benefit. To television networks, the Internet began as a threat. To Yahoo and Google, the Internet was an opportunity. It took television networks quite some time to explore how the Internet could be a boon to them as well. High gas prices were a threat to gas-guzzling vehicles but an opportunity for hybrids. At least, this was the case in theory early on; it took consumers and automakers longer than one might expect to respond to rising gas prices.

When United Airlines destroyed the musician Dave Carroll's $3,500 Taylor guitar and then refused to accept responsibility and pay for a new guitar, Carroll didn't just get mad; he made a YouTube video that went viral, reaching more than 1 million viewers at this writing. United had failed to recognize the power of consumers' newfound ability—through social media—to call out companies for failings and reach a wide audience; this large-scale failure made the airline vulnerable to an everyday, predictable problem that became a much bigger threat because of the power that the Internet had given to consumers. That same threat was a godsend to customers and to companies that did a better job of avoiding unfortunate incidents and owning up quickly and making things right when a problem occurred. Consumers' embrace of social media also became a major way of communicating and getting valuable feedback on products and services.

In health care, changes are both opportunities and threats, depending on how creatively we respond. Obesity has reached epidemic levels in the developed world, driving up health-care costs and threatening lives. For those who suffer from diabetes, heart attacks, or other obesity-related illnesses, and pay for treatment, this is a full-fledged crisis. For health-care companies, it is an area for business growth. For companies whose products contribute to the problem, growing awareness of obesity is a danger—or an opportunity.

If It Bleeds, It Leads

Much ink has been spilled and many trees felled to describe why crises happen and the sequences of events that precede them. Yet it is just as important to understand why they *don't* happen, or why they happen but are nowhere near as bad as they could have been. We can learn important lessons from the times when leaders get out of the way of a Gray Rhino. Unfortunately, we're not as likely to hear about them.

In the news, "if it bleeds, it leads." We all know about times when doing nothing or doing the wrong thing has escalated crises into catastrophes. Dangers averted don't make the headlines, yet those are exactly the ones we need to study in order to avoid future catastrophes.

A key lesson of a famous business school case study, based on the Challenger disaster, is that it can be calamitous to make a decision based only on known failures. In the case study, students have to evaluate whether or not to run a car race on an unusually cold morning, when they know that their engine gasket sometimes fails at low temperatures. They have data only on races in which the gasket failed. The stakes are high: if they race and win, they stand to gain significant amounts of sponsorship money on top of what they already have; if the gasket fails, however, they lose their current sponsor and destroy their reputation. When you look at the data points from the failed past races, it's unclear whether to race or not. But when you add in data from the successful races you see immediately that all the past successful races occurred at temperatures higher than those recorded for the morning of this race. It becomes obvious that the right decision is not to go ahead.

The engineers debating whether to launch the Challenger knew that the O-ring seals used in the solid rocket booster had a design flaw that allowed dangerous gases to escape and potentially destroy the space shuttle if it was launched at temperatures that were too low. The manufacturer had known about the problem since 1977, and shortly before the Challenger disaster it had been testing an alternative design. On the morning of the launch, several engineers warned that they did not have enough evidence that the O-rings would seal properly at temperatures lower than those documented at the time of any other launch. The NASA team pushed back, saying they saw no evidence of a link between cold temperatures and O-ring failure. "But, like so many of us, the engineers and managers limited themselves to the data in the room and never asked themselves what data would be needed to test the temperature hypothesis," the Harvard professor Max Bazerman wrote of the episode in his insightful book *The Power of Noticing: What the Best Leaders See*. If they had done so, they would have known that the odds of a successful launch were too low, postponed the launch until a warmer day, and those astronauts would still be alive.

The lessons from that case resonate, in particular, with me. On the morning of January 28, 1986, when the Challenger exploded, I was sitting in a student lounge at Rice University in Houston. Many of my classmates and their professors had experiments riding on the shuttle or had connections to NASA. The disaster hit the whole country hard, but for the Rice community it was personal.

Many years later, I studied the Challenger case, handily disguised in the cloak of an entirely different set of circumstances, in an exercise at the Harvard Kennedy School of Government with Professor Bazerman. Our group struggled with the conflicting emotions of a team wanting to win a contest in which the stakes were high, though hardly as high as the lives that were lost in the Challenger explosion. We focused too much on the chance that nothing would go wrong; on all the reasons that the low temperature outdoors was not the reason the equipment had failed in the past. If we'd requested a full set of data, we would have seen that every single one of the successful tests was above a certain temperature, and would have decided not to go ahead. We didn't ask ourselves the right questions about the data, which would have given us pause about proceeding. We failed to ask ourselves what made the difference when things went *right*.

In the real-life Challenger disaster, part of the problem was that the people making decisions weren't asking the kinds of questions that would have allowed them to see that the right answer was to abort the mission until the O-ring problem was fixed. There are many other reasons that we fail to respond in time to warning signals: the quirks and foibles of human nature, including the plain old impulse to procrastinate; cultural taboos against raising the alarm; our bias toward overweighting positive outcomes and discounting negative ones; groupthink, or the tendency of people to reinforce the prevailing wisdom and ignore information that counters the story they have come to recognize.

Much as we grasp intellectually that the sooner we recognize a red flag and deal with it, the better, all too often we come down against acting to head off disaster. We know that a stitch in time saves nine, but we also have internalized cautionary tales working in the opposite direction. Perverse incentives reinforce this inertia and make it unlikely that we will recognize and deal with the most obvious threats.

We have a name for those who predict bad things to come, and it's not meant to be complimentary: Cassandras. The word has come to imply someone who's perpetually gloomy about the future—generally, one not to be believed. In the original Greek myth, however, Cassandra's predictions came true. The daughter of King Priam and Queen Hecuba of Troy, Cassandra had the misfortune of catching the eye of the god Apollo. He gave her the power of prophecy, but when she did not return his affections he threw in a curse that prevented anyone from believing her predictions. She saw a Gray Rhino coming: the Greek attack on Troy. If only the Trojans had believed her, history might have turned out differently. The major lesson of Cassandra's tale, which has become a tenet of Western culture, is that naysayers are not welcome.

The Five Stages of a Gray Rhino

As we'll see in later chapters, cultural expectations are not the only obstacle to those who sound warnings. Human nature as well as organizational and social systems are set up to reinforce the status quo and a rose-colored view of what is to come. As we've already seen, denial is a deep-seated element in the lead-up to and aftermath of many crises. Denial, dangerous enough in the mind of a single person, becomes deadly when group dynamics come into play. If it's hard to persuade one person to pay attention to a warning, it becomes exponentially harder as you add group members to the equation. Behavioral economists warn of the phenomenon of groupthink, which leads groups to seek conformity, making them extremely vulnerable to ignoring information that contradicts conventional wisdom and, in turn, leading to bad decisions. People would rather be wrong together than be right alone.

Even if we get past groupthink and other barriers to sounding a clear warning, it's not easy to turn knowledge of a threat into action. If the first of five stages of response to a Gray Rhino threat is denial, the second and third stages include various reasons not to act. Usually, denial is followed by muddling, otherwise known as "kicking the can"; that is, finding ways to push the problem into the future. As it becomes clearer that muddling isn't enough, we try to gain control over the situation, very much along the lines of bargaining, the third of the five stages of grief famously laid out by Elisabeth Kübler-Ross, which also begin with denial. In this third stage, our responses to Gray Rhinos can be useful, if tardy, diagnostic exercises, yet they, too, often devolve into squabbles over what the right response is. In both of the muddling and the diagnosing stages, which involve much wasting of time and opportunity, an array of entrenched perverse incentives and challenges of collective action stand in the way of acting.

In 1429, Joan of Arc heard God's voice telling her to fight to save France during the Hundred Years' War. A mere teenager, she convinced Charles VII to let her lead the French army against England, turning the course of the war in France's favor and leading to a brief truce. After the truce ended, the Duke of Burgundy captured her and held her prisoner of war, then sold her to the English, who burned her at the stake for heresy at the age of nineteen. It was so rare for someone to hear and heed a warning that even the king, who owed her his crown, feared accusations of heresy and sorcery, which may have been why he did not do more to try to save her. The moral of the story: Act in time to save your people and get burned at the stake. For your troubles, you might eventually be made a saint a few centuries after your death.

In other words, no good deed goes unpunished. This is part of the reason too few leaders step up in time, unless it is on the off chance that they're hearing voices, have a teenager's sense of invincibility, feel that they have absolutely nothing to lose, or are a saint. It should not be as hard as it is for leaders to get out of the way of a Gray Rhino. But the odds are stacked against them standing up in time to prevent disaster.

Our financial, political, and social structures often encourage risky behavior and willful ignorance of threats. Being aware of these perverse incentives and ingrained biases is a first step toward changing the ones that we can change. The biggest challenge is the set of financial incentives and psychological predilections that favor short-term thinking over the medium and long-term strategies that could keep the danger at a safe distance on the horizon. Our system of rewards and punishments makes it easy to shirk responsibility for acting. The way we've set things up helps us to rationalize not acting. When this reason-based system collides with the irrational underpinnings of the decisions we make, it's a recipe for disaster.

The tricks our own minds play on us make it difficult to get out of the way of a Gray Rhino. As a growing number of investors and policy decision-makers are coming to understand, we are not always rational when we weigh risks versus rewards or in how we act based on what we know.

Even when the foibles of human nature aren't getting in the way, there are the genuine conundrums that make it hard to decide what to do. The trouble with many Gray Rhinos is that while there may be little doubt about whether a threat will materialize, the timing is far from certain. As John Maynard Keynes reportedly said, "The market can stay irrational a lot longer than you and I can remain solvent." It then becomes difficult to prepare and to prioritize, for there are costs to acting too soon in responding to a threat or an opportunity. Investors speak ruefully of the widowmaker trade: betting that Japan's rising national debt will crush the value of its bonds, a wager that for the past two decades has lured many investors to a tragic ending.

Michael Burry of Scion Capital saw the subprime crisis coming and began betting on it in 2005. But sticking with his bet cost him the support (and dollars) of investors who cared about short-term gain and complained that he wasn't making money fast enough. To stick with his conviction until the trade played out, he had to fire half of his staff and sell parts of other bets. By 2007, of course, subprime loans had begun to unravel and his wager paid off. When all was said and done, Scion's investment had returned 726 percent, generating nearly a billion dollars in profit. His story, brilliantly described by Michael Lewis in *The Big Short*, shows how hard it can be to act in time when there is an obvious threat—but also how profitable, if your pockets are deep enough.

Acting too soon on opportunities presents a similar challenge. The annals of Internet history are littered with the stories of early-stage companies that fell by the wayside after a new, more powerful generation of companies riding the Web 2.0 came along. Look at AltaVista, an early search engine that Yahoo later bought and eventually shut down in the summer 2013; or early Internet leader AOL, which Time Warner bought in 2000 for $164 billion, much of which Time Warner had to write off just two years later as nimbler players overtook AOL.

Another obstacle to our ability to deal with a threat is juggling which one to address first when we face many Rhinos at once. Given the uncertainty of timing and the scarcity of resources, it can be difficult to prioritize among competing Gray Rhinos. Sometimes the only choice is to face down more than one, because otherwise you'll be trampled from more than one direction. Sometimes, though less often than happens in reality, the right response is to let the trampling happen.

Regardless of the reason leaders fail to act quickly to head off a threat, that, unfortunately, is what tends to happen. Eventually, muddling, fretting, and squabbling over what to do fail to avert the inevitable. We move into the fourth stage of a Gray Rhino crisis: a state of panic. How we respond in the panic stage depends on how much preparation we've done in advance: how many other times we've seen and responded to similar situations, how well we've envisioned the possible options once we're required to act, and how many choices remain open or have closed to us as we muddled along and dithered over what to do. Good decisions help avert or minimize the impact of crises. Bad decisions lead to ca-tastrophe.

The fourth stage, panic, moves quickly to the fifth and final stage: action or a trampling, or sometimes both. Even when it is too late, there can be hope: when picking up the pieces, leaders can work to make it harder to repeat the same mistakes. In the Netherlands, for example, the terrible North Sea flood of 1953 killed nearly 2,000 people. The coun-try took the lesson to heart, embarking on a massive flood-protection public-works program to fortify itself against the kind of storm that comes along only once every ten thousand years. Cities like New York and New Orleans have turned to the Netherlands for advice on how to protect themselves from future catastrophic weather events—storms made more likely by our collective failure to respond to the Gray Rhino of climate change, which has raised sea levels and surface temperatures, making storms more violent and coastal areas more vulnerable.

Seeing the Rhino

We need a better way of thinking about Gray Rhinos: a framework for recognizing, prioritizing, and handling these highly obvious threats before it's too late.

First, we need to distinguish the Gray Rhino from other types of threats, particularly its companion, the Black Swan.

White Swans are highly probable but low impact, so not deserving the kind of attention we reserve for the Gray Rhino. Fat Tails or Black Swans are events that are improbable and high impact. Because they are so im-probable, and indeed largely unforeseeable in the case of Black Swans, the only way to respond is to create structures and systems that are generally resilient: strong foundations, ample reserves, flexible structures.

	Low Probability	High Probability
Low Impact		White Swans
High Impact	Fat Tails, Black Swans	Gray Rhinos

Gray Rhinos, by contrast, are both highly probable and high impact. The sooner we deal with them, the lower the cost. Unfortunately, the farther away they are, the lower the likelihood that we step up before they become more costly and our options become limited. This book is meant to shift that dynamic, to make us more likely to confront Gray Rhinos sooner, when the odds of succeeding are higher.

At each of the five stages of an approaching Gray Rhino, we have opportunities to change the course of events. You would respond very differently to a herd of rhinos on the horizon than you would to a rhino bull that's too close for comfort. Similarly, the options and strategies for each stage of a Gray Rhino threat are distinct.

We begin by denying or minimizing the existence of a Gray Rhino threat; muddle along, instead of acting decisively, once we've recognized the challenge at hand; play the blame game as we search for solutions; come to an alert, panicked state when the Gray Rhino is about to charge, but we do not always have the tools to act wisely; and, finally, we do something—occasionally before the trampling, but all too often after the fact.

Important lessons are to be found in the ways in which leaders, organizations, and countries have or have not responded successfully. The difference between being trampled or not is part character, part luck, part circumstances, part strategy, and part leadership. Those who can anticipate a major disruptive change stand to profit. They also can change the world.

If leaders hear a warning and decide to ignore it, or heed the warning and do the wrong thing, they will be flattened, and remembered as a Neville Chamberlain rather than a Winston Churchill or as a Herbert Hoover rather than an FDR. They must wait to act until a threat is real enough to create a sense of urgency and push people to action, but they must not wait until it is too late.

Leaders need to start by worrying more about Gray Rhinos than about Black Swans, and finding ways to shock themselves out of denial and change our incentive systems to make it easier to respond. They can draw from the examples of the systems set up to save people from recurring crises like tornadoes, tsunamis, hurricanes, and even the annual flu virus, which do a respectable job of saving lives. These include ways to recognize signs of an impending threat, sound a hard-to-ignore alarm to people in its path, educate people ahead of time on how to react, and provide shelters and clear instructions when the threat is on the way. They must create fail-safe measures ahead of time that can trigger automatic responses to short-circuit leaders who attempt to deny the existence of a threat. A prescient Gray Rhino strategy changes perverse incentives in order to encourage leaders to act sooner, and uses our understanding of the weaknesses of human nature to make us more likely to do the right thing.

Leaders intent on avoiding tramplings would inoculate societies against the dangers of groupthink and find ways to keep fresh ideas flowing into debates and decisions. They spend time looking ahead to Rhinos on the horizon, even if that means letting less important, short-term problems get worse. They listen to diverse voices to avoid being told only familiar thinking.

The leaders best equipped to outsmart a Gray Rhino have access to warning signals and pay attention when the alarm sounds. They know what to do to get out of the way, or, at least, they blunder through enough trials and errors to mitigate the rhino's charge.

By learning from examples of leaders who have faced down Gray Rhinos, whether they fail or succeed, we can do a better job of managing our countries, our companies, and our homes and families. The first lesson is that we can avoid being trampled only if we decide to do so. We need to recognize that Gray Rhinos are out there—and very, very dangerous.

2

THE PROBLEM
WITH PREDICTIONS:
UNLEASHING DENIAL

Every January, Byron Wien, the vice-chairman of Blackstone Advisory Partners, issues his annual Ten Surprises list. Wien defines a "surprise" as an event that he believes has a better than 50-percent chance of happening but to which the average investor would assign no more than a one-out-of-three chance. His predictions are among my favorites to watch every year because of the thought he gives to challenging conventional wisdom.

In 1985, Wien's first year at Morgan Stanley and his first as an investment strategist after years as a portfolio manager, he thought about how he could make an impact. A friend had challenged him on the wisdom of taking the job in the first place, asking him, "Why would you take that job when you're a successful portfolio manager? If you're wrong it will be very hard to go back to portfolio management." His friend had hit upon a truth: humans place unreasonable demands for accuracy on prognosticators, even though we know how uncertain predictions can be.

Wien knew that he couldn't be smarter than the other strategists, but he did think that he could do something nobody else was doing. He'd started out from nothing, an orphan growing up in the Chicago public schools, but got where he was for a very important reason: "All the money I had made I had made by having a non-consensus idea that turned out to be right." So he proposed to Morgan Stanley an annual Ten Surprises list for making predictions outside of the consensus view. "They turned it down because I could get all ten wrong and the firm would be embarrassed," he said. But eventually he convinced Morgan Stanley to give it a try. "Even if I got some wrong, I thought it was worth doing, because most people tend to think about the same things," he told me as we sat in Blackstone's Park Avenue offices. "People are very conservative. They are afraid to be wrong."

Wien looked at roughly twenty-five big predictions, easily culled from the announcements of the usual suspects. The simple exercise of identifying what the consensus was turned out to be tremendously useful in drawing attention to herd behavior that could be dangerous. He then thought about fifteen predictions that might unfold differently: either events that might dramatically overshoot in the same direction as conventional wisdom or things that were contrary to what people expected.

"At first, people thought the Ten Surprises were cute, a curiosity," Wien said. "Then one year I predicted that IBM would triple, and that put them on the map." The skeptics who had turned down the idea came up to him and now thought it was a brilliant idea. "At the beginning, I thought I'd be punished more than I was for being wrong. When I found out that I wasn't punished as much as I'd thought, I saw that people appreciated the Surprises for what they were, not for the score." He went back to the friend who had questioned his decision to take the Morgan Stanley job. "You said being a strategist is a slippery pole," he told him. "But I went to the bottom and there were no bodies, so maybe it's not as slippery as you think." His ideas got him recognized over and over as one of Wall Street's top thinkers. *Forbes* magazine has described him as an oracle. In March 2000, he was a leading voice on the Morgan Stanley team urging caution in a stock market badly overheated by a tech bubble.

In 2005, when Wien left Morgan Stanley, he assumed that the firm would continue the annual list because it was so popular. He was, in a word, wrong. "Nobody wanted to take the risk of being wrong," he recalled. So the Ten Surprises went with him to Pequot Capital and eventually to Blackstone.

In 2013, Wien predicted that Republicans would do an about-face on immigration as party leadership recognized the opportunity presented by a more open stance, and that immigration reform would pass. He told me a year later that he'd made that prediction with a particularly firm sense of conviction: "The Republicans lost the last election, but if they had taken the lead on immigration they could have won last year. Until they take the lead on immigration, Republicans will lose every election. Seventeen percent of the country today—and it's going to thirty percent—are Hispanic. They're natural Republicans—they're pro-life, they're Catholic, they're entrepreneurs. They could easily be a significant part of the Republican Party. The Republicans don't recognize that." As 2013 progressed, several leaders in the party did, in fact, embrace immigration reform. Wien's prediction didn't come true that year, but he wasn't completely wrong.

"Don't be afraid to be wrong," Wien says. "You're not punished for being wrong as much as you think you will be. Every year, some blogger will make fun of me—even a few bloggers." In fact, the PunditTracker blog called his 2013 prediction that gold would reach $1,900 per ounce and the S&P 500 would fall below 1300 "the worst financial prediction of 2013." But Wien is okay with being wrong sometimes. "Most people are wrong most of the time. Believe me, I've been wrong plenty of times," he said. "But people say here's a guy who has the guts to come out and be visibly wrong."

Wien's Surprises are useful for the way they identify the consensus and challenge it. By being willing to question prevailing views he opens our eyes to possibilities that are right in front of us but that we're unable to see, often because we're unwilling to open our eyes and break with the crowd. Wien is a Gray Rhino thinker: he is willing to challenge the conventional wisdom and thoughtfully analyze whether or not an event is likely to happen, how soon, and what it means.

Mandelbrotian Randomness?

Ask a room full of people what "highly probable" or "highly obvious" means to them, and you'll likely get a range of answers. Something that is obvious to one person may not be so obvious to the next.

For example, some Florida residents are deeply concerned about rising sea levels, but others are so sanguine about the possibility of increasingly destructive storms that they sink (pun semi-intentional) money into beachfront property. One person might think it highly probable that changing demographics will cause Social Security to collapse but doesn't worry about it because it's too hard to predict exactly when that might happen. Some problems—like the weaknesses in the market for collateralized debt obligations preceding the financial collapse of 2008—are highly obvious to people who follow them closely and were trained to spot problems. Yet they do not appear obvious to others because these people have not been educated in this field, because of deliberate attempts to hide the problems, or (as we will see in the next chapter) because of the way human nature masks what we don't want to recognize. Financial crises happen on a fairly regular basis and often have many predictable elements; what goes up must come down, after all. Yet, time and again, people fail to see them.

Other problems, like hurricanes, tornadoes, and epidemics, happen regularly, but where and when is hard to predict precisely. Nevertheless, there's enough certainty among a significant number of informed people to warrant categorizing all of these events as Gray Rhinos; these are instructive cases because of the systems that exist to warn people and because of the behaviors that are widely known to dramatically reduce the risk of injury, property damage, illness, or worse.

Though his book *The Black Swan* focuses on highly improbable, unpredictable events like World War I, Nassim Nicholas Taleb acknowledges the existence of crises that resemble Gray Rhinos. "Some events can be rare and consequential, but somewhat predictable, particularly to those who are prepared for them and have the tools to understand them (instead of listening to statisticians, economists, and charlatans of the bell-curve variety)," he wrote. "They are near-Black Swans. They are somewhat tractable scientifically—knowing about their incidence should lower your surprise; these events are rare but expected. I call this special case of 'gray' swans Mandelbrotian randomness." This was a reference to the mathematician Benoit Mandelbrot, known as "the father of fractals." Before his death in 2010, Mandelbrot popularized the use of fractal geometry to find and describe logical patterns in seemingly rough and random phenomena everywhere in our world, from nature to financial markets. Many traders use fractal theory to analyze seemingly random market movements in order to predict price changes.

Gray Rhinos are a broader category than these "gray swans." The difference between a Black Swan and a Gray Rhino is that a critical mass of people believe a Gray Rhino is sufficiently probable and are willing to say so. Once enough respected people predict an event, the question is whether enough others believe them to change the course of events.

Gray Rhinos are probable, high-impact occurrences that, to a certain extent, are predictable. Part of the challenge in facing down Gray Rhinos lies in the nature of our relationship with predictions themselves. If only a minority believe something to be highly probable, then how obvious is it, really? You might think that the number of people who accept that an event is obvious should not affect how probable it is. But predictions can be self-fulfilling or self-defeating; as a result, our beliefs in probabilities do affect how likely an event is to happen. An investor who bets on the markets going up, even though he knows that eventually they will tumble, doesn't want to be a party to crashing share prices before it's time—unless he's betting against the stocks.

Predictions are, of course, predictions: not inevitabilities. Their fickle nature gives decision-makers an easy excuse for failing to respond. They can blame the predictions for being unreliable, or they can point to other individuals who, similarly, failed to predict. Two all too familiar phrases—"Nobody saw it coming" and "This time is different"—are classic refrains in the unfolding of Gray Rhinos: predictions and hindsight based on wishful thinking. We need to question people who resort to these platitudes to defend themselves from criticism for failing to recognize and act on obvious dangers.

The Death Spiral

When we hear something but don't want to listen, we shut it out. Whether we recognize and respond to a prediction depends on how open we are to hearing it in the first place, and how much we respect the source. How others react to the prediction is important, too. As Wien certainly discovered with his Ten Surprises, we humans have a hard time disentangling ourselves from the desire for a consensus. Someone in a position of respect or authority—even simply a trusted peer, and, especially, a group of peers—can profoundly shape whether we heed a prediction or ignore it.

When I inadvertently stepped into a scientific hornet's nest at the 2014 Arctic Circle conference in Reykjavik, I both observed and experienced a clash of reactions to a prediction about the future of Arctic sea ice when an outlier provoked a heated debate by a group of scientists who disagreed with a speaker.

Viral images of disappearing Arctic summer sea ice circulating on social media in 2013 and 2014 captivated me. The numbers were one thing—2.50 million square miles of ice in 1984 reduced to 1.32 million in 2012—but the maps and visualizations (even more so than those photos of forlorn polar bears amid melting ice floes) were shocking for the way in which they showed that climate change was real.

I came to Arctic issues with a fresh eye and ear; not as an expert or as a scientist but as an observer keen to learn about a region that encapsulated one of the biggest threats to the planet, along with a fascinating set of policy questions. I sat fascinated, as did much of the audience, as Peter Wadhams, a professor of applied mathematics and theoretical physics at the University of Cambridge in England, posted a series of alarming graphs showing the steady decline of Arctic sea ice. He predicted an Arctic that was ice-free by 2020. One of the images was particularly compelling as a metaphor, if not particularly easy to read: the spiral-shaped graph that Wadhams called the Death Spiral of Arctic Ice. According to data from physicists at the Pan-Arctic Ice Ocean Modeling and Assimilation System (PIOMAS) at the University of Washington's Polar Science Center, it mapped ice levels in a circle rather than a straight line. The Death Spiral showed Arctic sea-ice volume falling from well over 30 million cubic kilometers in 1979 to just 3,673 million cubic kilometers in September 2013, the lowest on record.

I use Twitter as a way to take notes at conferences and to share the proceedings with others, so I took a picture of the graph and sent it out. As I was tweeting the Death Spiral graph, other conference participants were tweeting furiously to discredit Wadhams.

One of Wadhams's rivals from the University of Reading, also in the U.K., had this to say:

> **ArcticPredictability** @arcticpredict Nov 2
> **Peter Wadhams** views on both sea-ice & imminent methane pulse are inconsistent with IPCC AR5 consensus view #ArcticCircle2014
> **ArcticPredictability** @arcticpredict Nov 2
> What happened when **Peter Wadhams** views challenged by other climate scientists? Legal threats: http://ipccreport .wordpress.com/2014/10/08/when-climate-scientists-criticise -each-other/ . . . #ArcticCircle2014

The tweets put Professor Wadhams's remarks into context, so I re-tweeted them and searched the Web for more background. Both what I found and my own reactions to what I found made it clear that this was not just about a scientific disagreement and personal animosities but also about a much deeper dynamic around how we react to opinions that do not confirm prevailing views.

At first, I was slightly irritated and embarrassed at not having known that Wadhams had predicted in 2011 that the Arctic would be sea ice–free by around 2015, which clearly hadn't happened. (Complicating the debate further, it turns out that the definition of "sea ice–free" is not actually "free"; the National Snow & Ice Data Center considers an area to be "free" when ice coverage is less than 15 percent, not zero percent, which is what many would consider to be "free.") But then I was baffled. The conference had been thoughtfully organized and was excellent; I doubted that the organizers would have put a crackpot on the panel. After Wadhams's Arctic Circle presentation, an audience member continued the acrimonious debate. The questioner accused him of not including science or physics in his models. Professor Wadhams, visibly upset, responded indignantly that his predictions were not based on models but on data. Then he said that past complaints he had made about criticism of him were more about how Twitter was used. Curious, I did a bit of research.

As it turned out, the exchange I witnessed was actually an extension of a contretemps that had erupted weeks earlier, at a September Royal Society meeting on the Arctic. Further intrigued, I looked up a letter that Wadhams wrote to the heads of institutions of the researchers, alleging that they had actively ridiculed him. After the September meeting, Wadhams went on to complain that scholars shouldn't use Twitter to debate science. The Twitter thread and articles about the debate suggested that some of the problem is generational, in that this is a scientist who expects deference within the hierarchy of academe and is not familiar with the often cheeky nature of Twitter conversations. Mark Brandon, one of the organizers of the Royal Society conference and one of the scholars involved in the earlier dispute, then responded by publishing Wadhams's complaint with an annotation, in an attempt to refute it that took the whole confrontation into the realm of the near-comedic; it was worthy of an episode in a David Lodge novel subtly poking fun at the quirks of academic culture.

Nevertheless, the dispute brought home how complicated human emotions can be when it comes to views that lie outside the range of what is generally accepted. My own reaction was typical of all our responses to predictions and information that do not match commonly held views. Whether those outlier ideas turn out to be accurate or not, we instinctively recoil from them. Part of this is a natural defense mechanism to prevent us from being overwhelmed. We tend to search for, interpret, and prioritize information in a way that confirms our beliefs or hypotheses. Too little willingness to consider a wider range of predictions can be dangerous. Outliers are essential for challenging blind faith in forecasts.

Yet outliers are also very convenient for those who disagree with a particular prediction. That uncomfortable reality played into this particular debate, whose timing coincided with a much bigger conversation that had broader implications for the entire planet. The same day that Professor Wadhams spoke in Reykjavik, the United Nations' Intergovernmental Panel on Climate Change issued a new report, warning that climate change is irreversible. The fact that the panel represents the consensus of scientists is what makes it so powerful; it will be the basis for upcoming efforts in Paris to negotiate a new agreement for slowing the pace of greenhouse-gas emissions and the resulting changes in climate and increases in extreme weather.

Climate-change deniers stubbornly persist despite the abundance of scientific evidence. The very existence of these deniers may help to explain why scientists were so sensitive about Professor Wadhams's more aggressive predictions. The scientists wanted to remove any doubt that their findings are governed by scientific objectivity. An outlier made it harder for them to do so and easier for doubters to chip away at their case.

Monkeys Playing Darts

So many predictions are accurate on the "if" question but not on the matter of "when." When someone predicts that something will happen by a certain date and it doesn't, that person is often vilified. He doesn't receive credit if the predictions do come to pass later on. A perennial market joke is that economists have predicted ten of the last two recessions (that is, many more than have actually happened). When predictions are incomplete—for example, we know that what goes up must eventually come down, but the *when* remains up in the air—leaders are more likely to downplay the prediction and avoid doing anything to reduce the danger facing them.

The 2013 Nobel Prize in economics went to two economists who battled about whether we can predict bubbles. Eugene Fama of the University of Chicago made his name supporting the efficient-markets hypothesis; in other words, the belief that because stock prices absorb all relevant information they are unpredictable over short periods of days and weeks. The Yale economist Robert Shiller, by contrast, correctly called both the tech bubble of the 1990s and the housing bubble that began to deflate in 2007. His work supports the view that we can predict markets reasonably accurately over longer periods. The two views, though not entirely incompatible, raise the important question of how much we can trust our ability to predict.

These battling views of our power to predict shape our ability both to move past denial and to be able to respond appropriately to Gray Rhinos. If we cannot predict with a reasonable probability of success, we can hardly be expected to respond appropriately; there would be no such thing as a "probable" threat.

There are real reasons to be skeptical of predictions. It's not so easy to evaluate whether or not something is likely to happen. We know the predictions that come true. Many more do not. Sometimes it's because they were bogus in the first place. Sometimes, as we so often discover with weather forecasts, a high likelihood does not mean an absolute certainty. A 90-percent chance of rain means there's still a 10-percent chance of no rain—though many of us still subscribe, at least in jest, to the superstition that if you bring an umbrella it won't rain, and if you don't, it will. Sometimes it's because when we recognize a threat and do something about it the threat disappears. Often, it's hard to tell what's responsible for a particular outcome.

Remember the Y2K bug crisis that was supposed to bring millions of computers to their knees? We'll never know if that was just a huge overreaction to a minor danger or if it was the near-hysteria that set countless programmers to fixing a real problem. (By the way, start getting ready now; there is a Year 2038 bug lurking.) Debate still rages over what would have happened had the world not spent an estimated $400 billion preparing for it. Did the frenzied preparation for the most part fix the problem? Or did the lack of trouble in countries that did not carry out such extensive recoding indicate that it was all a waste of time and money? Some conspiracy theorists I met in Texas were profoundly disappointed that their predictions that the U.S. government and

Illuminati would use the Y2K bug to take over the country did not come to pass.

The *Wall Street Journal* famously makes the point that if you compare consensus market forecasts with results divined by a monkey playing darts the monkey generally does better. Wall Street forecasters are used to being wrong. As the blog PunditTracker pointed out, estimates for the performance of the S&P price targets are far off-target year after year: high by 9.6 percent in 2011, low by 7 percent in 2012, and more than 19 percent low in 2013. What's more, PunditTracker added, estimates tended to cluster together. Five of the six predictions it tracked fell within 100 points of each other within a range that did not include the actual price in a single case.

Look at the consensus of financial analysts' projections on stock-market performance each year and it's hard not to conclude that financial-market participants are eager to believe pie-in-the-sky stories of unprecedented prosperity and are too deeply skeptical of prognosticators of doom. That's true for many of the rest of us as well; we almost expect those who predict anything bad to be wrong. We're often right, yet when we're wrong it can be catastrophic. Meanwhile, Chicken Little gets hit by an acorn and runs down the road screaming that the sky is falling, becoming the laughingstock of a beloved childhood fable. Moral of the story: Don't assume that everything bad that happens is a harbinger of disaster. After all, even a broken clock is bound to show the correct time twice a day, isn't it? It's as if we all lived in Lake Wobegon, the fictional Minnesota boyhood home of radio host Garrison Keillor, where "all the women are strong, all the men are good looking, and all the children are above average." We know it's too good to be true, but we can't help buying in.

The neuroscientist Tali Sharot argues that humans are hardwired to see the world through rose-colored glasses. We are inclined to overestimate the likelihood of positive events and to discount the likelihood of negative events. In other words, we consistently demonstrate "optimism bias," a term coined by the psychologist Neil Weinstein. "Data shows that most people overestimate their prospects for professional achievement;

expect their children to be extraordinarily gifted; miscalculate their likely life span (sometimes by twenty years or more); expect to be healthier than the average person and more successful than their peers; hugely underestimate their likelihood of divorce, cancer, unemployment; and are confident overall that their future lives will be better than those their parents put up with," Sharot wrote in her fantastic book *The Optimism Bias*.

This impulse is so deeply embedded that it affects how well we can learn to recognize and adjust for our optimism bias. In a study that Sharot conducted at Israel's Weizmann Institute, volunteers were asked to estimate the probability of encountering various events (cancer, ulcers, being in a car accident). Later, they were told the real probabilities and then asked again how probable they thought the events would be. Showing just how deeply the optimism bias was embedded, they adjusted their expectations when information that the chances of a certain event's happening was better than they hoped but ignored information that wasn't in their favor.

While rose-colored glasses are not so helpful in processing information, especially recognizing dangers in time to do something to prevent them, Sharot believes that optimism does serve an important biological purpose. "Optimism may be so essential to our survival that it is hardwired into our most complex organ, the brain," she contends.

Optimism bias compromises our ability to judge which predictions are most likely to become a reality. That is part of the reason it's so hard to see the obvious. Our inherent optimism is a real obstacle to recognizing and acting to get out of the way of danger even when we have the information that should alert us. Sharot has recognized that underestimating health risks (for example) makes us less likely to seek preventive care and more likely to take risks.

Yet she makes a compelling case for the theory that our rose-colored glasses can come in handy: "Underestimating the probability of future adverse events reduces our level of stress and anxiety, which is beneficial to our health." She also noted that optimism can be a self-fulfilling prophecy, as long as it's embraced in moderation. A Duke University study she cited found that moderate optimists tended to work harder, save more, and smoke less than other participants in the study; the extreme optimists were at the opposite end.

As we'll see in later chapters, optimism can play a crucial role in re-framing our responses to Gray Rhinos by turning threats into opportuni-ties. And, if we're going to have a fighting chance of avoiding a trampling, we've got to believe that the odds of success are high enough to warrant making the effort.

Modern-Day Oracles

You might say that we are opportunistically optimistic in our complicated relationship with predictions. While we embrace predictions when we like them and disparage them when events take an unexpected turn, hu-mans pursue the holy grail of better predictions with the doggedness that only optimists can summon.

And, in fact, we are getting better at predicting some things. Chang-ing technologies and evolving systems are improving our ability to better understand the present and sometimes to divine the future through crowdsourcing, data aggregation, mapping, and prediction markets.

Big Data is the Next Big Thing. Google, Microsoft, Facebook, and other technology companies are working on ways to use information to predict consumer behavior and bigger trends. Tools like the Eurasia Group Global Political Risk Index and the Political Stability Task Force's recently created index are pinpointing global hotspots that are on the verge of eruption. Where data is unreliable—China's GDP growth, for example—analysts turn to proxies like electricity usage, which are more trustworthy. In other cases, like GDP itself, which some critics feel is too blunt a measure, policymakers are looking for alternative indicators of economic health.

Social media is creating new warning signals—some of them hit or miss, but others with the power to get results quickly. Google Flu Trends started out with the idea that people searching online for information about the flu could flag outbreaks. Unfortunately, most people who go to the doctor for the flu do not, in fact, have it. So far, despite Google's efforts to adjust its algorithms, the project has not yet been as accurate as its creators had hoped. Not long after the site was launched, it missed the 2009 H1N1 "swine flu" outbreak. A *Science* study calculated that Google Flu was wrong for 100 out of 108 weeks, consistently overreporting flu outbreaks in the period it studied, 2011–13. Nevertheless, as we learn more about how to interpret Big Data we will get better at predicting. Though Google Flu Trends hasn't gotten it right on the flu yet, its data may still provide an indicator of the combined cold-and-flu season, or of something we haven't yet determined.

Though individual predictions are erratic, aggregating them can make the combined results far more accurate, as James Surowiecki elegantly detailed in his 2004 book *The Wisdom of Crowds*. Technology is making it easier and easier to crowdsource opinions. Social media help us pull together a wide range of independent perspectives to come up with more accurate predictions. The strength of crowdsourcing lies in bringing together information from various viewpoints.

Nate Silver has applied this principle to Major League Baseball and to presidential elections, changing the rules of the game of forecasting. He warns of the limitations of his profession and alerts us to the danger that rapidly expanding information will outpace our ability to process it. The more humble we are about predictions the better we do, Silver suggests. As he pointed out in his important book *The Signal and the Noise*, many predictions fail. "We focus on those signals that tell a story about the world as we would like it to be, not as it really is," he wrote. "We ignore the risks that are hardest to measure, even when they pose the greatest threats to our well-being."

Silver has framed the 2008 financial crisis as a catastrophic failure of judgment and prediction, citing the ratings agencies as particularly egregious culprits. Standard & Poor's, he noted, estimated that there was only one chance in 850 that the collateralized debt obligations it rated AAA would default over the next five years; the actual rate turned out to be 200 times higher. S&P claimed that "virtually no one" saw the housing crisis coming. Yet, as Silver also noted, many people did see the financial storm coming, and said so publicly and repeatedly. By 2005, newspapers were mentioning the housing bubble ten times a day, even as Google searches for the term "housing bubble" rose tenfold in the previous year. In fact, he adds, citing an internal memo, S&P had considered the possibility that housing prices would fall by 20 percent over two years but brushed off the possibility that it would affect the securities enough to trigger a downgrade.

Why didn't the experts see it? It's hard to ignore the seeming conflict of interest inherent in ratings agencies being paid by the companies they rated. That problem no doubt helped create the perfect storm of conditions that led to the 2008 financial meltdown. But the bigger problem is that we are less likely to give serious consideration to outlier views before rejecting them; more often, we simply cast them aside outright.

Unknown Knowns

Attempting to extricate himself from the controversy raging over the lack of evidence that Iraq had the weapons of mass destruction that the United States government used to justify going to war, Defense Secretary Donald Rumsfeld in 2002 famously gave reporters a contorted explanation of the difficulties of knowing for sure what was out there: "As we know, there are known knowns; there are things we know we know. We also know there are known unknowns; that is to say, we know there are some things we do not know. But there are also unknown unknowns—the ones we don't know we don't know."

His tortured delivery provided rich fodder for pundits of every political persuasion. The Plain English Association roasted Rumsfeld with its Foot in Mouth Award for the most baffling statement made by a public figure. Perhaps the public derision would have been less had anyone pointed out that the categories themselves are well known to organizational-psychology students as the Johari Window, a tool developed in 1955 to help people assess relationships. All Rumsfeld did was change the context. In fact, the categories as he laid them out have since become a useful way for leaders to think of risks.

The unknown unknowns are the province of the Black Swan. Not being able to anticipate unknown unknowns is a major problem only in the rarest of cases. The "known knowns" and the "known unknowns" come into play, as we shall see, in our ability to deal with highly obvious threats.

A fourth category extrapolated by the philosopher Slavoj Žižek could be a synonym for the first stage of a Gray Rhino threat: the unknown known, or something that we intentionally refuse to acknowledge.

In defending Rumsfeld, the linguist Geoffrey K. Pullum cited a Persian proverb:

> He who knows not, and knows not that he knows not, is a
>   fool; shun him.
> He who knows not, and knows that he knows not, can be
>   taught; teach him.
> He who knows, and knows not that he knows, is asleep;
>   wake him.
> He who knows, and knows that he knows, is a prophet;
>   follow him.

The "unknown known" is the province of the Gray Rhino: the information we may have available in our heads but that we've refused to give its due.

Heeding Oracles

It's hard to, well, *know*, the original inspiration for the Persian proverb of the four known/unknown combinations. But it certainly applies to the story of the ancient Persian king Xerxes and his ambitions to conquer Greece.

In 481 BC, Xerxes attacked Greece despite having been warned of the possibility of an outcome far different from the one he anticipated; he knew but did not know that he knew. The Greeks knew what they knew and used their knowledge to fight off a far mightier power. The outcome of that epic battle turned on both sides having the ability to predict, respond to warnings, and react appropriately. The Greek historian Herodotus's account of the battles makes much of oracles, dreams, visions, and the importance of choosing which sources and advisers to follow.

Xerxes, king of Persia, son of Darius the Great, and grandson of Persia's first emperor, Cyrus the Great, set out in the fifth century BC to conquer Greece. When he took power in 486 BC upon his father's death, he was not yet known as Xerxes the Great. He had both his own reputation and his father's legacy in mind. Six years earlier, Darius the Great had invaded Greece, only for the ragtag Greek forces to expel Persian troops in the Battle of Marathon in 490 BC. Darius died before he was able to mount a new attack.

As Xerxes planned how he would conquer lands his father had not been able to seize before his death, his cousin and brother-in-law Mardonius, commander of the army, was the most vocal of a group of advisers who fawned over his plan to expand the Persian Empire across the Mediterranean. What force could withstand his army, the largest ever amassed, as it prepared to march on the Athenian peninsula? If their memories of the upset at the Battle of Marathon had not been so stunningly short, Xerxes and his advisers might have known the answer.

Two of Xerxes' trusted advisers sounded words of caution, but he refused to listen. His uncle Artabanus raised the possibility, "Suppose . . . that they engage us at sea, defeat us, then sail to the Hellespont and dismantle the bridge. *That* is where the danger lies, my lord." Xerxes flew into a rage, but later reconsidered and thought seriously of Artabanus's caution. By Herodotus's account, however, a tall handsome man visited Xerxes in his dreams, repeatedly threatening him that if he did not go forward with the attack he would lose his position of power.

After being deposed as the king of Sparta, the Greek Demaratus had fled into self-imposed exile in Susa, where he became a close confidant of Xerxes. Demaratus warned Xerxes that the Spartans would never give in to the Persian forces, even if the other Greeks defected to Xerxes. They would stand their ground and resist, no matter what: "Their master is the law, and they're far more afraid of this than they are of you." In contrast to the way he'd treated Artabanus, Xerxes "dismissed him civilly." Yet he did not heed Demaratus's counsel, and in 483 BC sent troops to begin the attack.

Later, when a scout reported to Xerxes that the Spartans had taken up defensive positions in Laconia, he summoned Demaratus, who repeated his earlier warning that the Greeks would not be easy prey. Not surprisingly, Demaratus turned out to be right. Xerxes went back to him a third time to ask what he could to do defeat the Spartans. Demaratus told him to send a convoy to the island of Cythera, off the coast, and use it as a base for distracting the Lacedaemonians and preventing them from helping the other Greeks. Otherwise, he warned, "What will happen, in all probability, if you don't do this? There's a narrow isthmus on the Peloponnese; all the Peloponnesians will form a confederacy designed to resist you, and then this isthmus will be the place where you should expect to meet far fiercer fighting than you have met so far." For the third time, Xerxes ignored him, and listened, instead, to his brother-in-law's advice to keep the fleet intact and support the main land army.

And so preparations continued for a full-out war to secure the vision of "dominion over the whole human race" that had appeared to Xerxes in yet another dream. Herodotus reports a set of conflicting oracles predicting quite the opposite. Shortly after his forces crossed the Hellespont, "a really extraordinary thing happened: a horse gave birth to a hare. Xerxes dismissed it as insignificant, though its meaning was transparent. It meant that, although Xerxes would walk tall and proud on his way to attack Greece, he would return to his starting-point running for his life." While it appears that Herodotus applied rather liberal poetic license to this particular moment in history, it is reasonable to believe that, given the eventual outcome of the war, there were numerous signs that things might not go as planned.

The Greeks, for their part, soon recognized that the invasion they had repelled in 490 BC was merely a warning of a far more intense assault. They consulted the prophetess of the Oracle at Delphi, who confirmed their fear of a Persian onslaught but offered hope in "a wall of wood" that would "stand intact and help you and your children." The

Greeks had abandoned what now appeared to be petty conflicts among themselves and instead united against Persia. In their planning, they made frequent use of the Oracle at Delphi, conferring widely (not leaving discussions to a tiny interior circle) about what, exactly, it meant. Eventually, they decided to take the advice of the Athenian general Themistocles, who had fought at Marathon and advised them to build a fleet of two hundred ships: the "wall of wood" prescribed by the Oracle. As Demaratus had predicted, the Greeks began to ready their fleet to meet the Persian aggressors at sea. In fact, things came to pass more or less as Demaratus had warned Xerxes they would. At the Battle of Salamis in September 480, a Greek fleet roundly defeated the Persians. Xerxes returned home, leaving Mardonius to continue the campaign against the Greeks. By the following year, the Greeks had destroyed what remained of the Persian fleet, Mardonius met his death in battle, and the Persians were forced to withdraw entirely.

The Greek peoples won the war against a much larger force because they recognized a crisis swiftly, acted decisively, and made the right decisions for overcoming the immediate threat. The stakes were high; they were anything but overconfident; they pulled together diverse opinions. Their enemy saw the possibility of losing as an unimaginable Black Swan, given the size of the Persian forces compared with those of the Greeks, while the Greeks saw the Persian attack as a Gray Rhino, a highly obvious threat that was bearing down on them.

Herodotus makes much of the Greeks' ability to read oracles. But their victory lay not only in their ability to interpret fanciful signs but in their willingness to act on them. King Xerxes had the warnings he needed. He just ignored them for many of the reasons common to all of us when faced with information we do not want to hear—information that we know but refuse to embrace.

"Information was available to Xerxes from his Greek advisers that could have made his invasion of Greece much more successful than it was, but insulated by his ambitious couriers and his own assumptions, he did not take advantage of it," Carolyn Dewald wisely writes in her notes to the 1998 translation of Herodotus's classic work *The Histories*. She notes the tendency of powerful men in his accounts—Croesus and Cyrus along with Xerxes—"to ignore the limitations that the world has placed on their power, and in particular to fail to hear information that would be useful but does not fit their own notions of the scope of their personal control over events."

We saw earlier that humans are likely to overvalue positive surprises and undervalue negative surprises. That helps explain why Xerxes resisted the more realistic scenario offered by Artabanus and Demaratus. The Persians had an example that should have shaped their decision: the defeat in 490 BC. But it was a negative example, so it didn't receive the weight it should have.

Xerxes weighed two opposing sides but ultimately went with the counsel of the adviser who was most like him: his brother-in-law, who shared his outsized ambitions for their family legacy. The Persians lost because King Xerxes remained in denial about the threats to his grandiose plan and ignored numerous signs and warnings. Alas, he did not appear to have learned from his failed Greek campaign: upon his return to Persia, he commissioned many elaborate building projects, draining the treasury, overtaxing his people, and eventually meeting his death at the hands of a disloyal minister.

Emorationality

King Xerxes exhibited many of the failures that are common to all of us when we fail to acknowledge and act on obvious threats. We base our decisions on what the French neuroscientist Olivier Oullier calls "emorationality": the mix of rational and emotional motivations that drive us. Oullier points out that we are overconfident; we follow or mimic others; we avoid recognizing losses even when that would save us more losses. "As human beings, we always make calls," he writes. "These decisions are biased for most of them and, at times, not appropriate for the context in which we are evolving."

These biases shape how much credence we give to predictions, and thus how useful they can be in preventing, or at least softening the blow of, crises preceded by warning signals. Recent welcome attention from behavioral scientists has helped to bring into the light reasons that we're not better at recognizing threats early on, even when there are signals. By being aware of these biases and compensating for them, we can act more like the ancient Greeks than like their Persian adversaries.

The first and most insidious of these biases is groupthink: the tendency of insular groups to miss signals of any threats outside their normal expectations. The research psychologist Irving Janis coined the term as part of a study of group decisions and behavior in poorly managed crises. Groupthink prevents us from seeing beyond the conventional wisdom, which is shaped by irrational human dynamics and keeps us from seeing what's in front of us. Closely related to groupthink, *confirmation bias* makes people less likely to consider and embrace alternative ideas that go against conventional wisdom. The more people around us believe the same thing, the more likely we are to go along with them whether or not their beliefs are sound.

Another bias that can warp the way we perceive information and react to predictions is *priming*: that is, the way we process information depends on who gives it to us. We're more likely to overweight information from "experts," a failing that can have disastrous consequences if we simply accept recommendations without question, as Noreena Hertz has shown in her best-selling 2013 book *Eyes Wide Open*. She cited a study of a group of adults who were monitored when asked to make a decision after hearing an expert's advice. An fMRI scan of their brain activity showed that the independent decision-making lobe essentially shut down. "An expert speaks, and it's as if we stop thinking for ourselves. It's a pretty scary idea," she wrote. It's especially scary given that many experts' records aren't so good, as Hertz details: that doctors misdiagnose one out of six cases, that market indexes beat 70 percent of mutual-fund managers, and that individuals are less likely to make errors on self-prepared tax returns than when they hire tax advisers.

Backfire effects further reinforce groupthink, priming, and confirmation bias. Hearing opinions contrary to our own can backfire when it makes us dig in our heels and hold even tighter to those views. The tall, handsome man in Xerxes' dream—his own ego—embodied this backfire effect.

Availability bias is a mental shortcut that frames our decisions in keeping with the most immediate examples that come to mind, especially if it involves near-misses that give us a faulty sense of invincibility. The Persians had defeated a revolt in Egypt in 485 BC, more recently than Darius the Great's defeat by the Greeks.

All of these cognitive biases combine to complicate our relationship with predictions, and thus our ability to respond to obvious dangers. Yet we can learn, and the better we are at coming to terms with predictions, the better our chance of responding appropriately.

Good Judgment

Being aware of our biases is an important step. I learned that by participating in the Good Judgment Project, which applies crowdsourcing to predictions on international affairs. Funded by the Intelligence Advanced Research Projects Activity (IARPA), Good Judgment pulled together hundreds of forecasters who have made hundreds of thousands of predictions since its inception. It has focused on questions ranging from North Korea to the eurozone to the Middle East to the economic growth rate of China to Russia. Its attention to the process of making forecasts sheds light on how we might improve our own estimates of how accurate our predictions are, which could significantly change whether or not we decide to act on those guesses.

The four-year research project based at the University of Pennsylvania creates teams and asks them to make forecasts, with team members judging both the likelihood of an outcome and their confidence in their score. Its system calculates what's called a Brier score, which measures the accuracy of predictions, including confidence in a prediction for each forecaster and for each team. (The technical definition is the squared deviation between probability judgments and reality.) The goal is to keep your score, which ranges from 0 to 2, as low as possible. By example, someone who predicts correctly all the time would get a zero;

a dart-throwing monkey, averaging half-right and half-wrong predictions, likely would score 0.5; someone who predicted a 100-percent probability of something that did not occur would get 2. The system harshly punishes extreme overconfidence and extreme underconfidence.

People tend to be overconfident of their ability to predict, a tendency to which I discovered I was susceptible when I took an initial assessment test. Having an ironclad taskmaster to judge my predictions made a big difference in the probabilities I assigned each outcome. It was tempting to look at my teammates' predictions for each question, but I forced myself to wait until after I had made my choice so that groupthink wouldn't skew my answers. As the season progressed and world events unfolded (or failed to unfold), I could track my progress against the group. Paying close attention to my confidence level systematically made me ask questions about my sources and possible biases that might have shaped the predictions I made. As each deadline passed, determining whether or not a prediction had come to pass, I saw my scores improve.

The project directors, Barbara Mellers and Michael C. Horowitz, studied the results and concluded that three factors determined how accurate the forecasters were. First were psychological factors: "inductive reasoning, pattern detection, open-mindedness and the tendency to look for information that goes against one's favored views, especially combined with political knowledge." Second was the forecasting environment, including training in probabilistic reasoning and team discussion of rationales. Finally, not surprisingly, effort made a difference; the more time forecasters spent deliberating their predictions, the better they did.

The Good Judgment project has shown that people can learn to make better predictions by being aware of when they are most likely to be overconfident or underconfident. "If I were President Obama or John Kerry, I'd want the Penn/Berkeley predictions on my desk," David Brooks wrote of the project in his *New York Times* column. "The intelligence communities may hate it. High-status old vets have nothing to gain and much to lose by having their analysis measured against a bunch of outsiders. But this sort of work could probably help policy makers better anticipate what's around the corner. It might induce them to think more probabilistically."

As our ability to measure and predict improves, will we get better at heeding what modern-day oracles tell us? Being aware of our biases and our shortcomings allows us to correct at least some of them and get better at anticipating what might be coming at us. Yet that is only part of the problem. Sometimes we fail to head off crises because our rose-colored glasses or other biases blind us to seeing them coming.

Yet sometimes the problem isn't with the quality of the alarm systems or with our ability to predict. As we'll see shortly, sometimes our biases and decision-making systems get the better of us. And sometimes the problem is one of willful denial.

CHAPTER 2 TAKEAWAYS

- **Don't be afraid to be wrong.** Most predictions are wrong. We're particularly likely to make mistakes when we look to those around us to shape our views, which, given human nature, is far more often than not. Outlier predictions are crucial in bucking the herd and seeing things that are obvious but not recognized.
- **Curb your enthusiasm.** Humans are more likely to believe an optimistic prediction than a negative one. So if you find yourself wearing rose-colored glasses, try another filter and see if it fits better.
- **Predictions are complicated.** Our relationship with predictions can get in the way of recognizing highly probable events.
- **Seek the wisdom of crowds.** Pulling together predictions from independent sources creates a more accurate picture of reality.
- **We can learn.** Practice makes perfect; applying what we know about our biases can help us make better predictions.

3

DENIAL: WHY WE MISS
SEEING RHINOS
AND DON'T GET OUT
OF THEIR WAY

Thor Bjorgolfsson was once the 249th richest man on Earth and Iceland's first billionaire. He had made nearly $4 billion before he was forty by investing in a Russian brewery, then in industries from pharmaceuticals to telecommunications in the frontier markets of Eastern Europe, borrowing heavily for every deal. For his fortieth birthday in 2007, he hired a Boeing 767 filled with business seat flat beds and took 120 of his friends on a surprise trip to Jamaica, where 50 Cent and Bob Marley's son Ky-Mani performed. He continued investing in deal after deal, increasingly aware that he was following what he now recognizes as a siren song. "We all know that bubbles burst, but what an opportunity before that inevitably happens," he later commented.

That same year, Bjorgolfsson became the largest shareholder in Actavis, a generic pharmaceuticals company that went from $50 million in revenue in 2002 to $7.3 billion in 2008, fueled by mergers and acquisitions. In 2007, when Bjorgolfsson borrowed the money to take over the company, he recalls urging bankers to consider bringing in other partners to diversify the $4 billion in risk they were taking on, but his suggestion fell on deaf ears. They wanted the fees for themselves, and counted on being able to syndicate the loan so that it would only be on its books for a short time.

Trouble similarly lurked around his bank holdings. During the boom from 2002 through 2008, foreigners (mostly Europeans) were depositing billions of dollars in Iceland's banks, which paid a better rate than those in their home countries. Bjorgolfsson and his father were the largest shareholders in Landsbanki, Iceland's second-biggest bank, whose value increased tenfold during the boom. But nobody seemed to notice that the money in Iceland's three largest banks was eleven times the size of the country's entire economy, or that there were more Disney dollars in circulation than Icelandic krónur.

"I had criticized the Icelandic boom but when I tried to do something about it in 2006 and 2007, I was proved wrong. I looked at the figures and thought the market would crash but nothing happened," he told me years later, after he had gone bankrupt—from billionaire to bust, as he liked to put it—and back again. "I relied on information that confirmed everything would work out just fine and dismissed the facts that undermined my beliefs," he said. So even though things were getting worse, he cast aside his earlier conviction. Still, he'd never imagined that Iceland could lead to a crash on a global scale.

Nor, as an investor whose biggest successes had come from going where others feared to tread, did he imagine that he would fail to rely on what he saw as an important part of his personality, which he had thought helped to insulate him from making lemming-like mistakes. "I have always been more of a loner and a contrarian, so following the herd was not natural to me and proved to be very costly and dangerous."

In 2008, everything came crashing down. The first domino was Actavis. Deutsche Bank's grand plan to syndicate the loan fell through when financial markets seized up, just as the company itself was dealing with regulatory problems and a management shake-up: a perfect storm of sorts. As the value of Actavis plunged, its shareholders' equity evaporated, prompting Deutsche Bank to exercise its right to require shareholders to pony up more cash if they wanted to keep their stakes in the company. In a controversial move, Bjorgolfsson borrowed the money from Landsbanki, keeping Actavis afloat but increasing the bank's exposure to companies in which he was an investor and, many observers believed, weakening it at a catastrophic time.

When Landsbanki collapsed in 2008, taking Iceland's banking system and economy down with it, Bjorgolfsson became one of Iceland's most hated men. In a matter of months, his net worth went from $4 billion to his being a billion dollars in debt. He lost his stakes in many of the companies in which he'd invested. His home and vehicle were vandalized.

"There wasn't a Eureka moment when I saw how everything would play out. It was more like a puzzle; the last days before the Icelandic banks fell all the bits started to fall into place at a rapidly increasing pace until the picture was clear enough to send chills down my spine," he told me.

After the crash, it became a personal obsession to repay his debts, to rebuild, and to share what he learned in the hope that others would not make the same mistakes.

He began with a public apology that appeared on the front page of newspapers. Bjorgolfsson acknowledged his failure for the part that he had played in the market bubble that led to the collapse of the country's banking system. "I apologize to you all for complacency in the face of the red flags that were going up all around. I apologize for having not followed my instincts when I became aware of the risks. I apologize to you all."

He liquidated many of his assets. Actavis had recovered from the 2008 crisis and attracted the interest of the U.S. generic drug manufacturer Watson Pharmaceuticals, which bought it for $6 billion in October 2012. The deal put Bjorgolfsson firmly on the path toward repaying the rest of his debts, which he did in October 2014. In 2015, he landed back on the Forbes World's Billionaire's List.

His once bright-red hair and beard now tempered by salt and pepper, Bjorgolfsson has gone over and over in his head how he could have acted differently if he knew before the crisis what he knows now; if only he had not consciously ignored the warnings. "I have tried to imagine what I would have done, had I known: what could have been done, when I would or should have done it and so on. Of course, there were times when I cursed myself for getting into high-risk situations that threatened to bring it all tumbling down," he told me.

"Everyone who's been in a dangerous situation will tell you, after the fact, they should have gone out while they could. In many instances they have the freedom to leave, but they just don't believe everything will go south. People who have a lot to lose are usually people who don't give up easily. They have weathered many storms and believe they will ride this one out as well. So most of the time, people don't get out in time. It's inevitable. It's also due to inertia, just laziness and an aversion to making tough decisions.

"I should have paid more attention to what I *knew* and not what I *wanted*. The two didn't match," Bjorgolfsson said. "I had enjoyed unbelievable success, but I had the education and experience to know that the system was not sustainable. Wishful thinking is a dangerous thing." He quoted the American actress, Mary Martin: "Stop the habit of wishful thinking and start the habit of thoughtful wishes." He keeps her words in mind. "I should have known better, and I *did*, but on an almost subconscious level I wanted to believe. We all did. We were a cult and our religion was the opium that kept us happy. I'm not a part of that cult anymore. I rely on my knowledge, not wishful thinking."

Denial Is Not Just a River in Egypt

Bjorgolfsson wasn't alone in ignoring the warnings, though he did stand out for apologizing publicly. The signals leading up to 2008 were there, not just in Iceland but in the United States and across Europe, but the people with the power to do something different didn't act on them because they refused to recognize that these signals were real.

Why? The reasons range from unconscious biases to wishful thinking to miscalculations and far more sinister drivers: self-interest and perverse incentives that feed willful denial and sometimes outright deception designed to keep others from seeing the obvious and acting on it. As we saw in Chapter 2, predictions don't always come true and, given the choice, we'll choose to believe the most optimistic outcome.

Denial, a defense mechanism deeply embedded in human nature, is the first phase of a typical response to a threat. It kicks in to allow us to deal with shocks without shutting down. Denial can protect us by preventing us from becoming so overwhelmed by daunting problems that we lose the energy and motivation needed to deal with them. In some cases, denial can help us focus on fixing problems as long as we have enough time to adapt to an unpleasant new reality, adjust our behavior, and set about correcting it.

It is a blessing and a curse that humans are the only animals that can anticipate threats in advance. We have the opportunity to minimize threats if we act in time, but if we're constantly revved up in anticipation of a threat we'll exhaust ourselves. "Viewed from the perspective of the evolution of the animal kingdom, sustained psychological stress is a recent invention, mostly limited to humans and other social primates," the neuroendocrinologist Robert M. Sapolsky has written. "Sometimes we are smart enough to see things coming and, based only on anticipation, can turn on a stress-response as robust as if the event had actually occurred." That is the ideal scenario if you have the ability to anticipate and act. But if a crisis is prolonged, that anticipation takes a severe physical and emotional toll.

When a problem is seemingly too big to grasp, or the thought of marshaling the necessary resources seems impossible, or when there appear to be too many competing threats, we compensate by ignoring the issues for too long, following the lead of the Gray Rhino's avian cousin, the ostrich with its head in the sand.

Denial is supposed to be temporary, as described by Elisabeth Kübler-Ross in *On Death and Dying*, her landmark work on grief. "Denial functions as a buffer after unexpected shocking news, allows the patient to collect himself and with time, mobilize other, less radical defenses," she wrote. "Denial is usually a temporary defense and will soon be replaced by partial acceptance." Later on, she says, denial comes and goes. The end stages of denial coincide with the beginnings of anger and, importantly, hope. These last two elements are key if we extrapolate her framework to all the kinds of shocks and threats that humans face. She recommends allowing patients their denial, for very few do not move on. I wonder if hope and anger are the causes or the effects of the shift from denial to reality for dying patients and their families; in either case, they are essential motivations for leaders to move out of denial in other types of crisis or shock.

It is astonishing to see the complex strategies that humans have developed to avoid recognizing information that could reduce the costs of a likely threat—or even create an opportunity. Some of those strategies are the product of the unconscious mind; they are auto-pilot defense mechanisms like those Kübler-Ross identified. Most of us are unaware of them. When we recognize their existence, we can use some strategies to counteract their effects in order to move past denial toward finding and implementing appropriate responses. Being aware of these aspects of our nature can make us less vulnerable to missing signals or being taken in by others who have a vested interest in preventing us from recognizing obvious dangers. Failing to compensate for our biases once we are aware of their existence is a form of denial: willful ignorance.

Unforeseen, Quote-Unquote

Pick up the newspaper any day and you'll find examples of repeated warnings that have been ignored. Look at the Affordable Care Act website, which crashed within hours of being launched on October 1, 2013. Days earlier during testing, the system was still freezing up under the pressure of as few as five hundred users. Team members downplayed the problems as typical, despite the fact that there was significant evidence to suggest that holding off on the launch would have been the most prudent course.

The escape of two convicted murderers from a New York prison in June 2015 similarly took place following years of unheeded warnings. "No single lapse or mistake in security enabled the two men to break out of the Clinton Correctional Facility, long considered one of the most secure prisons in the nation. But it now appears an array of oversights, years in the making, set the stage for the prison break a little over two weeks ago and for the ensuing manhunt," The New York Times reported.

When news broke that two passengers had boarded the doomed Malaysian Airlines Flight 370 with stolen passports, Interpol officials said that only three countries regularly checked its database of more than 40 million lost and stolen passports. Yet Interpol and many diplomats had repeatedly warned member countries of the danger that fraudulent travel documents posed. Though it likely will never be known if the stolen passports were related to the plane's disappearance, the tragedy should be a warning signal to the many countries and airlines not using the database.

After the rainiest March in the history of Washington State, 7 million cubic yards of mud cut loose from a mountainside in 2014, taking down trees a hundred at a time, crossed the Stillaguamish River, and buried the town of Oso, Washington, fifty miles or so north of Seattle. It was another example of a problem denied or ignored. "DON'T tell me, please, that nobody saw one of the deadliest landslides in American history coming," the columnist Tim Egan wrote in *The New York Times* after the death toll hit twenty-five as emergency crews continued to search for ninety missing people. "Unforeseen—except for 60 years' worth of warnings, most notably a report in 1999 that outlined 'the potential for a large catastrophic failure' on the very hillside that just suffered a large catastrophic failure," Egan continued. "It is human nature, if not the American way, to look potential disaster in the face and prefer to see a bright and shining lie." Despite the warnings and despite the occurrence of major landslides in the valley roughly once a decade—the most recent one eight years earlier—people continued to build on the hill. Logging, carried out more aggressively than allowed under legal limits designed to prevent just such a catastrophe, had stripped the hill of many of the trees whose root systems held the earth in place. And the public officials charged with emergency management continued to claim that nobody saw it coming.

What part of these failures resulted from willful denial and how much was the result of human nature and of bureaucratic decisions and political obstacles? We could debate this for a long time. But the pattern is (so to speak) undeniable: those who could have done something denied either the existence or the importance of the warning signals.

The organizational theorist Ian Mitroff argues that it is essential for organizations to calibrate their signal detectors to recognize the difference between normal signals and indications of potentially dangerous conditions, and to make sure those signals reach the ears of people who have the ability to do something about them. He cites research by Judith

Clair of Boston College, who identified several typical ways in which organizations fail to detect important signals. "While many of them are perhaps obvious, they are all important nonetheless. Indeed, their obviousness may prevent us from realizing their true importance," Mitroff noted. That's what Gray Rhino thinking is all about: understanding why we fail to recognize the obvious. Clair's first point: you need to have a mechanism for detecting signals. "As obvious as this may be, it is apparently not obvious enough, since most organizations do not have signal detectors," Mitroff wrote. Even when they do have signal detectors, they do not always heed them. In one example Mitroff recounted, a power brownout started a chain reaction that disabled the systems that provided information to airport traffic control at LaGuardia and Kennedy. The brownout triggered a backup generator, which then failed but triggered a battery and sounded an alarm. But nobody heard it, because, ironically, all the operators were out at a training session for a new backup system. (This calls to mind the thought experiment "If a tree falls in a forest and no one is around to hear it, does it make a sound?") People need to know how to respond to signals effectively, which includes being aware of who has the authority to act in which ways. Finally, signal systems need to be able to connect signals from various parts of the system.

As discussed in Chapter 2, we're getting better at creating the warning signals we need. Far more complicated is honing our ability to hear them. Mitroff describes a set of defense mechanisms that make us prone to willful ignorance, playing on the warped sense of our invulnerability: disavowal (minimizing the likely impact), idealization (it can't happen to us), grandiosity (an outsized sense of our power to fend off crisis), projection (blaming a crisis on others), intellectualization (minimizing probabilities), compartmentalization (imagining limited impact). By identifying the defense mechanisms that organizations use when responding to unwelcome information, we can more easily test our reactions and more effectively counteract these tools of willful denial.

Johns Hopkins University developed a simple, hard-to-ignore system designed to sound the alarm and trigger immediate action: a five-step checklist intended to prevent hospital infections from infiltrating

central-line catheters. These infections cost $3 billion nationally and
kill as many as 60,000 patients each year. The checklist is simple: wash
hands; clean the patient's skin; wear sterile clothing and use a sterile drape;
avoid the groin; and remove the catheter as soon as possible wherever it
is located. Crucially, the checklist also requires teams to stop work if the
procedure was not followed to the letter. In initial tests, it virtually
eliminated infections. Within three months of putting it in place in more
than one hundred intensive-care units in the Michigan hospital system,
bloodstream infections fell from above the national average to zero. Three
years later, the results continued. The surgeon and writer Atul Gawande has written of the power of checklists for everything from airplane cockpits to skyscraper construction sites and operating rooms; in
these high-stakes environments, where missing or dismissing key indications can be fatal, checklists are an essential tool for flagging problems
and giving the whole team the authority to step in if it appears that
something important is not receiving the attention it deserves. When
an organization faces an impending crisis, whether the threat appears
to be moving slowly or quickly, using a similar system can make it harder
to deny the urgency of acting.

A constant stream of economic indicators drives movements in
the financial markets and, in turn, the decisions of central banks and
economic-policy decision-makers. One might think that these indicators
could provide a similar checklist to help flag problems and provoke cor-
rective decisions; indeed, automated trading programs use signals in the
prices of securities to trigger buying or selling. Yet when it comes to the
choices that bankers and policymakers face, we're far less successful at
turning alarms into action. The signals are there, but we've proved to be
less than nimble at recognizing them.

If It Had Been Lehman Sisters . . .

When seemingly obvious signals go unheeded, there are two reasons:
there is something wrong either with the signal system or with our ability to hear and respond to them.

Alan Greenspan, in his 2013 *Foreign Affairs* essay explaining why "nobody saw it coming" in 2008, suggested that the problem was that the warnings were weak. He argued that the answer is better predictive models that incorporate such aspects of human nature as risk aversion, time preference, and herd behavior. But the problem was not a matter of weak signals; it was a lack of both the willingness to see them and the will to act. This suggests that we need much more than a better signal system. We need a better way of translating signals into responses. The first step in this process is finding a way to defeat denial. Our ability to grasp the seriousness of a threat depends as much on our willingness to see it—a culture of openness—as on the quality of the signals.

The transcripts of the 2008 Federal Reserve Board debates over how to handle the slowing economy and the eventual collapse of Lehman Brothers show a perfect storm of confirmation bias, priming, and backfire effects in action as U.S. officials tried to face down the intensifying financial crisis in 2008.

In an unusual emergency meeting on January 9, 2008, prompted by a sharp increase in the unemployment rate, Ben Bernanke, the chairman of the Federal Reserve, and Janet Yellen, the vice-chair, who would later become chairman, both spoke out with pessimism, warning that a much sharper economic downturn was highly likely. Bernanke cited falling stock prices, slower manufacturing growth, increasing borrowing costs, rapidly rising unemployment, consistently slow GDP growth, and a wonky but critical indicator—the federal funds rate (the rate at which the most creditworthy banks lend to one another through the Federal Reserve overnight) being far above two-year interest rates. Arguing that the odds of a potentially very nasty recession had risen, Yellen recommended that the bank lower interest rates that day. "The severe and prolonged housing downturn and financial shock have put the economy at, if not beyond, the brink of recession," she said.

"None of the thirty CEOs to whom I talked, outside of housing, see the economy trending into negative territory," said Richard Fisher of the Dallas Fed. "Some of them see much slower growth. None of them at this juncture—the cover of *Newsweek* notwithstanding, a great contraindicator which by the way shows 'the road to recession' on the issue that is about to come out—see us going into recession."

When the Fed released the transcripts of its 2008 meetings, the news media characterized the record as showing an out-of-touch body that was in deep denial. "Fed Misread Crisis in 2008," read a *New York Times* headline.

In January 2008, the Fed did act. On January 21, in a dramatic surprise move in between its regular scheduled meetings, the Fed cut its benchmark rate by seventy-five basis points, the biggest amount in more than twenty years. On January 30, it slashed another fifty basis points. Yet through the rest of the year there were questions about the Fed's ability to affect the economy, the severity of the crisis, and the possible unintended consequences of more aggressive action.

The problem came in September, after Lehman Brothers failed, when the central bank sounded out of touch and appeared (with the benefit of 20/20 hindsight, to be sure) to be very slow to move. In September 2008, Federal Reserve officials said the word *crisis* 13 times but mentioned inflation 129 times. They were looking for inflation, so they didn't see a recession.

Eric Rosengren of the Boston Fed pointed out that the unemployment rate had risen 1.1 points in barely five months; this was a major alarm signal, along with the failure of one major investment bank, the forced merger of another, the largest thrift and insurer teetering, and the collapse of the federal housing-finance institutions Freddie Mac and Fannie Mae. "The degree of financial distress has risen markedly," he warned. Rosengren was one of eleven Reserve Bank presidents among whom four voting spots rotated a year at a time, though all of them attend meetings, and thus did not have a vote at that meeting. As a result, he could not directly affect the outcome. Ignoring Rosengren's concern, the twelve Fed governors voted unanimously against cutting rates that September, even though clear alarm signals were there.

Reality did not set in firmly until October. "The downward trajectory of economic data has been hair-raising," Yellen said at the October 28–29 meeting. "It is becoming abundantly clear that we are in the midst

of a serious global meltdown." Notably, Yellen was among the most vocal in support of stronger action by the Fed to prevent a recession.

The chaos triggered by Lehman's collapse had finally shocked the Fed
away from gradualism and kicked it into an aggressive stance. Fed chairman Ben Bernanke's scholarship on the Great Depression put the crisis
at hand into the context that the U.S. central bank needed to do everything in its power to stabilize the markets. By the end of the year, the
Fed would cut rates to zero, a total of eight reductions since January.
Nevertheless, doubts remained within the Fed about the nature of the
situation. As 2008 drew to a close, Richmond Fed president Jeffrey Lacker
was still characterizing the situation as a "moderate-sized recession."

Why had the Fed been so slow to act? And why were some of its
members so reluctant to recognize the enormity of what had happened?
Some of the explanation lies in the governors' familiarity with the most
recent problems, which had stemmed from loose monetary policy. Former chairman Alan Greenspan had responded to financial turmoil in the
1990s by keeping interest rates extremely low. For quite a while, he had
practically been revered for shepherding a period of prosperity, especially
for anyone with money invested in the markets. Yet by the time the
2007–08 crisis hit, he was being blamed for having created the financial
asset bubbles that led to the troubles in the subprime and other markets.
Many of the governors were still looking at the problem in the rearview
mirror, rather than in the mirror that was in front of them. That made
it harder to take in new information and delayed their response to a problem that was much bigger than the one they were still battling in their
minds.

The More Things Happen . . .

Our ability to recognize warning signals and respond effectively in the
present depends, in part, on our history with past dangers.

The policy analysts and scholars Carolyn Kousky, John Pratt, and
Richard Zeckhauser have argued that people are not as rational as we
might like to believe. In their analysis, people who experience a "virgin

risk," such as a car crashing into their living room, are likely to overestimate the possibility that it will happen again. The more emotionally vivid a scenario is, the more inclined you are to overpredict the likelihood of its happening. As a corollary, people who are dealt an "experienced risk"—that is, one they've thought about or seen before, like a fender bender or a computer crash—are likely to underestimate the likelihood that it will repeat.

Though the odds are far greater that you will die in a car accident than in a plane crash, the dramatic coverage of airplane disasters has left an emotional impression that makes many people terrified of flying. That's how the "shoe bomber" attempted airplane bombing combined with the emotional impacts of terrorism and fear of flying to create a widely hated get tolerated requirement to take off our shoes at the airport.

The virgin-risk phenomenon also explains why the Black Swan crisis concept received so much attention; it piques the curiosity and the imagination. We spend too much time on the emotionally powerful risks that are least likely to happen to us, and are thus blinded to the highly probable dangers to which we ought to be responding. We look for what we want to see, so we often miss seeing the important things. If we're only looking for Black Swans, we won't see a Gray Rhino.

Financial crises are an example of experienced risks, as the economic historians Carmen Reinhart and Kenneth Rogoff have so clearly demonstrated: no matter how many crises happen, there's always a chorus of people saying that "this time is different"—a classic example of denial. Long periods without a particular type of crisis—like the financial euphoria of the 1920s, late 1990s, and early 2000s—should be warning signals. The banking and debt crises in Mexico, Russia, and Asia in the 1990s may, paradoxically, have made developed countries less aware that they could encounter such problems. Swans can't be black, right? No more or less so than debt crises can strike wealthy countries.

Seeing a Rhino for What It Is

What could the Federal Reserve Board have done differently in 2008? Its failure to act was hardly malicious, and it has since been praised for providing essential liquidity when the markets needed it. (To be sure, it has attracted its fair share of criticism, as well, for the unintended side effects of its policies of low interest rates and aggressive bond buying, known as "quantitative easing.") The question is why it didn't recognize important evidence sooner, especially when some members of the Fed raised their concerns. One area of clear weakness lies in its decision-making structure: a group of people who are very similar to one another.

The board at Lehman Brothers was made up of nine men and a single woman. The Fed officials making decisions were mostly men. The two members of the group who were clearest about the risk facing the economy were Chairman Ben Bernanke (an academic, not a career banker), and a woman, the San Francisco Fed chief Janet Yellen. Christine Lagarde, France's finance minister at the time, famously quipped, "If Lehman Brothers had been a bit more Lehman Sisters we would not have had the degree of tragedy that we had as a result of what happened."

In Iceland, in 2007, a year before the collapse, two women, Halla Tomasdottir and Kristin Petursdottir, formed their own financial firm, Audur Capital. It was Iceland's only financial firm to weather the financial crisis without direct losses to its clients. That may have been because it was still small and hadn't amassed the huge foreign deposits that the other banks had; and also because its services—wealth management, private equity, and corporate advisory services—were neither highly capital-intensive nor speculative. Nevertheless, the firm's founders have an important perspective on the voracious risk appetites that led to the crisis. Tomasdottir, who likes to repeat Lagarde's "Lehman Sisters" witticism, doesn't believe it was a coincidence that a woman-owned firm, founded on different principles, distinguished itself from Iceland's troubled banks. She and Petursdottir were "overwhelmed by testosterone," as she put it. That was her shorthand for highly risky behavior and short-term investment objectives. She has cited the firm's founding values—risk awareness, straight talk, emotional capital, profit with principles, and independence—as antidotes to the mind-set and activities that led to the crisis. When I heard her speak at a conference for women corporate board directors in New York, she placed a large part of the blame for the disaster that befell Iceland on the lack of diversity among decision-makers.

And, in fact, the more diverse a corporate board is, the better the company performs. A 2007 report from the not-for-profit organization Catalyst found that companies with the highest percentage of women board directors outperformed those with the least by 53 percent. A 2013 Thomson Reuters study found that companies with no women on their boards performed worse than gender-diverse boards. Yet only 17 percent of the companies analyzed report having a board consisting of 20 percent or more women.

Women are often the disruptive voices, willing to say what others won't say: Sheila Bair, the chairman of the Federal Deposit Insurance Corporation, who challenged the concept of "too big to fail"; Meg Whitman, who sounded the alarm on municipal bonds; Erin Brockovitch, who refused to ignore groundwater contamination; Cynthia Cooper, who uncovered a $3.8 billion fraud at WorldCom; Elizabeth Warren on consumer rights. And let's not forget Cassandra and Joan of Arc. Many of the journalists who predicted elements of the 2008 financial crisis were women: Gretchen Morgenson and Diana Henriques of the *New York Times*, Gillian Tett of the *Financial Times*, and *Fortune's* Bethany McLean.

But women are hardly the only source of diverse ideas. Had the members of Lehman Brothers or the Federal Reserve looked harder for diverse opinions—whether from gender, ethnic or age diversity, or from wider sets of disciplines—they might have seen the obvious sooner. This is true for any organization. One of the first questions leadership should ask is whether the organization has set up a structure that brings in a mix of perspectives and gives room to opinions that challenge the status quo. Does it have the combination of expertise it requires? Is it willing to consider the possibility that it may be unpleasantly surprised? Is it willing to invest an ounce of prevention to save a pound of cure?

Down with Groupthink

Groupthink and conformity are pervasive. In a series of experiments conducted in the 1950s, Solomon Asch found that significant percentages of subjects in groups went along with majority opinions even when the majority was visibly wrong. (Paradoxically, given the high-profile women who have sounded alarms on financial crises and fraud, the studies showed that women conform more than men do.) Other researchers, notably Stanley Milgram, took a similar approach in other countries, where they found some differences across national borders (Norwegians conform more than the French, for example; and Asians more than Americans). Nevertheless, Milgram remained skeptical about exactly what role culture played in these differences. "One may ask whether or not national borders really provide legitimate boundaries for the study of behavioral differences," he wrote. "My feeling is that boundaries are useful only to the extent to which they coincide with cultural, environmental, or biological divisions. In many cases boundaries are themselves a historical recognition of common cultural practice."

I asked Frank Brown of General Atlantic, a former dean of the international business school INSEAD, what role culture played in how well companies in different countries recognized and responded to obvious threats. Were different countries or regions more or less likely to deny the existence of threats because cultural barriers stood in the way? His answer was intriguing: the main issue is not culture itself but how culture affects the mix of people in the room when decisions are made. "Diverse groups make better decisions and have more fun," he said. A highly homogeneous, hierarchical society is unlikely to be able to handle challenges or opportunities as well as others. "Surround yourself with people who are from different backgrounds, who look, think, talk, and act differently," he said. "If you put six people in a room, if they are all from different countries, you have a better than even chance of coming up with a better answer than if they are all they same."

Steve Day, the CEO of Wowprime, one of Taiwan's biggest restaurant chains, with brands that include Wang Steak, has earned a reputation for innovation and for thinking outside the box—not necessarily what you might think of from a Taiwanese service-sector firm. Founded in 1993, the firm's market capitalization had risen above $1 billion in 2013 and got Day named to *Forbes* magazine's list of the top twenty Taiwanese businessmen to watch. Day has credited his success in part to Confucianism's emphasis on humanity and to Taoism's principle of non-action by rulers, which he has incorporated into collective management and "people-oriented management" styles. He earned a reputation for being an atypical CEO not just because he once impersonated Lady Gaga at a company year-end party but because of an inclusive management style that actively solicits diverse voices.

The company's management team of twenty-five brand and division heads solicits ideas monthly from more than two hundred outlets, relying on diverse ideas to help it identify both opportunities and threats. Those ideas include everything from not using disposable chopsticks, a major contributor to deforestation in Asia, to including "no superstition" and "no use of endangered species" among its mandates. Wowprime's decision-making process is designed to encourage new ideas and discourage groupthink. It invites experts from diverse fields, from academia to medicine to technology and fashion, to present. It allows management team members to veto proposals anonymously, a practice it has not been afraid to observe. Only rarely does he resort to his privilege of dictating 5 percent of policies, which allows him to overturn vetoes sparingly.

The best business leaders are well aware of groupthink and its kin: confirmation bias, priming, and backfire effects. They recognize and confront the cognitive biases that prevent us from acknowledging problems, and they respond by bringing fresh voices to the decision-making process.

"Countless studies and experiments have found that when group members are actively encouraged to openly express divergent opinions, they not only share more information, but consider it more systematically and in a more balanced and unbiased way," Noreena Hertz has written. She cites an executive who sees one of his primary roles as being "Challenger in Chief." What a powerful concept for shaking off the biases inherent in group decision-making. She asks, "Who, at work or at home, can serve as Challenger in Chief for you?"

While stronger company performance is correlated with more diverse boards, there is a big chicken-versus-egg question. "It's not like companies all of a sudden are enlightened and add women to their board and then performance goes up," Irene Natividad, the president of Corporate Women Directors International, told me. Often, the reverse is the case: companies recognize their market and then add women to the board because they know they need diverse gender perspectives, and thus create a virtuous cycle.

As Japanese companies have opened their boards to independent directors, the percentage of women on corporate boards in Japan has risen to 3.1 percent from 1.4 percent in 2009, more than doubling in five years, but from a very low base. In 2014, Prime Minister Shinzō Abe pledged to create 250,000 day-care openings, offer companies tax incentives to increase the number of women in executive and board positions, and extend family leave. There's still a long way to go, but it's a start.

Having the right systems in place is crucial to recognizing the obvious. Having diverse perspectives around the table can counteract confirmation bias. Bringing into the room a range of sensitivities to different risks can help overcome availability bias. These are especially important when we're not just confronting our natural failure to see what we don't want to see. In some cases, we have to fight efforts to deliberately keep us from seeing what's important.

Manufactured Denial

The line between the simple flaws of human nature and willful denial can be thin. Look at the case of the Fukushima nuclear disaster in Japan, a classic example of ignoring the obvious. Not far away from Fukushima Daiichi (Big One), the plant that melted down because its backup generator was flooded, was another nuclear plant. Daiini (Big Two) was only eleven kilometers to the south. Daiichi had been built ten meters above sea level; Daiini was only three meters higher. Daiini also was damaged by the tsunami, but there was one key difference: unlike Daii-chi, Daiini's backup power was located high enough that the waters did not damage it. This was not a case of a weak signal: Daiichi and Daiini were very similar and had access to the same information. Yet Daiini's operators took a preventive measure that Daiichi's did not.

William Saito, who participated in the Japanese government's com-mission that investigated the incident, calls this a willful failure to per-ceive. As with the failure of the Fed to recognize and react soon enough to the subprime financial crisis, we could argue ad infinitum about the mixture of reasons for this. In both cases, key lessons include the fact that those with the power to change things would have benefited from different decision-making structures and also from making crisis preven-tion a higher priority. Yet there are cases of willful denial that go far beyond the biases and blind spots inherent in groupthink and poor orga-nizational design.

These cases involve people who take advantage of the fact that denial is a fundamental part of human nature. They work actively to prevent others from recognizing problems; that is, they manufacture denial.

The Stanford professor Robert N. Proctor and the linguist Iain Boal coined a term—"agnotology"—to describe the study of the cultural pro-duction of ignorance. "Ignorance has many friends and enemies, and figures big in everything from trade association propaganda to military operations to slogans chanted at children," Proctor wrote. He detailed the efforts of the tobacco industry to persuade people to doubt the haz-ards of smoking, from 1950s campaigns arguing that the dangers of smok-ing had not yet been proved to later efforts that suggested other causes for lung cancer. The thrust of his argument was that correlation does not imply causation. For a time, it worked: in 1966 not even half of those questioned in a Harris poll thought that smoking was a "major" cause of lung cancer.

From the tobacco industry to acid rain, asbestos, and climate change, those with interests in preserving the status quo have preyed on our susceptibility to denial. They co-opt experts and authority figures, who often have their own conflicted interests, to encourage others to doubt inconvenient truths.

Naomi Oreskes and Erik Conway have detailed many of these campaigns in their book *Merchants of Doubt*, which later became a documentary film. "The industry had realized that you could create the impression of controversy simply by asking questions, even if you actually knew the answers and they didn't help your case," they wrote. "And so the industry began to transmogrify emerging scientific consensus into raging scientific 'debate.'"

By the 1950s, Oreskes and Conway reported, the tobacco industry knew the dangers of smoking. In 1964, the surgeon general's report distilled the results of more than seven thousand scientific studies to announce that lung cancer had reached epidemic rates and that the cause was clearly cigarettes. Oreskes and Conway pointed out that the surgeon general was challenging the vested interests of the federal government, which subsidized tobacco farming and reaped significant tax revenues from it. "To argue that tobacco killed people was to suggest that our own government both sanctioned and profited from the sale of a deadly product," they noted. It took decades, a lawsuit leading to a more than $200 billion settlement with the four largest tobacco companies to reimburse states for tobacco-related health-care costs, countless more deaths, and dedicated efforts by many antismoking activists to bring smoking rates down to a third of their earlier levels.

Similarly, on climate change Oreskes and Conway paint a grim picture, from the early days of emerging scientific evidence in the 1960s through the repeated recent affirmations by the Intergovernmental Panel on Climate Change that human activities are affecting the world's climate. In one example, they describe the deliberations of the Climate Research Board of the National Academy of Sciences leading up to the National Academy letter report submitted in 1980, which focused on uncertainties rather than on the accumulated body of research. "Rather than confront their own caveat that changes might happen much sooner than their model predicted—and thus be much more costly than prevention—the economists assumed that serious changes were so far off as to be essentially discountable," they wrote. Here is a classic example of the collision of the optimism bias with our tendency to discount the future, pushing even scientists to downplay more dire possibilities.

If the early days of climate-change debate revealed the influence of cognitive biases that lead us to deny the obvious, as time progressed a conscious campaign emerged to downplay the evidence. Major fossil-fuel companies spent hundreds of millions of dollars, some of it masked through third-party channels, to fund climate-change denial.

Attitudes toward climate change vary widely throughout the world. A 2013 Pew Research survey showed that only four out of ten Americans believed that climate change was a major threat to them, the lowest out of thirty-nine countries surveyed, and significantly lower than the global average of 54 percent. While the study does not correlate opinions with spending to affect public opinion one way or the other, it makes clear that there are widely varying relationships between scientific consensus and malleable public opinion.

Another technique for manufacturing denial is to manipulate data. Investors have long been skeptical of China's national economic indicators, which they see as broad approximations. Greece's financial problems worsened when the world learned, in 2010, that it had been masking its true debt load, with the help of Goldman Sachs.

When I wrote about Latin American economies in the early 1990s, it was hard to get economic data from many countries. As governments raised more and more money on international bond markets, however, they learned that better data meant better market access. In most places, there's far more and far better data than there was two decades ago. Yet there are exceptions, and the reasons are obvious. In recent years, Argentina has gone backward. Seeking to camouflage the economic troubles that followed its 2001 default, the government began applying a heavy hand to manipulating economic data and, alarmingly, threatening to fine or prosecute independent economists for publishing their own statistics. It got so bad that in February 2012 *The Economist* announced that it would no longer include data from Argentina's once respected official statistics office in its tables of indicators. The government recognized that data can be a powerful tool for change—in this case, change that would be unlikely to benefit the Argentine government.

Part of having the right systems for flashing alarms when something goes wrong is setting up the right incentives for people to take notice. We now know how tangled financial incentives and conflicts of interest kept auditors from taking as hard a look as they should have at Enron and WorldCom.

"Under current law, auditing firms have financial incentives to avoid being fired and to be rehired by their clients," the Harvard University professor Max Bazerman wrote in his 2014 book, *The Power of Noticing: What the Best Leaders See*. Apart from auditors losing business if they do not approve their clients' books, they profit from selling other consulting services that add to the conflicts of interest; in addition, many auditors and client firms have the same revolving-door dynamic as Washington politicians and lobbyists. "All of these conditions that act against auditor independence were in place between Arthur Andersen and Enron. Again, consider this simple fact: Arthur Andersen was able to successfully maintain Enron as a client from 1986, soon after the energy company was founded, until the death of both organizations," Bazerman added.

In studies designed to test the impact of auditor conflicts of interest, Bazerman and his colleagues found that both role-playing participants in an analysis of a fictional company *and* actual auditors and found sobering evidence: "Simply being in a purely hypothetical relationship with a client distorted the judgment of those playing the role of auditor." Bazerman blames the accounting industry's long denial of the problems stemming from conflicts of interest on its reluctance to assume the inevitable costs of change. Yet in the case of Enron, a classic example of perverse incentives combined with a short-term mind-set, these conflicts of interest together destroyed the long-term interests of both the auditor and the audited. The same could be said of the 2008 financial crisis. These real-world examples—instances of what Bazerman has called "predictable surprises"—perhaps played a part in a growing recognition of the importance of these insights. "Only recently did accounting scholars become open to the obviousness of our work," Bazerman wrote.

Bazerman makes a set of sensible recommendations: hire auditors under fixed contracts that allow neither firing during the term nor re-hiring afterward; prohibit personnel from moving to the new firm when a client changes auditors and from moving to the client's employ; and pro-hibit auditors from providing any non-audit services.

Other researchers have similarly uncovered ways in which systems get in the way of recognizing the obvious and promoting denial. A team of investigators, including Esther Duflo and Michael Greenstone of the Massachusetts Institute of Technology and Rohini Pande and Nicholas Ryan of Harvard University, tested new pollution auditing rules in the state of Gujarat, India. The control group stayed within the traditional system under which the plants being audited chose and paid the audi-tors. For the test group, by contrast, auditors received payment from a third-party pool of funds; some of the auditors had their findings re-examined; and auditors received bonuses for accurate reports. The dif-ferences were impressive. Auditors using the new system were 80 percent less likely to make false reports that readings were in compliance. Their pollution readings were 50 to 70 percent higher than in the old system.

When those who are supposed to be catching problems have con-flicted motives, it's much easier to deny that problems exist. If auditors have certified that there's no problem, it's that much easier to avoid dig-ging deep enough to discover one.

The lesson? If you're not sure how seriously to take a piece of infor-mation, consider the source.

From Denial to Acceptance

How do we move from denial to acceptance? Kübler-Ross, through her conversations with the dying and their families, came to believe that this transition was best managed by allowing it to happen naturally, rather than pushing it.

"Defeat may serve as well as victory to shake the soul and let the glory out," the American poet Edwin Markham has written. Indeed, shock can lead to insights and motivate us to action, as it did for Al Gore and his climate change activism. The former vice president often tells the story of how nearly losing his six year old son after a car accident woke him up to the urgency of acting to protect what's most important. By forcing him to imagine something unimaginable—the possible death of his child—the rawness of the experience opened his eyes to the possibility of losing other things that were dear to him. It allowed him to recognize the beauty and majesty of the earth, and experience what previously he could not: the fear that we could lose the planet where we live. "It was because of my son's accident and the way it interrupted the flow of my days and hours that I began to rethink everything, especially what my priorities had been," he wrote in his 2006 book, *An Inconvenient Truth*. "When you've seen your reflection in the empty stare of a boy waiting for a second breath of life, you realize that we weren't put here on earth to look out for our needs alone; we're part of something much larger than ourselves," Gore said of the experience during his speech at the 1992 Democratic National Convention. His awakening to the urgency of combating climate change led him to the quest to raise awareness and earned him a Nobel Peace Prize.

What is the difference between the leaders who successfully face down a Rhino, the ones who get trampled and fall, and those who get trampled but pick themselves up again? It's the speed with which they recognize and act on the threat, their ability to look ahead, and their con-viction to distinguish themselves from others.

People who think about how to solve problems tend to be wonkish, detail-oriented, and, frankly, are often considered boring when they try to convince others. They want to see the facts and figures and sort through things rationally. Policy is the province of logic, not emotion. But over-coming denial, whether it is willful or unintentional, is about emotion. It's about breaking through our tendency to hold on too hard to what we know or wish and to keep wearing those rose-colored glasses.

Once we are aware of the reasons we fail to recognize Gray Rhinos, we can start to get past our denial and move toward action. We need to break down our cognitive biases, starting with groupthink. We're making progress in improving our signal mechanisms, and we can do even better.

The companies, governments, and organizations that survive are the ones that are willing to listen to voices that are not the usual suspects saying what everyone wants to hear. By being aware of our blind spots, questioning our thinking, and building systems to sound alarms that are harder to ignore and may even set into motion responses that our denial reflex might keep us from making, we can see Gray Rhinos in time, prioritize them, and act not only to avoid getting trampled but, often, in such a way that we end up better off than we were in the first place.

Harvard's behavioral economists have generated insights that have informed authors from Malcolm Gladwell to Daniel Kahneman to Ori and Rom Brafman, even as they have influenced government and business efforts to employ social psychology and behavioral economics to improve policy. Listening to Max Bazerman, Mahzarin Banaji, Iris Bohnet, Dutch Leonard, and their colleagues in a Harvard Kennedy School course on global leadership and public policy helped me frame my thinking about what makes the difference between leaders who recognize and act on highly obvious threats and those who don't.

In one session, Banaji had our class watch a video of people playing dodge ball and count the number of white balls and black balls. When the video was over, we were asked if we'd noticed anything unusual about it. Only a couple of classmates had noticed a woman with an umbrella walk across the screen. When we watched a replay, we all saw the woman without any problem. This was, of course, a variation of the famous "Invisible Gorilla" experiment devised by Christopher Chabris and Daniel Simons, which has become a classic study taught widely in psychology and business classes around the world.

In most cases, as Chabris and Simons rightly point out, not spotting the unexpected carries little or no consequences. But when the Federal Reserve, looking for inflation, failed to see the coming meltdown, companies collapsed, the economy plunged, and people lost their jobs. When politicians cynically whip up fury over immigrants, or social issues on which reasonable people can disagree, or over geopolitical foes, you should ask: What is it that they don't want you to see instead?

For Gray Rhinos, where we know what to look for but deny its existence, our failure to see can be catastrophic. It's the opposite of the Elephant Game. If someone tells you not to think of the word *elephant,* you'll have a hard time: that pesky word will keep popping up in your head. With important information that you know you should pay attention to but don't want to hear, it's far too easy to push the matter out of your head.

CHAPTER 3 TAKEAWAYS:

- **Look in new places for warning signals.** New technologies and data streams give us new abilities to predict and to identify patterns.

- **Question conventional wisdom.** Recognize how susceptible we all are to groupthink and respond by systematically challenging yourself to listen to alternative explanations. By being aware of cognitive biases and collective blind spots, and questioning whether we are thinking clearly, we can see Gray Rhinos in time, prioritize them, and avoid getting trampled.

- **Bust up Groupthink.** Nurture a culture that is open to recognizing warning signals. Make sure that decision-makers include diverse voices who are less likely to accept the conventional wisdom and to be complacent in the face of threats. Within a government, business, or organization, make sure there are systems in place to prompt people to recognize, respond to, and, ultimately, act on danger signals.

- **Beware of manufactured denial.** Sometimes our own nature unintentionally deceives us. At other times, people looking out for their own interests intentionally do so. Know the difference.

4

MUDDLING: WHY WE DON'T ACT EVEN WHEN WE SEE THE RHINO

"Our lives are not only defined by what happens, but by how we act in the face of it, not only by what life brings us, but by what we bring to life. Selfless actions and compassion create enduring community out of tragic events." These words are etched in pale letters against a backdrop of polished black granite at the I-35W Bridge Remembrance Garden in Minneapolis. In front of the granite wall, thirteen steel I beams stand sentinel, one for each of the people who died when the 35W bridge dropped sixty-four feet into the Mississippi River during rush hour at 6:05 PM on August 1, 2007. The beams are adorned with poems and memories, many referring to roads and highways: a boy with Down syndrome and his doting mother, a Mexican immigrant, a woman rushing to teach a dance class at her Greek Orthodox church, an American Indian woman from the Thunder clan of the Winnebago tribe, a father of four, a fan of Minnesota's Vikings and Twins, a refugee from the Khmer Rouge. The memorial is dedicated to "those who were lost, those who survived, and those who responded."

In the summer a solid sheet of water cascades over the inscription on the memorial and over the names of the 171 survivors engraved on the dark granite blocks that make up the wall. I was there on a winter day just as Minneapolis was beginning to thaw out from its worst winter in fifty years. Three streams of water dripped from a melting icicle on the top of the monument—an impromptu fountain—down to the ground, where unswept autumn leaves still skittered about. The day I visited the memorial, the Mississippi River behind and below the monument was iced over, except for a small patch of running water near the foot of the bridge. Plumes drifted out of the top of four smokestacks into a crisp blue sky over a stately redbrick building across the river.

To the left are two bridges, including an old stone railroad bridge for carrying grains from the mills. Off to the right, behind a stand of trees, you can see the new bridge erected where the old one collapsed. The old bridge was the casualty of warnings gone unheeded and of a decision to put off needed repairs for years: a decision that might not have ended in tragedy had it not been for an undetected design flaw in the gusset plates that connected the steel girders. Even if the design flaw had not existed, however, the timing of plans to replace the bridge was stunningly slow. The I-35 bridge had received a "structurally deficient" rating from the U.S. Department of Transportation in each inspection since 1990. In 2006, inspectors noted cracking and fatigue: a disaster waiting to happen for the people riding in the 140,000 vehicles that crossed the bridge each day. Yet it was still not a candidate for replacement until 2020. The new bridge went up astoundingly quickly, as if to make up for the lack of response that might have prevented the tragedy. It opened on September 18, 2008, just over a year after the collapse. The city lights up the new bridge at night in different colors depending on the occasion, much like the Empire State Building.

I visited the bridge memorial to reflect on the cost of choosing not to act even when the people with the power to do something had gotten past their initial denial that a problem existed. They recognized it, yet decided to do nothing. The decisions that led to the bridge's failure were typical of the second phase of a Gray Rhino: muddling, when we are aware of the nature of a problem yet cannot or will not face it.

What intrigued me was the memorial's location, just down the road from the incongruously modern Mill City Museum, which was built amid the ruins of what was once the world's largest mill until it was closed in 1965 and nearly destroyed by fire in 1991. It was fitting that the bridge memorial was in the city's old mill district, whose very architecture and history spoke to an industry that similarly had faced a threat and had all but disappeared in the city but survived in a new form elsewhere. The mills, powered by water from Saint Anthony Falls, had helped make Minneapolis into a thriving city. The Washburn Mill itself had been the site of a major tragedy of its day. On May 2, 1878, airborne flour dust exploded, killing eighteen workers and destroying the Washburn A Mill and four other factories, in what came to be known as the Great Mill Disaster. As so often happens after a disaster, this one catalyzed major reforms to improve safety.

When fuel-powered mills became the industry standard after World War I, the industry as Minneapolis knew it all but disappeared. Milling moved to other cities, Minnesota turned to higher-value food processing, and the mill district all but shut down. The bridge collapse and the milling-industry decline were part of a bigger story not just of one city but of all cities that face stark choices in dealing with major changes. The decline of the mills, and their replacement by other industries, represented creative destruction: the process by which new ideas and technologies destroy older ones, and by doing so create wealth. Creative destruction succeeds when we make wise decisions about what to maintain and reinforce, what to repair, and what to let go so that something better can take its place. When a better option is in sight, allowing collapse to happen is as much a view of the future as it is a view of the past.

Decisions about infrastructure sometimes involve creative destruction. The abandoned streetcar lines near my hotel and the traffic congestion on highways even on Saturday nights encapsulated all cities' struggle with finding a way to transport many people at once over varying distances to the center of commercial and social activities. Indeed, the I-35 bridge itself and the vehicles that crossed it daily represented part of an evolution of transportation choices, from the horse and buggy to horse-drawn cars traveling on rails to streetcars to motorbuses and automobiles.

Traffic congestion costs Americans $101 billion each year in time and wasted fuel, according to the McKinsey Global Institute. That will only increase not just in America but around the world as people continue to move to cities. Today, just over half of the world's population, or 3.9 billion people, lives in cities, according to the United Nations. By 2050, it estimates, 66 percent of people will live in cities, bringing the total to 6 billion, because the world will have added 2.5 billion people to its population.

Even if Americans were to embrace a more radical shift to public transportation, it would not remove the need for much of the infrastructure that has been built so far, nor for the necessity for upkeep and upgrades. Despite the changes that have taken place over the centuries, most of our infrastructure—roads, bridges, ports, railroad tracks, and sewer systems—is unlikely to succumb to the creative destruction that makes them obsolete anytime soon. They will require extensive investments just to keep doing what they have been doing, and much more to be able to meet the demands of fast-growing urban populations.

McKinsey estimates that maintaining and building the world's transportation and energy infrastructure through 2020 will cost $57 trillion, more than the value of what already exists. The price tag is steep, but McKinsey argues that planning ahead, upgrading existing infrastructure in time, and evaluating and choosing projects based on how they fit into a bigger picture, could save 40 percent, or $1 trillion, each year. Without investing in roads, ports, telecommunications lines, and other infrastructure, we will face paying an even higher price tag of disasters and missed growth created by congestion, power outages, unsafe water, and sudden collapses.

The United Nations estimates that the number of megacities, with 10 million or more inhabitants, will rise from twenty-eight now to forty-one in 2030. Those cities need to be thinking about and investing in transportation infrastructure now, while there is still time to reserve the space and lay the groundwork for rail routes that can expand to be able to bring millions and millions of people from their homes to work.

Alongside the challenges lies a tremendous opportunity for increasing productivity and building economies. McKinsey calculates that investing just 1 percent of GDP more in infrastructure would create 3.4 million new jobs in India, 1.5 million in the United States, and 1.3 million in Brazil.

The costs of failing to invest in our infrastructure may come in the form of reduced productivity that we all but ignore because it happens incrementally, lost opportunities that we do not actively miss because we can't measure what has not happened, or catastrophic failures that take a heavy toll in human lives and economic costs, like the I-35W bridge collapse. The costs are well documented and obvious. So why don't we act more aggressively on what we know we need to do?

Why We Muddle

Infrastructure, particularly in cities, is a telling example of the third stage of a Gray Rhino: muddling, or the ways in which you avoid dealing with a problem you know you have. Also known as kicking the can, muddling is the easy way out. It usually comes with excuses of some sort: no budget, not politically feasible, doesn't matter what we do, because we're doomed anyway. . . . The list goes on. It's familiar in business, governments, personal lives, and finance. It played a role in the 2008 financial crisis. In the now classic excuse for inaction given by the Citigroup chief Charles Prince, "As long as the music is playing, you've got to get up and dance. We're still dancing."

Even when decision-makers get past denial, they are likely to contort themselves to do anything but act decisively. For every example of a leader who acted in time to prevent a crisis, there are dozens more who kicked the can down the road. We muddle because of poorly designed systems, lack of resources, weak leadership, difficulty prioritizing seemingly overwhelming problems, and lack of accountability; all play a role. We muddle for cognitive reasons, like misperceptions of risk, misinterpretations, and poor motivations for acting on available information.

We muddle because it's easier to ignore the cost of not acting than it is to ignore the smaller sacrifices necessary to prevent much larger consequences: the harm of inaction versus the harm of action. We muddle because we perceive the pain of hurting a few as more significant than avoiding greater pain to others. In the famous Trolley Problem, psychologists ask people if they'd be willing to push one person in front of a runaway trolley to prevent it from killing several people. The vast majority of subjects won't do it, revealing a key tenet of human nature: we are reluctant to sacrifice one person in order to save many more. In other versions of the experiment, subjects were more likely to agree to push a gorilla—crucially, a nonhuman—in front of the train, or to flip a switch: both ways of removing them one step from the consequences of their action. When a solution requires choosing between winners and losers, people prefer not to act, unless they're able to dehumanize the losers. If, instead, we could find ways to offset the losses for a few in order to benefit many, we'd get further.

We muddle because of a culture of magical thinking that makes it too easy to imagine that a solution will somehow appear. In Hollywood movies, the hero escapes from dire straits in one of three ways: Luke Skywalker and the Jedi Knights defeat the Death Star in an epic battle through sheer strength and skill; Batman gets help at the last minute from an unexpected ally, Catwoman, who he thought had betrayed him; or an antidote appears—in *Mars Attacks*, a Slim Pickens song on a tinny radio just happens to make the brains of Martian invaders explode into green goo. But life isn't the movies.

Indeed, the home of Hollywood itself, the state of California, faces any number of Gray Rhinos: water scarcity, poverty, housing shortages, budget chaos. *The Economist* highlighted two new studies showing that California's poverty problem was even worse than previously thought, with one placing the percentage of Californians living in poverty at 23.8 percent, the highest level in the United States. Yet John Husing, an economist quoted in the article, acknowledged, "Everyone knows it's an issue. But no one is talking about it."

Diet is now the biggest risk factor for disease and death, having risen rapidly to that dubious distinction and leaving smoking a distant second in 2010. More than one-third of American adults are obese, costing each of them $1,429 more in annual medical bills than healthy people and nicking the economy a total of $147 billion each year. The medical evidence is clear: eat more vegetables and fruits, and you will lower your risk of heart disease, lower your blood pressure and your "bad" cholesterol, and possibly even reduce cancer risks.

The psychologists and leadership consultants Robert Kegan and Lisa Lahey point to research showing that only one in seven heart patients heed warnings from their doctors that they will die if they don't change their habits. This phenomenon, Kegan and Lahey contend, emerges from humans' "immunity to change": powerful habitual behaviors and mindsets that get in the way of dealing with matters as serious as life and death.

Is there anyone who doesn't know that a diet of too much sweets and fats is bad for you? Yet obesity rates in children have tripled in a generation, increasing the risk of diabetes, asthma, and other health problems. Only one in twenty children gets enough vegetables. Overall, Americans eat only half as many vegetables as they should. We haven't yet figured out how to change. "Health messages are simply overwhelmed, in volume and in effectiveness, by junk-food ads that often deploy celebrities or cartoon characters to great effect. We may know that eating fruits and vegetables is good for us, but the preponderance of the signals we get— and especially the signals children get—push us in the direction of junk food," Michael Moss wrote in a powerful *New York Times Magazine* article. "It also may be undeniable that the crunch of a piece of broccoli is never going to be as satisfying as what food-industry scientists refer to as the 'mouth-feel' of a potato chip." He also points out how the incentives are stacked against consumers who can't afford healthier food, and against farmers for whom the economics of growing for fresh-produce shelves doesn't match up with growing livestock feed crops or selling to food processors or ethanol producers. Subsidies and insurance and research dollars just don't flow to produce. "The agricultural system offers precious little incentive to farmers wanting to grow more of the crops that would be better for us," Moss concluded.

Perverse incentives embedded in our financial and political structures, both focused on short-term profits and election cycles at the expense of long-term (and potentially much greater) gains, encourage muddling. Paradoxically, success in preventing a crisis doesn't get you credit. In keeping with our cultural condemnation of Cassandra, helping to prevent a crisis by calling attention to it often backfires. If enough people change their behavior because of your message, you're likely to get pilloried because your predictions didn't come to pass.

We muddle because we perceive that we'll be worse off for making a wrong decision than we'll be for the consequences of not acting. We remember the times when people did the wrong thing: Herbert Hoover decided that austerity was the right path out of the Great Depression and made things worse. He got the blame for a serious misstep, but no credit for acting.

Organizations are particularly bad at responding to threats. Responsibility slips through bureaucratic cracks; organizational cultures promote extreme risk aversion and dilution of personal responsibility. Natural risk aversion, calibrated to our fear of doing the wrong thing, heightens the risk of things going very wrong.

How do we move from kicking the can to acting? Policy advocates know all too well that reason and facts are not enough to push decision-makers to change: they need to find the right emotional trigger or the right subconscious "nudge." To do that, they need to define the crisis in a way that resonates with the people who have the power to do something about it. We need also to change the underlying financial and political incentives that get in the way of acting in time. If we were to account properly for avoided costs, it would make a big difference.

The trade-off is as clear as choosing to change the oil in your car now or replacing the engine because of neglect: failing to address obvious threats because of expense only creates greater costs down the road.

Fracture Critical

The Minneapolis bridge was hardly alone among bridges and other key infrastructure in posing catastrophic risks: there are 77,000 bridges rated structurally deficient; just under 8,000 of them are, like I-35W, both structurally deficient and fracture-critical—that is, in danger of collapse if even a single element fails. Fixing one creaking bridge is one thing. When cash-strapped states face hundreds of them—even dozens—at once, the task becomes an overwhelming challenge.

Muddling spares us immediate pain but makes it harder and more expensive to deal with a threat later on. Rebuilding after a catastrophic failure costs significantly more than it does to build on a planned schedule, and the costs in human lives and in lost economic activity can be devastating.

If federal and state budget debates were required to include regular assessments of the cost of inaction versus the costs of maintenance, that would be a start toward drawing needed attention to infrastructure Gray Rhinos. The new I-35W bridge, designed to last a century, cost $251 million to build. The bridge collapse cost Minnesota about $400,000 a day—$17 million in 2007 and $43 million in 2008—in time and other expenses caused by detours.

"I hope that we can continue to keep this tragedy in mind as we go forward into the future," Minnesota Representative Keith Ellison said at a news conference to announce the new bridge opening. "We've got to use this as a call to action to rebuild the bridges, the dikes, the roads, the transit systems, the water systems in our nation so that they will be safe and serve the needs of the people, and also put Americans to work."

In its 2013 four-year report card on infrastructure in the United States, in sixteen categories from solid waste to ports and aviation to highways and levees, the American Society of Civil Engineers rated the country at a dismal D+. "Forty-two percent of America's major urban highways remain congested, costing the economy an estimated $101 billion in wasted time and fuel annually," it warned. The ASCE estimates that America needs to invest $3.6 trillion in infrastructure by 2020 just to get it up to an acceptable level. Yet in early 2013 only about $2 trillion in infrastructure spending was projected over that period.

The Goldman Sachs economist Alec Phillips, in a note to clients in January 2015, warned that America's failing infrastructure was a major economic risk but that any improvements likely would occur only very slowly, even though investment in them could provide a major economic boost.

Infrastructure is a challenge to countries around the world. When I first started going to the Dominican Republic in 1988, the power went out regularly, and the running joke was that the lights went out but the president didn't notice because he was blind. The part about him being blind was true, not a joke; however, the power circuits around the National Palace and the president's home were never cut. Nearly three decades later, the country still can't provide enough electricity to keep the power on twenty-four hours a day.

India's highways are so congested that the maximum speed for trucks and buses is less than forty kilometers per hour. By some estimates, India's poor transport—that is, its power and water infrastructure—costs the country 2 percent of GDP each year. Whenever investors compare India and China, India's poor infrastructure comes up at the top of the list of reasons that so many prefer China. The World Bank estimates that Africa, where 90 percent of people and goods move by road and which has the highest rate of traffic fatalities in the world, could save $48 billion by investing $12 billion in road repair.

For rapidly growing cities, the costs of muddling rise with time, as homes and businesses spring up on land that will be harder to reclaim for public use in the future. Visiting China in 2011, I marveled at the nearly empty multilane highways that ran through vast fields, seemingly in the middle of nowhere, even though we were just an hour outside Dalian, a city of more than 6.5 million people. At the time it seemed incongruous, though there was logic behind the construction. The roads had been built as part of China's infrastructure splurge to keep the economy growing throughout the economic crisis that followed Lehman Brothers' collapse. So rather than simply reserving the land to accommodate future growth, the government built for the future.

On the opposite side of the spectrum is Chicago, where I moved in 2014. After living for many years in New York City, just off of an express subway line, I find Chicago's Red Line subway (the "El" to Chicagoans) maddening for its lack of express service. But it's hard to see how the city can expand the line, with buildings practically hugging the tracks on both sides, without a major political fight and huge expense to reclaim those buildings. So people suffer the longer daily commute by train or take their cars, adding to congestion that's already maddening and will only get worse with time.

How to Remove the Band-Aid

Recounting his days as a teenager in a hospital undergoing regular disinfectant baths and changes of his wound dressings while being treated for severe burns he suffered during an explosion, the psychologist Dan Ariely experienced excruciating short bursts of pain when nurses ripped his bandages off quickly instead of slowly. The nurses believed that this reduced the total amount of pain, though they had no hard evidence to support it. Ariely disagreed, to say the least. "Their theories gave no consideration to the amount of fear that the patient felt anticipating the treatment; to the difficulties of dealing with fluctuations of pain over time; to the unpredictability of not knowing when the pain will start and ease off; or to the benefits of being comforted with the possibility that the pain would be reduced over time," Ariely recalled in his 2008 book, *Predictably Irrational.* This led him to an early experiment as a psychology student that helped inspire a lifetime of research in behavioral economics. Using volunteers and friends as subjects, he tested the responses to various types of physical and psychological sources of pain. (They must have been very good friends, indeed, to agree to undergo this, and to stay friends afterward!). He returned to the hospital to tell his nurses and doctors what he had found: "People feel less pain if treatments (such as removing bandages in a bath) are carried out with lower intensity and longer duration than if the same goal is achieved through high intensity and a shorter duration." This seemed an apt metaphor for, and even an explanation of, the reasons so many countries muddle through financial and other problems rather than solving the problems quickly, to exchange less total pain for longer periods of suffering.

Similarly, Daniel Kahneman and Don Redelmeier compared groups of patients who had colonoscopies before anesthetics and amnesiac drugs were administered as widely as they are now. Patients, some of whom underwent procedures that took a matter of minutes and some more than an hour, reported levels of pain at intervals throughout the procedure and at the end estimated the total amount of pain. Kahneman and Redelmeier discovered that two things mattered more than the total time: pain at the worst moment and at the end of the procedure. As a result, some patients whose "total pain" was at the high end, as measured by intervals, nevertheless reported less pain than others whose total pain should have been much less. "We cannot fully trust our preferences to reflect our interests," Kahneman concluded.

These insights into the psychology of distress go part of the way toward explaining why leaders are so likely to kick the can. It's a core reality of human nature. Yet that is only part of the picture. The systems we've set up make it harder than it should be to overcome our natural resistance to change.

Reasonable Muddling?

There are reasonable political and economic reasons for muddling. Some economic explanations appear to provide evidence that backs up our psychological preferences for gradual changes. The Russian economist Vladimir Popov argues that what makes the most difference to a country's growth prospects is not the speed with which it reforms but the strength of its decision-making process. His study of gradualism versus shock therapy compares five Central European countries—Estonia, Turkmenistan, Uzbekistan, Belarus, and Kazakhstan, all of which underwent reform slowly—with the Baltic nations that moved quickly to liberalize their economies in the early 1990s. The Baltic economies contracted earlier, more deeply, and for longer than those of the so-called "procrastinators." Two years after the bottom of the recession, sectors of the economy were still down 31 percent to 58 percent from their peak, compared with Uzbekistan, which contracted by "only" 18 percent and began growing again within two years. In other words, speed is not necessarily the answer: the prerequisites need to be in place.

Latin America's shift from a dictatorship to a democracy took decades, and is still not complete. Nor have its economies grown as quickly as Eastern Europe's. Popov explains this by pointing to Latin America's weak political institutions, combined with a rapid increase in inequality that added to social tensions and prevented state institutions from building the legitimacy they needed.

Popov cited the rule of law—which he defines as strong state institutions, not necessarily including respect for human rights—as a crucial prerequisite for change. Popov pointed to China as a successful example of gradual reform not only since the reform period began in 1979 but also from Liberation in 1949 forward (the Great Leap Forward and the Cultural Revolution, notwithstanding). He attributed China's success to the country's ability to maintain continuity through strong state institutions and efficient government, improve its infrastructure, increase its pool of human capital, and make changes gradually rather than through economic shock.

"A wrong sequence may be worse than no reform, because implementing some programs may block other more fundamental reforms," Weiying Zhang wrote in *The Logic of the Market: An Insider's View of Chinese Economic Reform*. As a research fellow of the Economic System Reform Institute of China under the State Commission of Restructuring Economic System, he was deeply ensconced in Deng Xiaoping's extensive economic reforms. I spoke with him when he was visiting Chicago as the Dr. Scholl Foundation Visiting Fellow at the Chicago Council on Global Affairs.

When I asked Zhang what made it possible for China to reform the economy and head off an impending crisis, his answer was that timing played an important part: if Mao Zedong had died sooner or later, the political dynamic would have been quite different. Deng's leadership, of course, was crucial. Yet so often even the most skillful leaders need the right environment to succeed.

"Changing the status quo generates tension and produces heat by surfacing hidden conflicts and challenging organizational culture," the management theorists Ronald Heifetz and Marty Linsky have written. "It's a deep and natural human impulse to see order and calm, and organizations and communities can tolerate only so much distress before recoiling." Their "adaptive leadership" model explores ways to address the challenges of getting people to feel enough of a sense of urgency that they will deal with the challenges facing them, while lowering the temperature when necessary to keep the inevitable tensions manageable. "The heat must stay within a tolerable range—not so high that people demand it be turned off completely, and not so low that they are lulled into inaction."

How societies perceive change, and how closely leaders' understanding of what their constituents believe, is crucial to whether muddling and gradualist strategies can succeed. Leaders must weigh their available options according to how much they cost and how much their voters or citizens will accept. This certainly has been the case in the European Union and in China as well, despite Westerners' fondness of arguing that authoritarian structures have explained China's ability to push through important reforms. At times, what appears to be denial or short-sightedness may be political astuteness; for me, the difference lies in whether leaders acknowledge the need for bigger changes even if they do not immediately implement them. The success of such a strategy depends, however, on how accurately leaders perceive the threshold beyond which the failure to change may send events careening out of control. Louis XVI in France in 1789, the czar of Russia in 1917, and the shah of Iran in 1979 all made this mistake, failing to address long-simmering problems soon enough to prevent revolutions spiraling out of control.

I've heard many people credit China's authoritarian style of government with the dramatic changes in that country's economy over the past few decades, which a Western-style democracy might not have been able to achieve. That may be true, but I suspect that the reasons are somewhat different from the way I've heard it expressed. It's not that an authoritarian government necessarily has an easier time pushing through changes because it has the power to stifle dissent. Instead, its advantage may lie in the freedom to better control the timing of the changes in a way that the often messy echo chamber of a democracy does not allow. And there are risks to attempting to silence protests: without the important signals that freedom of expression provide, leaders can miss essential cues that can alert them that they need to change course.

Of course, public dissent can create a feedback loop that accelerates change as more and more people become aware of the extent to which their dissatisfaction is shared. In Russia, Mikhail Gorbachev lost control of the timing of the changes that he presciently had set in motion with perestroika and glasnost. His initial instinct of the need for reforms was correct, and the pace of many of the changes he instituted was far swifter than what we might consider muddling. Yet just like the leaders in the earlier French, Russian, and Iranian revolutions, he lost control of timing in part because he misread the signals near the threshold of discontent that ultimately led to the collapse of the regime.

Too Big, Too Far, Too Soon

A combination of our preference for lower pain over a longer period—think of Ariely's bandages—and the importance of prerequisites help explain why Europe has taken a gradualist approach to fixing its economic problems. It's abundantly clear that without reforms to handle the growing imbalances within the eurozone, the European Union will face seismic internal rifts, both political and economic. Yet to many investors the pace of change has been maddeningly slow, prolonging pain and keeping Europe at risk of further problems far longer than is necessary.

The Institute for New Economic Thinking convened seventeen economists who issued a stark statement in July 2012: "Europe is sleepwalking toward a disaster of incalculable proportions." There was a solution at hand, but European leaders were not taking it.

But why? Was it possible to act? Over coffee outside a conference hall at Davos in 2013, Katinka Barysch, a fellow Young Global Leader of the World Economic Forum who at the time was the deputy director of the

Centre for European Reform, told me she strongly believed that muddling was, in fact, the only thing that Europe *could* do in the face of its economic crisis. In her view, Europe was simply not ready to act as a unit to make the kind of big, top-down reforms–like banking, political, and fiscal unions—that many analysts argued the euro needed to survive. By creating a common currency before the process of integration had gone far enough for it to work properly, Europe already had taken a step that was too big, too far, too soon. Now, faced with a crisis, it had to play catch-up trying to forge political consensus at the most difficult possible time. Small steps and muddling through were the only options at hand.

With the benefit of hindsight, Barysch and I caught up at another World Economic Forum meeting in August 2015. She had moved on to a post as director of political relations at Allianz SE, the German financial services company. Europe's policy dilemmas had evolved as well. Economic growth had resumed across the eurozone as a whole. Most of the countries that had experienced the biggest impact of the economic crisis had stabilized. The economies of Spain and Ireland were growing robustly. Portugal and Italy had emerged from recession as well. Greek and European policymakers, however, were still embroiled in bitter recriminations over where to lay blame for Greece's deepening economic crisis, and how to fix it.

Barysch ticked off problems that had accumulated over hundreds of years: few exports (or even potential exports), a clientelist system that created a bloated public sector, hundreds of protected professions, corruption, and a private sector with entrenched interests that prevented it from growing. Private sector wages had fallen farther and faster than public sector salaries. The headline debate over austerity versus fiscal stimulus, she felt, didn't do justice to the complexity or extent of Greece's problems. "You can't solve Greece at one go," she said.

She remained skeptical about Europe's ability to create the sweeping changes that would be needed for the euro to work long-term. And without such needed but unlikely European-wide reforms, all the European Union could do was work on one country at a time. Yet she appreciated the importance of keeping in mind the ultimate goal of broader reform. "There's a lot to be said for doing what is feasible at the time," she said. "However, we still need people to come up with the grand solutions so that we have a yardstick. The problem is that we don't always realize that the big solution is in our own interests. But if you do step-by-step changes, it might change your perception of your own interests."

It was unfair, Barysch felt, to compare the European Union, a group of sovereign nation states, to a unified nation like the United States. "Analysts and politicians kept calling for the eurozone to supplement the currency union with a fiscal and political union. But there was no agreement on what that means," she noted. When France and the Southern European nations talk about a fiscal union, for example, they mean transfers from richer to poorer countries. For the Germans and other North Europeans, fiscal union means stronger central powers of fiscal oversight. Because Germany was the biggest creditor and strongest economy, it had an outsized say in any outcome. "So if we had thrashed out a fiscal and monetary union at the height of the crisis, as many demanded, it would probably have ended up looking rigidly German and rules-based," Barysch said. "For the other countries that would have been just as unacceptable as it would have been for the Germans to set up automatic transfer mechanisms at a time when there was no way of knowing how much money would be needed in the end." In other words, until countries with very different approaches and economic realities broadened their views of what served their own interests, a solution remained elusive. Yet she remained a guarded optimist: "Now that things have calmed down in the eurozone, the chances of finding workable and acceptable compromises for strengthening the euro look much better."

And it was true that at times of greatest apparent threat, European leaders did act when it appeared that they were staring into an abyss. The bigger the sell-off in the markets, the more likely European leaders were to do something to calm their fears by loosening credit or, however reluctantly, providing rescue funds to the weakest among them. Being on the brink was the only force stronger than the resistance from a group of countries whose economic policies had not yet fallen into line with each other.

As I write in September 2015, Europe's decision to muddle is coming full circle. After a rocky several months, the possibility of an imminent Greek exit from the euro has receded, yet the country's situation is far from resolved. Full banking, fiscal, and political integration remain pipe dreams, though neither the need for it nor the recognition of that need has gone away.

It may still turn out to be the case that muddling, albeit a rational strategy as European leaders repeatedly decided not to act more decisively, was not enough to prevent a bigger catastrophe. It may have simply postponed the inevitable. Or, as Barysch has argued, it may end up being the compromise needed to get Europe where it had to go. Or the answer may fall somewhere in between.

Embracing Uncertainty

There's a strong cultural element to how well any person or leader responds to shocks, affecting whether they muddle or take action and how well they adapt to changing circumstances. "It's about how unwilling you are to accept uncertainty," Dana Costache, a cross cultural leadership consultant who has worked with Western companies in Eastern Europe and in the United States, told me over coffee in midtown New York. Costache grew up in Romania, which after the Iron Curtain fell went through twenty-four governments in twenty-four years. "Talk about uncertainty!" she said. "Living in a chaotic environment gives you an extra advantage in thinking about how to solve problems. The party that has the most flexibility in a chaotic environment will do best."

Having a certain level of comfort when facing uncertainty is a huge asset in environments where frequent changes happen, especially when the only easily predictable aspect of those changes is that unexpected obstacles will appear regularly. The differences between individualistic

cultures like the United States and Western Europe, where there is less
uncertainty, and collectivist cultures like Latin America or Eastern
Europe, where uncertainty is rampant, are profound, she said.

Western business leaders tend to approach problems with a specific
outcome in mind, and tend to single mindedly pursue that goal even when
it is clear to others that other possible scenarios are more likely. Overconfidence in a particular strategy can make it harder to respond when
events take an unexpected course; it blinds leaders to the need to change
as conditions evolve and demand new strategies. Costache believes that
this lack of flexibility explains, in part, why many American and Western
European executives have a hard time operating in environments
where there is high uncertainty, like Romania and other Eastern European countries.

It also can explain why people muddle. "If you believe destiny is in
your hands, you're more likely to succeed," Costache said. "If I make a long-
term plan and believe it's only up to me to make it succeed, is that more
likely to succeed than one where 10 percent is up to me and 90 percent
is up to others?" If a leader has no confidence in the surrounding environment or in her own ability to create the outcome she wants, there's
much less chance that she'll act. On the other hand, leaders who are
overconfident in their approach can blindly pursue the wrong strategy,
which in hindsight might make muddling look like a far more attractive
option.

The Costs of Muddling

Infrastructure is one example of how muddling creates an opportunity
cost from failing to invest in maintenance or in improvements. Health
care is another, with preventable diseases costing more than $260 bil-
lion in productivity losses each year. Most medical care focuses on preventing further complications once an ailment has been diagnosed. In
the 2014 Ebola outbreak, for example, Congress approved more than
$6 billion to contain the outbreak, nearly as much as the entire regular
annual budget of the Centers for Disease Control and Prevention.

The CDC estimates that, in most cases, preventing an outbreak of a disease costs a tiny fraction of the cost of treating it. Nevertheless, debate rages over whether preventive care overall saves money. The answer to the question depends on how broadly you define "preventive care" and how many expensive tests you include in the calculation. Still, there is a consensus that certain preventive actions—childhood vaccines; quitting smoking; screening for high blood pressure or cholesterol; obesity reduction and diabetes prevention and control—can save a significant amount of money.

The Trust for America's Health has estimated that investing $10 in each American could yield more than $18 billion in health-care savings in the next ten to twenty years, not counting gains in worker productivity and quality of life. Each dollar invested in preventive care, if calculated, could nearly double the value of the investment within two years; the return over a decade or more could rise to more than six times the investment. For example, the organization estimated, reducing Type 2 diabetes and high blood pressure rates by 5 percent could save the United States more than $5 billion in health-care costs. Another study found similar results. Reduced tobacco use and a decline in obesity alone could lower national health expenditures by $474 billion over a decade, according to the Commonwealth Fund.

Too many simple measures to reduce the costs of health care languish. We know what works, yet it proves to be devilishly difficult to put these proposals into action. When Paul O'Neill, who later became U.S. treasury secretary, joined Alcoa in 1987, he immediately put in place a system to report within twenty-four hours all injuries and accidents, their causes, and ways to keep them from happening again. In the thirteen years during which he was at Alcoa, its lost-workday rate dropped from 1.86 to 0.23, and by 2013 was 0.085, resulting in huge cost savings and productivity gains. Charles Duhigg, in *The Power of Habit*, credits that change with having helped to quintuple Alcoa's net income during O'Neill's tenure there.

O'Neill later adapted the practice and tested it at Allegheny General Hospital in Pittsburgh, with stunning results. The hospital invested just $85,607 and nearly eliminated three costly types of infections that patients acquired there, improving the hospital's bottom line by $5,634,269 over two years. It was an astonishing return for a surprisingly small outlay. In 2004, Pennsylvania began requiring all hospitals to upgrade their reporting procedures and reduced errors by 27 percent. O'Neill has estimated that hospital-acquired infections and errors cost as much as $600 billion each year. "One thing that's perplexing to me is how difficult it is to get organizations across American medical care to adopt practices that are proven life-savers and money-savers," he told the *Pittsburgh Post-Gazette*. "The things I've been talking about for 15 years would create vast improvements in outcome—and save trillions of dollars a year."

In 2012, O'Neill urged the United States to require all U.S.-based Veterans Administration and military hospitals to adopt a simple but powerful practice: reporting all hospital-acquired infections, patient falls, medication errors, and caregiver injuries within twenty-four hours of their occurrence. The V.A., of course, turned out to have even bigger problems: it wasn't accurately reporting wider problems in the system, much less within twenty-four hours. An internal audit found that more than 120,000 veterans had been left waiting indefinitely for care. The V.A. is a particularly egregious example of lack of accountability. Yet its particular problems do not negate the question of why the country has been so slow to adopt the practices that have been so helpful in Pennsylvania.

A case study of the Allegheny experiment placed the problem in a context that wasn't easy to dismiss: two million hospital-acquired infections were costing $5 billion annually and affecting as many as one in ten patients. "There is no controversy about whether such harmful conditions are value-less in health care, and no argument that health-care workers do not intend such harm to occur," wrote Dr. Richard Shannon in the report. "Rather, there is the lack of a systematic approach to the provision of care and of organizational accountability when such harmful conditions exist or are allowed to persist once recognized." His study asked why there was so much resistance to change—and started with underlying cultural barriers and misplaced incentives. "First, we believed that HAI [hospital-acquired infections] were simply collateral damage, the inevitable price that must be paid for sophisticated, complex care," Shannon wrote. "Second, we believed that HAI were benign and readily treated with antibiotics without untoward consequences. Third, in an era of public reporting, average results were the goal, and there was little reason to aspire to high performance. Fourth and last, was the little-mentioned fact that HAI are a common accompaniment of complex care and are covered in outlier payments, such that doctors and hospitals were probably paid more when care was complicated by an HAI."

A perverse incentive had come into play. While behavioral and cultural reasons help to explain why we muddle, our distorted incentive systems bear a huge part of the blame. Hospitals simply don't get rewarded for doing the right thing. When they're judged by total income, they focus on generating more income, even when the revenue doesn't catch up to the costs, and they end up losing money in the end. Pennsylvania was lucky to have the leadership to push its hospitals to get past the distorted incentive structure that stood in the way of doing the right thing. The story of the state's success draws attention to the need to properly account for both revenues and costs in order to form a clear picture of a serious problem and respond appropriately. It also shows how important leadership is to shocking people out of their inertia and bad habits.

The People and the Politicians

The cases of inertia that bother me the most are the ones in which majorities of citizens repeatedly support changes, but political decision-making structures stand in the way. In the U.S. political system, for example, only the most active turn out for primaries, giving radical and polarized candidates more weight than they deserve.

Immigration reform is a prime example. Poll after poll after poll has shown solid majorities of Americans support immigration reform that would formalize the legal status of millions of people who have been living and working here, and in the process make the economy more competitive. A Gallup poll fielded in summer 2013 showed 87 percent of Americans in favor of a path to citizenship.

So why don't things change? Too often, it takes a perceived crisis to make things change. A crisis is personal. First, for most of those nearly nine out of ten citizens who support changes to a system that people on both sides of the issue agree is broken, the status quo is not an acute crisis. For many of the eleven million people without legal papers, the lack of a legal path represents a crisis, but they're not the ones making a decision. People in the Congressional districts opposing immigration reform feel that immigrants challenge a key part of their identity. Until recently, the only people who saw immigration as a crisis *and* felt they had the power to do something about it have been the people who oppose what the majority of Americans have said they want. The benefits of immigration are spread broadly, while those who feel threatened by immigration experience that fear as acute and urgent, regardless of whether the facts justify their beliefs.

More recently, however, supporters of immigration reform have reframed the issue in terms of the future of the Republican Party, just as Byron Wien had predicted in the Ten Surprises discussed in Chapter 2. Unless the party supported immigration reform, many argued, the party would lose the fastest growing demographic in the country; and along with it, crucial swing votes would disappear and deny the party the victories at the polls that it needed. Recognizing this new danger, moderate Republicans began to step forward in support of legalizing undocumented immigrants under certain conditions. In 2013, a bipartisan group of eight U.S. senators came to an agreement that reflected the desires that Americans had expressed in polls. Though the proposal had majority support in the House of Representatives, it could not get past procedural obstacles to a vote.

In messy democracies, by design small groups can subvert the wishes of the majority. Democracies also do a poor job of reconciling conflicting interests—for example, when everyone recognizes that there is a problem, but every constituency digs in its heels to keep from having to pay to solve it.

When I moved to Chicago in the autumn of 2014 amidst a mayoral election campaign, it was hard to ignore the consequences of years of muddling: skipped pension payments, a near doubling of the city's debts over a decade, and political near-paralysis. By early 2015, Chicago Public Schools hit a budget impasse, the state's highest court had rejected a proposal to cut pension benefits, and Moody's Investors Service downgraded the city's debt to junk-bond status. "Chicago is in deep, deep yogurt," Governor Bruce Rauner declared, to the great delight of the media. He warned the city that the rest of the state was not willing to bail it out. This was practically a moot point, given that the city represents around 70 percent of the state's economic output and so essentially would be bailing itself out, but the words sounded good.

Though Chicago's glittering lights, success-attracting Fortune 500 companies, and relatively stable population were a far cry from the images of dilapidated houses and abandoned blocks in Detroit, the fellow Midwestern city's recent bankruptcy was hard to ignore. Sparring columnists debated whether Chicago and Detroit were comparable, in an indication that some Chicagoans, by insisting that they were not in the same ballpark, hadn't even achieved a muddling mentality. They were still solidly mired in denial that the problems of over-spending, corruption, and under-investment had too much in common for Chicago to be complacent. It took bankruptcy to force Detroit to start making critical changes. Once Detroit capitulated, turning over financial powers to the state, and its creditors (including pension holders, who are crucial to Chicago's fate) agreed to restructure its debt, investment and people began to return to the city.

Chicago is still muddling, despite Mayor Rahm Emanuel's efforts to bring its budget into balance through a combination of tax hikes and, so far unsuccessful, efforts to reduce pension costs. Can Chicago make enough headway on its fiscal troubles without falling into a situation as dire as Detroit's? Can it spread the costs of cleaning up its finances fairly, with every single constituency giving according to its ability? Can it find a way to trade short-term pain in return for longer-term gain? These are exactly the kinds of questions at the heart of many Gray Rhinos. They are challenging in both democracies and authoritarian states and communities. Finding and implementing the solutions often is a thankless task; leaders around the world face a choice between muddling and falling on their swords.

Chronicle of a Death Foretold

Like the murder of a young man at the hands of a jealous lover in Gabriel Garcia Marquez's *Chronicle of a Death Foretold*, many crises unfold in slow motion as observers stand by and do nothing to stop them. There are, nevertheless, ways to get past the muddling stage. Sometimes we muddle because we think we have more time than we really do to get out of a mess. Scientists in the nineteenth century claimed that if you drop a frog into a pot of hot water he'll hop out right away, but if you heat the water gradually enough the frog will allow itself to be boiled to death. While more recent studies suggest that this is not, in fact, how real frogs behave, the original version still works as a metaphor. Just as you don't see how quickly a child is growing because you see him or her day by day, it's easy to be blind to changes as a situation gradually gets worse. This is part of why people muddle for so long, often until it's too late. Frequently, it takes a shock to make you realize that you have to deal with a crisis.

Sometimes it is possible to alter the calculus of the cost of muddling and the benefit of action. One way is to change how we account for costs so that families, organizations, or governments accurately recognize the benefits of a penny saved being a penny earned. When it comes to expensive fixes or investments, like infrastructure or education, it's too easy to put things off. You've heard the argument: We don't have the money, because we have pressing short term needs. This kind of logic creates a perpetual downward spiral. As we've seen, the costs of not making the decision to invest leave us constantly vulnerable to sudden shocks, and to forever muddling.

Reframing the ability to successfully affect the outcome of a threat is an important strategy for moving past the muddling stage. When a problem appears to be so big that the impact any individual could make might seem negligible, framing problems in manageable, relevant sizes can help to give people the confidence to believe that taking action to change things is worth it. Take climate change, for example. How much does any one of us believe that our individual actions will affect the future of the planet? But if you frame the issue differently, in terms of something that we can affect, the response may be different. When any one of us decides to switch off a light before leaving the room, we unconsciously make a calculation that it is worth it, but it may not have anything to do with climate change. I may not be able to stop global warming by turning out the light, but I can reduce my electric bill.

Sometimes muddling is the only choice that makes sense, though not nearly as often as politicians would like us to believe. Muddling works only if in the meantime, change is happening, however slowly. If Europe is indeed lurching toward a more unified system, muddling will prove to have been the right choice. But the continent has been racing the clock, and it's not at all clear that the euro will outrun the Gray Rhino chasing it.

Sometimes you have to make a choice: if there are too many Gray Rhinos at once, you may have to let some go, or choose to muddle through on smaller dangers. At other times, when dangers are interconnected, the only way to avoid any of them is to adopt a grand strategy of fighting on several fronts at once.

Muddling can be the right answer if it is part of a strategy of gradual change, as long as it is accompanied by a bigger vision. (One could argue that this approach is not merely a failure to act, but a strategic approach that lays the groundwork for action. However, since such gradual approaches include a significant element of trial and error—feeling our way through the dark—it's a close enough cousin to muddling to include alongside it.)

Defining the crisis and creating a sense of urgency are as important as correctly reading the appetite of employees, customers, or citizens for those changes. If there's a sense of urgency for change but lack of consensus on what changes to make, muddling or gradualism can help to put a transition in motion. It's completely reasonable to accept that sometimes we muddle because we're not sure what to do. As we've seen above, knowing the right thing to do is a start, but it's not always enough to get you there. That's why it's essential for leaders to diagnose the nature of a Gray Rhino both to decide what to do, how to prioritize multiple dangers, and how to make the changes they need to avoid a trampling.

CHAPTER 4 TAKEAWAYS:

- **Muddling is expensive.** The old saw "an ounce of prevention is worth a pound of cure" applies here, whether in delayed infrastructure investments, preventive health care, financial crisis, or wherever any number of other obvious dangers are involved.
- **Consider timing.** There are costs to acting too soon as well as too late, though we are less likely to act too soon than we are to act too late. Include opportunity cost in your analysis of whether to wait or act.
- **Change incentives.** Make it worth people's while to solve problems using carrots or sticks. In a company, set key performance indicators to reward employees for addressing problems early on and to penalize them if they get out of hand. *Increase rewards for preventing problems* in order to remove some of the obstacles to acting in time in the face of likely disaster.
- **Spread costs fairly.** If you know that you'll have to throw one group of people under a trolley for the sake of the greater good, find a way to ease their pain.
- **Account properly for costs, savings, and investments.** Change accounting systems so that policy decision makers can take credit for investments that create savings or profits in the future. Include an "avoided costs" budget line.
- **Sometimes muddling is the only choice,** though not nearly as often as many politicians would like us to believe.

5

DIAGNOSING: RIGHT AND WRONG SOLUTIONS

Once leaders recognize a threat, they have a choice of doing the right thing, the wrong thing, or nothing. As we saw in Chapter 4, the deck is stacked against acting in time to get out of the way; our incentive systems discourage doing what we need to do. But even when you get past the denial and the muddling stages, it's not always obvious what is the right thing to do. To get from denial to action, it is essential to diagnose the type of Gray Rhino and the source of the problem so that you can find your way to the answer.

In other words, you need to know what species of Gray Rhino you're dealing with. There are five species of rhinoceros in the wild: black (*Diceros bicornis*), white (*Ceratotherium simum*), Sumatran (*Dicerorhinus sumatrensis*), Javan (*Rhinoceros sondaicus*), and Indian (*Rhinoceros unicornis*). While they are all gray in color, each species has distinguishing traits. The black rhino, native to Africa, has a pointy lip used for browsing and is considered to be more solitary and ill-tempered than the white rhino. The white rhinoceros, also native to Africa, is often said to have gotten its name from the Dutch or Afrikaans for *wide*, because of its wide, square lip suited to grazing. Scholars have debunked this explanation but have not agreed on alternate theories. The Sumatran is the smallest of the rhinos and has hair that is rather sparse, but more than other rhinos have. The Indian rhino has just one horn, and skin folds that look like armor; unlike its forest- and bush-dwelling cousins, it prefers wetlands.

Javan rhinos, the rarest species, of which only about sixty are left, is smaller than the Indian rhino and has less prominent skin folds.

What would a taxonomy of the Gray Rhino look like? It would reveal several subspecies with a variety of distinct traits. Is this a recognized challenge whose solutions are clear but are acted on only halfheartedly? Is this the real challenge, or one hiding a deeper, root issue? Is it a widely recognized problem for which the solutions are unclear and all the answers seem bad? Is it an emerging Rhino for which the previously unimaginable begins to be imagined? Or is it a problem for which there may be no solution other than to bow out, and in which the bigger Gray Rhino is the damage done by clinging to the impossible or the obsolete?

Inconvenient Truths

The easiest type of Gray Rhino to identify is an Inconvenient Truth: a threat that most of us recognize but for which there is no silver bullet, and to which significant resistance remains. These Inconvenient Truths require sacrifices by everyone. Generally, some people (by no means everyone) have started to do something about them, but it is nowhere near enough.

Climate change is the most obvious example. The temperature of the globe is rising at alarming rates. NASA scientists reported that the year 2014 was the warmest since records began in 1880, and nine of the ten warmest years ever have occurred since 2000. Scientists have formed a solid consensus that the cause is humanity's emissions of carbon into the atmosphere. Though governments have agreed to keep the temperature rise of the planet under two degrees, it's highly unlikely that they will meet that goal. If the current rate of change continues, the temperature on earth will rise six degrees by the end of the century, bringing enormous changes in weather, sea level, ocean acidity, and the survival of many species. Our options are grim: dramatically reduce our greenhouse-gas emissions, protect against increasingly frequent extreme weather events caused by climate change, and plan for the millions of people who are estimated to be at risk of being displaced. Some people have chosen another option: denial, as we saw in Chapter 2. If we are to survive, we need to do more.

The big challenge with Inconvenient Truths is that too many people want to push responsibility on someone else. Each of us might think that a problem is too big for us to have a meaningful impact. Or we might assume that the problem is the government's responsibility—which it may be, but it may also be likely that the government lacks the capacity or the political will to assume responsibility and take action. A business might want to do something to solve the problem but may not have the data or the ability to make the case to shareholders.

"CEOs clearly recognize the scale of the global challenge—but may not yet see the urgency or the incentive for their own business to do more and to have a greater impact," Accenture and the United Nations Global Compact reported in 2013. Interestingly, the main issue that CEOs blamed for the lack of progress was that businesses had a hard time recognizing a link between sustainability and business value. Many saw sustainability as a charity or a regulatory issue, as opposed to a way to improve their bottom line. Yet many of those surveyed were more likely to view their own efforts as satisfactory than to rate others' efforts the same way.

Recurring Rhinos and Charging Rhinos

Sometimes Inconvenient Truths quickly morph into a new form. Charging Rhinos are the smoldering issues that all of a sudden flare up into focus. Usually, these fast-moving crises have been lying in wait for some time. Because they create a sense of urgency, these events can provoke fast responses that may not solve the underlying problem and may even make things worse. If their root causes are deep—for example, the deep governance issues behind the troubles in the Middle East—they can be incredibly dangerous. Youth unemployment and food scarcity in Africa combined to create the protests that led to the Arab Spring; the failure of governments to transition to democracy and generate economic growth will lead to more of these Charging Rhinos.

When problems quickly turn from chronic to acute, they shorten the amount of time we have to fix them, increasing the odds that circumstances will overtake us. They raise the odds that we will act, but also increase the likelihood that the responses will be incomplete and lead to more problems, as is likely in the Middle East.

Other Charging Rhinos are also Recurring Rhinos: the hurricanes, tornadoes, and epidemics that we know will happen, though the when and the where remain unknown until the last minute. For many of these Recurring Rhinos—with the unfortunate exception of financial crises—there are systems in place for warning people and getting them to safety.

Meta-Rhinos

Meta-Rhinos are structural problems that create symptoms, which often get more attention than the root cause. We're often more likely to recognize the symptoms as the major challenges and treat them one at a time, but unless we get to the deeper issues we can't fix the symptoms.

A case in point is the economic gender gap, which is widely recognized as a waste of potential and an untapped opportunity. Yet the decisions that need to be made to close the gender gap are often a major problem that is at the root of the undervaluing of the potential of half of the world's population. The gender gap in economic and political leadership is also a culprit in the decision-making flaws—the groupthink and the blinding effects discussed in Chapters 1, 2, and 3—that lead to so many other Gray Rhinos.

Leaders recognize the problem the gender gap creates, and there have been changes. Many European countries have put in place quotas on corporate boards; others have mandated that companies report the number of women on boards and in leadership; still others have put in place quotas in their parliaments. There are organizations dedicated to closing the gender gap in business, politics, education. Yet resistance remains strong and progress painfully slow. Catalyst, which tracks women in business, has reported only negligible growth in the percentage of women on corporate boards for nearly a decade. The World Economic Forum, whose Global Gender Gap report is a powerful tool for measuring and tracking the problem and pushing for change, nevertheless takes a beating every year for the low percentage of women at its annual meeting in Davos, Switzerland. The Forum has tried to encourage companies to send more women by offering a fifth spot at the meeting to companies that bring four delegates, yet the representation of women remains stubbornly stuck at around 17 percent.

Political polarization is another meta-Rhino. As we saw in Chapter 4, our political structures may make it impossible to solve looming problems. Were the protests in 2014 over Michael Brown and Eric Garner just about the deaths of two men at the hands of the police? Or were they about the rule of law and deeper socioeconomic problems that must be solved? Are conflicts between Islamists and the West only about religion? Were the thousands of deaths in Haiti's 2010 earthquake just about the earthquake, or were they about the lack of resources for safe buildings and the lack of building codes that could be enforced?

The hacking of Sony Entertainment in December 2014 was an example of several layers of problems that led to an embarrassing and costly failure for the company. A *Forbes* reporter obtained a security audit that showed that Sony had not been monitoring as much as 17 percent of the systems. "It's rarely a good idea to keep IT teams that are supposed to protect a single business in silos. It opens up gaps, as it did at Sony," the reporter, Thomas Fox-Brewster, noted. Sony employees went to the media claiming that Sony's security procedures were lax and that it repeatedly ignored warnings from employees, even when an earlier hack happened. An April 2011 hack attack on Sony PlayStation cost the company at least $171 million. Sony responded by improving its protections against data breaches and distributed denial-of-service attacks. Yet, a *Fortune* magazine article pointed out, Sony Pictures Entertainment—a different division of Sony—did not coordinate with PlayStation to benefit from the attacks and apply the lessons it had learned. In this case, the hack was a symptom of a bigger problem: corporate silos. The Sony hack also revealed a host of other issues at Sony, which created tremendous embarrassment for the company. But that's another story.

Still, the FBI estimated that nine out of ten companies could not have avoided a similar attack. Was that a commentary on the power of the attackers, or on how widespread complacency is? The examples of companies failing to protect themselves from cyberattacks are widespread. We've heard the stories of the attacks on Target, Neiman Marcus, and many others, all of which involved unheeded warnings.

One group took an extreme approach to letting a company know that there is a big price to be paid for not responding to warnings. Snapchat is a popular smartphone application that allows users to exchange messages or images that it claims disappear ten seconds after they are opened. Hackers regularly alert Snapchat—and the world—of problems in its code. In fact, they did so at least three times publicly in 2013 before the company raised $60 million in financing in June 2013.

Gibson Security, which describes itself alternately as an Internet security firm and as a group of "poor students, with no stable source of income," and which the website ZDNet calls a group of Australian hackers, says it warned Snapchat in August 2013 of its vulnerabilities. The oversight in the code allowed hackers to access users' names, phone numbers, and aliases and to create bogus accounts. When, by late December, Snapchat had not responded, Gibson published a Christmas surprise: information about the security holes that would allow hackers to stalk the sites' millions of users. "Given that it's been around *four months* since our last Snapchat release, we figured we'd do a refresher on the latest version, and see which of the released exploits had been fixed (full disclosure: *none of them*). Seeing that nothing had *really* been improved upon . . . we decided that it was in everyone's best interests for us to post a full disclosure of everything we've found in our past months of hacking the gibson."

When Snapchat finally responded, it neither apologized nor made a convincing show of having addressed the problem. "We want to make sure that security experts can get ahold of us when they discover new ways to abuse our service so that we can respond quickly to address those concerns," the company wrote. "The Snapchat community is a place where friends feel comfortable expressing themselves and we're dedicated to preventing abuse."

Conundrums and Gordian Knots

Many of the Gray Rhinos we've seen so far have had obvious solutions. The most difficult kind of Gray Rhino—and the one to which we respond least well, and understandably so—is the Conundrum: the one to which the answer (or answers) is not completely clear. At the top of this list is inequality: the topic that made the French economic historian Thomas Piketty a runaway best-selling author in 2014.

As the year opened in late January 2014, the Korean pop star Psy, whose hit song and video "Gangnam Style" parodied the residents of a wealthy Seoul neighborhood with a dance that looks like a child pretending to ride a horse, made an appearance at the annual meeting of the World Economic Forum in Davos. Surprisingly unassuming in person despite his goofy Gangnam Style persona, he stood with Korean dignitaries around an elaborate display of Korean delicacies separated from the room with a velvet rope. The Belvedere Hotel, where the event took place, reportedly served guests sixteen thousand bottles of bubbly and three thousand bottles of red and white wine during the week that the world's business, media, academic, government, and NGO élite convened in the Swiss Alps at the foot of Thomas Mann's Magic Mountain.

An Oxfam report released a few days earlier estimated that the net worth of the eighty-five richest people in the world was $1.7 trillion: as much as that of the 3.5 billion poorest combined. Pope Francis sent a welcome message to delegates drawing attention to the problem of inequality and urged the business leaders there to take an inclusive approach to their decisions and to put their skills to use in the service of those still living in dire poverty. "I ask you to ensure that humanity is served by wealth and not ruled by it," he implored.

Gathered for a few days in a secluded alpine town, the global élite was talking about what people on Main Street already knew: that the average U.S. CEO's pay was more than three hundred times that of the average worker and nearly eight hundred times that of a minimum-wage worker. While it's impossible to have economic growth without some inequality, the gap between the rich and the poor had become so vast that it threatened growing economies. Inequality between countries was shrinking, thanks to globalization, but within countries it had increased to new heights.

Even leaving the justice issues aside, the business and government leaders assembled at Davos recognized that inequality was a problem because it made it harder to find customers, created social tension, protests, and upheaval, and otherwise threatened their prosperity. Inequality reduces economic growth, though economists argue about how much, and can cut short growth spurts, making inequal countries fall behind and hurting both the poor and the rich.

While there are disagreements about the exact relationship between inequality and economic growth, most people agree that inequality causes problems. But getting agreement on the sources of the problem is harder. How do we address it? Whose responsibility is inequality? What policies can change it?

Piketty proposes a global wealth tax. Others propose education, or minimum wage, tax cuts or tax hikes, more government services or fewer, insurance to prevent catastrophic financial failures, more subsidies or fewer subsidies. How do we turn recognition of the problem into concrete goals and measurable steps to get there? There's no easy answer.

Conundrums taken to the next level are Gordian Knots, where the best options are merely the least worst. Look at Syria, or the Israel-Palestine question. These cases are even harder. It's easy to see why leaders muddle in the face of conundrums. It's hard to see through to the way out. Even when there may be some plausible options, the payoff likely won't come until the long run, leaving today's leaders stuck with the blame for making trade-offs while their successors far down the road get the credit.

In conundrums, we often end up treating the symptoms—if we treat anything at all—and leaving the root causes intact.

Creative Destruction

Sometimes the best response is not just to get out of the way of a Gray Rhino but to transform completely or to fade away gracefully. This is the case for companies in the path of creative destruction.

Kodak invented the first digital camera in 1975 but shelved the innovation, to protect its core film business, until the 1990s, when it finally faced the inevitable as its film business started to decline. It spun off its chemical business in 1994 to pay down debt as it moved firmly into the digital world. Once it did embrace digital cameras, it led the business from the late 1990s until the mid-2000s. It was the top digital-camera producer in 2005, selling nearly $6 billion worth. But cheaper cameras from Asia began chipping away at its market share as digital cameras became a commodity instead of a rarity. By 2007, Kodak had slipped to fourth place, and then just kept falling. As digital photos switched to phones and tablets, the company's market share eroded further.

There are all sorts of explanations for Kodak's woes, which basically boil down to the fact that its executives didn't recognize and embrace change fast enough. But the question remains whether even such recognition would have changed its fate.

"For all purposes, the old Kodak had to die because it had run its course of usefulness and meaning," Erik Sherman wrote on Money-Watch. He pointed out that the average life span of a Fortune 500 corporation is only forty to fifty years. Kodak already had outlived that by a long shot; George Eastman and Henry Strong had founded the Eastman Dry Plate Company in 1881 and placed the Kodak camera on the market in 1888, marking the birth of snapshot photography.

Kodak filed for bankruptcy in January 2012. It has switched to digital printing, sold many of its patents, and moved to the imaging business. In 2014, it was relisted on the New York Stock Exchange under the ticker KODK, with a new CEO and a new vision. Its corporate history on its website is two sentences long: "The Kodak name is recognized around the world for its long heritage of delivering imaging innovations.

The company is now writing its next chapter as a technology company focused on imaging for business."

Is the business threat your company is facing one that will lead to obsolescence? If so, is there another direction it could take that would be true to its purpose? Or are the forces of creative destruction too strong? A company facing either scenario must change or collapse. Some Gray Rhinos are so powerful that it's nearly impossible to get out of their way, and the sooner you recognize them the less it will cost to fight the inevitable.

Unidentified Rhinos

In thinking and talking about Gray Rhinos, I've been surprised by how often people default to what are more like Black Swan events. One friend mentioned the danger of a giant asteroid's hitting the earth. The extinct cretaceous-era dinosaurs might beg to differ; but that did not sound highly likely to me; nor was it something that anyone could do anything to avoid.

Other problems baffled me, and I wasn't sure how to judge how likely they were. Artificial intelligence is another puzzle. The first time someone suggested that robots were a highly probable, high-impact threat, I ignored it. But then Stephen Hawking and Elon Musk came out with their warnings, and I reconsidered. When it was a friend warning about artificial intelligence, that was one thing. But Hawking and Musk know a lot more about this topic than either of us does. Hawking, whose work in theoretical physics and the framework for understanding the general theory of relativity and quantum mechanics is rivaled in impact only by his skill at making science accessible to a broader public, told the BBC that artificial intelligence could spell the end of the human race. Similarly, Tesla founder and technology investor Elon Musk has called artificial intelligence "our biggest existential threat" and has even gone so far as to put a five- to ten-year timeframe on the risk of something dangerous happening. "The leading AI companies have taken great steps to ensure safety," he wrote on the website Edge.org. "The[y] recognize the danger, but believe that they can shape and control the digital superintelligences and prevent bad ones from escaping into the Internet. That remains to be seen."

The World Economic Forum, in its 2015 Global Risks report, also wrestled with the issue, taking a more measured stance. "Contrary to public perception and Hollywood screenplays, it does not seem likely that advanced AI will suddenly become conscious and malicious," the report concluded.

I still don't know what to make of the nature of the threat that artificial intelligence poses to humans. While he was visiting Chicago to speak at a conference, I raised the question with Vivek Wadhwa, who oversees research at Singularity University, about the exponentially advancing technologies that are soon going to change our world. He raised his eyebrows, then came up with a thoughtful description of a challenge that is yet to take clear shape. "We're not ready for the size of the changes that will come about," he said. "We're creating a whole new species without knowing what it means. We are not mentally capable of keeping up. As computers get faster, they will be building new computers. Will they be building themselves? Will they be grateful we created them? Will they leave us alone?"

Wadhwa painted a picture of robotic surgeons that are far more skilled than humans; of genome sequencing that will cost no more than a cup of coffee; of self-driving cars that are safer than humans; of vertical farms; of digital tutors driven by artificial intelligence; of presentations given via holodeck; of medical sensors that constantly update telemedicine services and diagnose us. He sees technology democratizing the world by lowering the cost of medical care, communications, energy, transportation, and so many other things.

At the same time, he draws a potentially darker picture as robots take over many of the repetitive tasks that are now performed by lower-skilled humans. "My worry is that we're headed into a jobless future," he said. The rich will get richer, but what jobs will be left for the poor? Wadhwa draws possible scenarios of robots going on strike because 3-D printers are taking jobs away, or of a new Luddite movement in which people burn down technology companies. "The only thing that is for sure is that it is happening," he said.

Roombas are already taking over some house-cleaning chores; most of us are more likely to get money from ATMs than from tellers; and it seems that every day technology automates more and more of the things we do.

For me, the jury is still out on the threat that artificial intelligence poses to the human race. But I do think there is a Gray Rhino in the impact technology has on jobs and on society that we need to face. An Oxford University study published in 2013 estimates that around 47 percent of U.S. jobs could be lost to computers in the next two decades. The question is what new jobs automation can create, how it changes the way we value skills that are unique to humans, and whether we are prepared to educate people in those skills.

Getting It Wrong

We don't always properly diagnose the Gray Rhino in front of us. Sometimes getting it wrong leads us to getting it right. In the early 1980s, executives at Coca-Cola found themselves practically underfoot of a Gray Rhino: Pepsi had driven Coke's share of the soft-drink market down from 60 percent at the end of World War II to 24 percent in 1983. Younger drinkers preferred sweeter drinks like Pepsi. Coke did blind taste tests of regular Coke, Pepsi, and a secret new formula that beat out both of the established tastes. Nearly nine out of ten focus-group participants said they would drink the new formula if it were to become Coca-Cola. Based on the research, the company changed the formula in April 1985, only to be met by a huge public backlash from brand loyalists. Within three months, Coca-Cola brought back the original formula, which soon outstripped New Coke and gained back market share from Pepsi. The company saw a threat, researched and analyzed its options, and acted; was hit by an entirely new crisis because it failed to understand its own biggest strength; and then recovered because of the attention it drew. This shows just how hard it is to make the "right" decision in the face of a Gray Rhino.

Coke got it right by first getting it wrong. Other companies have gotten things wrong not long after getting them right, reacting early and wisely, only to become overconfident. Netflix, for example, saw early on that it would have to contend with the switch from DVDs to streaming video, and acted boldly and strategically to face the challenge. It was, then, a complete surprise that the company stumbled badly in 2012 by announcing that it would charge subscribers separately for DVDs and streaming. The mistake cost Netflix a third of its subscribers, raising the question of why such a seemingly sure-footed company would make such a misstep.

Widowmaker Rhinos

Though people are highly likely to ignore Gray Rhinos that need attention, they also are prone to paying too much attention to problems that are not the most likely threats—a tendency that interferes with handling the real challenges. Gray Rhino strategy often involves choosing between diametrically opposed possible outcomes and the strategies to deal with each; recognizing a Gray Rhino also depends on deciding what is not the danger that others think it is.

The world's central banks, for example, have faced a dilemma as they have tried to maneuver between two diametrically opposed Gray Rhinos: inflation and bubbles, versus deflation and recession. If they keep interest rates too low for too long, they risk inflating asset bubbles, which could create a bigger financial crisis down the road when the bubbles collapse. (Think of the early 2000s.) On the other hand, if they raise interest rates too soon, too fast, they risk choking economic recovery and adding to deflationary pressures, which some economists believe are more dangerous than inflation; they also will add to national budget deficits by raising the cost that governments pay when they have to roll over maturing debt. Both arguments have compelling elements and carry high stakes. There is little room for error. Yet discussing monetary policy in a vacuum, as if it is the only way to solve complex economic challenges, makes it harder to choose the correct answer. It's essential to relate the key economic questions behind interest rate decisions to what others can do, or to other ways of popping asset bubbles that are more precise than the blunt tool of interest rates. The same is true of national debts, or of many other economic policy challenges: the answers turn out very differently if you look at a question in isolation from other, related factors.

Not everyone who sees a Gray Rhino is out to solve it; some are out merely to make a buck off of a disaster they are sure will happen. Dan Alpert, founder of the New York investment bank Westwood Capital, knows a thing or two about debt owed by distressed companies and governments, and about the importance of recognizing it, restructuring it, and getting back to growth. The author of *The Age of Oversupply: Overcoming the Greatest Challenge to the Global Economy* and a fellow at the Century Foundation, Alpert also has spent considerable energy thinking about and advocating for ways to solve public policy Gray Rhinos, from debt hangovers to infrastructure.

Alpert arrived in Tokyo in spring 2000 to set up a new office for Westwood. The next morning, Japan's prime minister passed away, a somber event that set the tone for the depth of the problems the country was facing. Over the course of the year, the Nikkei stock market index would fall by 26 percent. "This was the point where Japan hit the wall," he recalled at his light-filled Fifth Avenue offices. After the economy had collapsed eight years earlier, nothing the government tried seemed to work. Neither loose monetary policy nor infrastructure projects had succeeded in kick-starting growth. It tried to reactivate its once booming export economy but failed because Japan was no longer competitive in many of the areas it had pioneered. It took over six teetering banks, a policy that expanded the national debt, which today is one of the highest in the world at roughly twice the size of Japan's economy.

Japan's yawning debts catalyzed the Widowmaker trade: the bet that Japan's national debt would sink the country's bond markets. For investors who sold short its bonds—that is, selling borrowed securities on the hopes that the prices would fall before they had to pay for the borrowed paper—Japan was a disaster waiting to happen. Unfortunately, the collapse of the government bond markets on which investors had counted never happened, costing these investors fortunes. Some observers still believe the diagnosis was right, but the timing was off. Alpert disagrees: he thinks people lost so much money because the diagnosis was entirely wrong. He pointed out that unlike many other highly indebted countries, Japan enjoys the advantage that the vast majority of its creditors are its own citizens; in other words, stakeholders in the country's economic success. "If you take the entire household and corporate savings of Japan and offset it against bank debt, you get a donut," he said. "The country is not insolvent. Japan's not in a credit crisis. It just has funny looking books."

A Crack in the Wall

Sometimes it is eminently clear what we need to do to get out of the way of a Gray Rhino. Not sending workers into a dangerous building is one of those times. The collapse of a Bangladeshi building on April 24, 2013, injuring 1,800 factory workers and killing (by the official count) 1,132 people, was one of the worst industrial disasters ever. Yet it was no surprise: four other factories and a bank in the building had closed the day before when giant cracks appeared in the walls on the seventh floor. Industrial police had asked Rana Plaza to keep the building closed until it could be stabilized. At first, bosses told workers to stay out of the building, but later, after the building's owner insisted that the cracks were "nothing serious," ordered them to report for work. Many workers feared losing their jobs more than losing their lives, and paid the ultimate price for persuading themselves to ignore a clear and present danger.

Government officials had for years been turning a blind eye to illegal construction, in a system that provided little incentive to follow the law. It turned out that the original six-story building went up without permits, and that two additional floors were built, also illegal, as well as a ninth floor that was being built at the time of the collapse. Garment factories in the building produced clothing for major U.S. and European companies, many of which denied that they had authorized production there. Nineteen companies acknowledged a relationship with a Rana Plaza factory. A half-dozen others refused to admit that they permitted production at the building; two others refused to comment on whether the factories produced their garments, though their labels were found in the rubble. There was no system in place for holding factory owners or their clients accountable.

From 2005 to 2013, more than 1,800 workers died in preventable tragedies in Bangladesh: a 2005 collapse of the Spectrum garment factory after building cracks appeared killed 64 workers; a 2010 fire at a factory that supplied Gap, JC Penney, and Target killed 29 workers; a 2012 fire at Tazreen Fashions, a supplier of Walmart and Sears, that killed 112 people; and the Rana Plaza collapse. "We avoid using the word 'accidents' because we acknowledge that these tragedies could have been prevented with proper fire and building safety measures and with respect for workers' right to refuse dangerous work," wrote the authors of a report by the Clean Clothes Campaign, taking stock six months after the Rana Plaza collapse.

It became clear that See No Evil, Hear No Evil was the operating principle behind an industry that employed more than four million garment workers, seven out of ten of them women, in Bangladesh alone.

It's not as if Bangladesh has no laws. Tuba Group, the owner of the Tazreen factory, stated in a company profile that it is "strictly maintaining safety, health and hygiene provisions as per ILO's and Bangladesh labour law's rules and regulation."

Walmart reportedly performed an audit at Tazreen in May 2011, giving it an orange rating, flagging violations, and requiring the factory to draw up a plan to fix the issues. (It is unclear whether the factory ever did so.) The company had been certified by the Worldwide Responsible Apparel Production's Certification Board.

Nothing compares to the consequences that befell the workers who lost their lives. But the companies that did business with Tuba Group, either directly or through contractors, did not escape unscathed.

Fourteen major international companies—from Europe, the United States, and Hong Kong—risked serious damage to their reputations. Some of them claimed that the contractors had subcontracted to Tazreen without their authorization, so they were not responsible.

The Clean Clothes Campaign estimated that it would cost $71 million to provide full compensation to the families and survivors at Rana Plaza and $5.7 million at Tazreen. It's hard to calculate the brand damage to the companies involved, as much as many of them tried to deny responsibility.

Eight of the brands involved met in Geneva with the International Labor Organization and agreed to set up a fund to compensate the families who lost relatives and the survivors; other companies balked at taking any responsibility. Weeks after Rana Plaza, thirty-five initial companies signed the new Accord on Fire and Building Safety in Bangladesh; by the end of 2013, more than a hundred had signed on. During the same period, another sixteen garment workers died in building fires.

Shifting the Diagnosis

One company is trying to prevent future Rana Plazas by changing the diagnosis: turning a problem into a solution. Tau Investment Management is a fund built on the premise that it will be harder for companies to decide not to address obvious threats. Companies can either see that as a threat or recognize that the companies least vulnerable to possible future Rana Plazas will have a distinct advantage in a world where it's becoming increasingly hard to paper over worker abuses, shoddy products, and other black marks on their reputations. Tau's plan is to bring Western-style management to the global garment industry, making factories more productive and profitable by upgrading working conditions and equipment and connecting them with buyers who don't want to take the risk that they will have to deal with the fallout of another preventable disaster.

"Right now we have a flawed system built on a lack of transparency," Tau's CEO, Oliver Niedermaier, told me. Yet the speed and reach of social media is rapidly changing that. It is becoming harder and harder for companies to hide unscrupulous behavior and get away with it without significant consequences.

More and more companies see increasing transparency as an opportunity to do well by doing the right thing. "The more transparency you get on a superficial level, the more you connect the consumer with the worker in Bangladesh with investor and 401K holders," Niedermaier said. "The best corporations are getting ready for that level of transparency."

The kinds of corporations he means are the ones that have acknowledged not only the Rana Plaza tragedy but also what had happened with Nike, Kathie Lee, and Disney in Haiti and elsewhere: three strong brands that took heavy hits from campaigns against the sweatshop-labor conditions in which workers produced shoes and clothing. They recognize that dangerous working conditions represent a Gray Rhino far bigger than the economic cost of a building collapse.

"Things are going to change with the rise of Chinese and Indian consumers and the increasing sophistication of all consumers," said Ben Skinner, Tau's director of research, whose work as an investigative journalist has uncovered egregious human-rights abuses in supply chains around the world. (I met both Niedermaier and Skinner because they are fellow Young Global Leaders.)

"Governments increasingly are recognizing that people are fed up with having to drink bottled water because rivers are choked with pigs," Skinner said, noting that companies can no longer count on operating in the dark. "What is probable is that when the curtains open, I, as a large downstream consumer company, will have something that hurts my brand that I'll have to get rid of after the fact. For most companies, that's a high-probability event."

Skinner cites the example of New Zealand, which for three decades knew that its fishing industries were rife with slavery. Industry leaders tried to explain it away. Then they tried to claim that they couldn't do away with it without losing competitiveness. When the story came to light, one business that had been ignoring the problem went bankrupt. Another's market cap fell by millions, with the result that its CEO was forced out. New Zealand's parliament banned the types of vessels that had allowed slavery. "The CEOs who had seen it coming soaked up the opportunity—and new contracts," Skinner said. "Those other vessels thought they heard the Gray Rhino of China swamping them with cheap labor. What they didn't understand was that you can't cheapen the brand of New Zealand fish in an attempt to stay competitive with fish caught by Chinese vessels, or you're going to lose millions of dollars doing it."

A similar story of a garment-industry company that saw a threat and turned it into an opportunity is MAS Holdings, one of the largest companies on the Colombo Stock Exchange. Founded in the 1980s, the Sri Lankan company had built a steady business around making dresses out of synthetic fabric for a handful of companies in the United States, which at the time gave favorable treatment to some countries under the Multi-Fiber Arrangement. Those quotas were set to expire in 2005, which would force MAS and other Sri Lankan companies, with hourly wages at thirty-five cents, to compete with China (twenty-five cents) and Bangladesh (sixteen cents), with their much lower wages. Here was a real threat, with 100-percent probability, that had the potential to destroy MAS. It responded by moving its plants to the countryside to lower costs and marketing itself to big international firms based on the fact that it had working conditions far above what was typical for developing countries: onsite health care and child care, limits on overtime, a safe work environment, respectful interactions among managers and employees, free transportation, education, respect for women, and other socially responsible business practices that were not common. That helped it land contracts with consumer giants like Victoria's Secret and Marks & Spencer. Though its labor costs were not as cheap as China's, MAS won higher-end customers by showing that you get what you pay for.

Companies like MAS and Tau operate on the same principles that the legendary automaker Henry Ford did: "There is one rule for the industrialist and that is: Make the best quality of goods possible at the lowest cost possible, paying the highest wages possible." They understand that costs aren't just day-to-day expenses but the much greater potential costs and losses that come from being penny wise and pound foolish.

Ignore or Invest

Portuguese cork producers represent another industry that saw a clear path forward when faced by a clear and present danger: competition from synthetic bottle closures. As has been the reality for so many businesses, it took a crisis to jolt cork producers out of complacency. Through the 1990s, cork had close to 95 percent of the market share for bottle closures: more than 17 billion bottles worldwide. For centuries, it was the only closure acceptable for wine, despite the fact that it wasn't always perfect. Oenophiles had long been wary of "cork taint," caused by a cork fungus that can make wine smell like a wet dog, even at the most minute levels. Wine drinkers had long complained that they found cork taint in more bottles than they would have liked, but the cork industry turned a deaf ear. Its monopoly on bottle stoppers gave it a false sense of invincibility.

Past attempts to create alternative closures had failed; rather than recognizing rapidly changing technologies as a real threat, the industry remained complacent. And it relied on importers and distributors to get its products to market so did not have a good sense of what its customers wanted. Besides, as new wine producers were emerging in Australia and New Zealand, South Africa, and South America, the total market was expanding, increasing demand for bottle stoppers. Paradoxically, the rosy outlook hurt the industry by making it harder for deeply traditional producers to face the need to change.

In the 1980s, however, scientists identified the cause of cork taint: the chemical 2, 4, 6 Trichloroanisole, more commonly known as TCA. That discovery refocused attention on the problem. The timing could not have been worse for the cork industry, whose long neglect of the problem had driven innovators to pursue a viable alternative. Solid plastic had never worked as a substitute because it was too hard to put in and take out, and too prone to air leaks. But, as technology improved, this changed. In 1993, a Washington State company succeeded in producing the first injection-molded synthetic cork that was good enough to replace the real thing. Plastic stoppers started coming on the market soon afterward, and other producers jumped in. Then, in 2004, screw caps began eating away at the market. These new competitors used the TCA issue to aggressively chip away at cork's market share. Supermarkets, which had become increasingly important as wine sellers, seized on the cheaper alternatives. Cork's dominance of the bottle closure market came under serious fire, falling to under 70 percent.

In the 1990s and 2000s, the industry finally came to recognize the threat from the new competition. Cork producers faced a stark choice: ignore the challenge or invest. They had chosen the former for centuries; it was time to embrace the latter.

Corticeira Amorim is the world's biggest cork producer. Founded in 1870, Amorim is based in Santa Maria de Lamas, Portugal, a country that controls over 50 percent of the global cork market. Portugal relies on its more than $1 billion in annual cork exports to generate 60,000 jobs, the highest paid in the agricultural sector, because they require skills to harvest cork from trees by hand without killing the tree.

As head of the Portuguese Cork Association, Amorim's chairman and CEO, António Rios de Amorim, has been credited with playing a major role in pushing the industry to face up to the threats that it had been able to ignore for so long. "We had lots of internal debates: Either we stay with cork or we engage in whatever flavor of the month, becoming closure specialists and not cork specialists," Amorim told me.

To rise to the challenge from synthetic bottle closures, cork producers had to make sure that they had diagnosed the issues properly. They no longer were in denial about the need to treat cork taint and the possibility of lower-cost competitors as real threats. Amorim also realized that a key issue was that the cork industry had never connected with the end consumers of its product and so did not understand their desires, nor its own value proposition as well as it needed to if it was to win them back. It needed to do better than supermarkets in shaping its customers' preferences.

First, industry leaders had to deal with the TCA scare and convince bottlers that their corks were safe. In the mid-1990s, after the first synthetic corks appeared, Amorim invested in completely redesigning its factories, one the size of eleven football fields, in the south of Portugal, to new standards that helped it to win the fight against cork taint. Because factories are not built overnight, responding took time. Amorim opened the first factory in 2000 and the second in 2001.

Portuguese cork industry leaders worked together to create a code of good manufacturing practices, requiring every single cork producer to be approved. They brought in researchers and partners, including wine companies, to understand how they could improve the quality of their product. And they put that new knowledge to use developing new cork products, whether to better compete with alternative closures or to find new uses for cork. The transition was painful for many cork producers; the number of members of the Portuguese Cork Association has fallen to 267, only about a third of what it once was. The crisis thus had ushered in an era of creative destruction, creating casualties among companies that would or could not abandon old practices.

Once cork industry leaders were confident that they had defeated TCA, it was time to get the message out if it was to win market share back from the synthetic stopper manufacturers. Given the importance of the industry to the country, the Portuguese government agreed to help finance a €21 million marketing campaign in 2011 focused on communicating the value of cork to creating value and sustainability. Amorim and other European cork producers worked to address the cost issue by making a simple argument: that wine in glass bottles with cork stoppers fetched a much higher price than with synthetic stoppers. Maybe a plastic or screw top was cheaper, but if a cork allowed a winery to sell at a higher price, it was worth it.

They added the message that cork was a sustainable product from trees; it was good not only for the wine and for the environment but also for the bottom line. Amorim commissioned PricewaterhouseCoopers to study the total greenhouse-gas emissions of cork versus other kinds of bottle stoppers. The consulting firm concluded that its synthetic competitors emit between ten and twenty-four times as much greenhouse gas as cork, and use as much as five times more energy to produce. That study became part of its new messaging: "Artificial plastic wine stoppers or screw caps consume fossil fuels, and use at least five times more energy per ton to produce, before millions of them end up in our landfills and oceans. It may seem like a little thing, but demanding natural cork in your wine stopper is something we can all do."

Finally, the cork producers made the case that for a barrel worth $700 to $1,000, part of the value was the flavor from the oak, but that cork improved the taste of the wine even with the tiniest amount of contact with the stopper in a way that synthetics did not. Advertising aimed at California wine producers proclaimed, "Any wine worth its grapes deserves natural cork."

Amorim credits high end winemakers, especially champagne makers, with continuing to trust in cork and thus helping cork makers to understand its real value to oenophiles and to occasional drinkers. "If we could run a poll around the world and ask what people considered to be the five happy sounds of mankind, I bet the pop of a bottle being opened would be one of them," Carlos de Jesus, Corticeira Amorim's director of communications, added. "If you are going to throw that out the window for a metallic crackling sound, you had better know what you are doing."

The first marketing campaign, from 2011-13, helped to stabilize cork's share of the market and has been renewed twice. Cork's share of the global bottled-wine closure market is steady at around 70 percent. Major wineries, including Michel Laroche and Lurton in France, along with several California producers, have announced that they are returning to cork. In the United States, which had adopted synthetics more broadly than other countries, cork's share of bottle closures for premium wines had risen to 59 percent in 2015, up 9 percent in just five years.

I asked Amorim if the cork industry's near death experience had changed the way he and the company responded to possible future threats. He responded that the biggest impact was to keep the company on permanent alert. "We have not won any war. We keep winning battles but the war is always going to be out there," Amorim said. "We got through to have a dynamic that will allow us not to fall into that trap again."

Market Disruptions

The road is littered with companies and industries that failed to respond to market disruptions. Given the speed of technological change, there's a lot more where that came from.

The media industry offers a still unfolding example of the threat and the opportunity that the digital world has presented, and the double challenge of making the right move at the right time. Act too soon, and waste your investment; act too late, and become a has-been. AOL and AltaVista were early movers that were then overtaken by nimbler competitors. The *Wall Street Journal* invested early in digital but neglected the content that was its heart and soul, until its owners sold it to News Corp.

The troubles of Yahoo are well known. After a revolving door of CEOs—four from 2007 through 2012, with the most recent being Scott Thompson, who was fired for lying on his résumé—Yahoo brought in Marissa Mayer from Google. Mayer was widely respected as a dynamic, strategic leader. "Several wondered how Yahoo, a company so many had written off as mortally wounded, had nabbed such a well-regarded executive from rival Google," the *New York Times* noted at the time.

Her strategy was to make Yahoo's mobile offerings the best in class, improve the search engine, and acquire start-ups that might give it the Next Big Thing. But the strategy didn't produce change as big or as fast as investors wanted. Shareholders were calling for Yahoo to divest its biggest asset, a stake in Alibaba, and to merge with AOL, another onetime Internet innovator that had become a shadow of its former self.

A devastating profile appeared in *The New York Times Magazine* in January 2015: "Yahoo grew into a colossus by solving a problem that no longer exists. And while Yahoo's products have undeniably improved, and its culture has become more innovative, it's unlikely that Mayer can reverse an inevitability unless she creates the next iPod. All breakthrough companies, after all, will eventually plateau and then decline." The same month, Yahoo announced that it would divest Alibaba.

In hindsight, perhaps it would have been prudent to break up Yahoo earlier. But Gray Rhinos are more about foresight than about hindsight: seeing them is a matter of quickly recognizing that change is needed, and deciding what kind of change is called for. In Yahoo's case, there has never been a silver bullet. Yet change was coming.

In March 2015, *Fast Company* published a profile of Mayer titled "Don't Count Yahoo Out: How CEO Marissa Mayer Will Defy Her Critics." The article argued that Mayer had made significant changes in the company's culture and in the way it approached its business. "For the first time in years, Yahoo is positioned for some kind of future success, whether mild or bold," wrote Harry McCracken. The trick for Yahoo has been to define success, which may turn out to be a much smaller version of itself. Or it may be something bigger—but different.

Many companies have faced the same dilemma: Polaroid, BlackBerry, Barnes & Noble, whose stories are all still playing out. But there are also examples of companies that stumbled and then reinvented themselves, picking up the pieces after being trampled, so to speak: IBM, Apple, Ford, GM, and Chrysler.

What is the difference between the companies that successfully face down a Gray Rhino, the ones that get trampled and fall, and those that get trampled but recover? It's the speed in recognizing, prioritizing, and acting on the threat, the ability to look ahead, and the conviction to distinguish themselves from others. These abilities come back to the need to avoid groupthink. The companies that survive are the ones that are willing to listen to voices that are not the usual suspects saying what everyone wants to hear.

We have much to learn from both companies that have succeeded and those that have failed to manage an obvious threat, and from how each made decisions that shaped their futures.

Taxonomy of the Gray Rhino

Gray Rhinos, like real rhinos, come in many species. Inconvenient Truths, Recurring and Charging Rhinos, meta-Rhinos, Conundrums, Gordian Knots, Creative Destruction, Unidentified Rhinos—all play out in their own ways and require distinct strategies.

That's not even including the ones we misdiagnose. The strategies described in Chapters 2 and 3 can help us to make the right diagnosis, whether that leads to giving more consideration to the dangers that cognitive biases and homogeneous decision-making structures compel us to ignore, or to rejecting siren-like scenarios that draw us to them only to prove to be mirages.

Domino Rhinos catalyze or increase the impact of other related rhinos. Subprime mortgages coupled with lax risk management at banks combined with a liquidity crisis became the crash of rhinos of the 2007–08 global economic meltdown. Water and food scarcity combined with unemployment, governments' failures to acknowledge their populations' voices, and corruption all joined together to create the mess that is the Middle East today, a Gray Rhino mixed together from distinct beasts (a Chimera-Rhino, perhaps). These Domino and Chimera Rhinos should be at the top of our priority list, and we need to develop strategies to address them jointly. The advantage of these complex challenges is that the set of stakeholders is wider, potentially building a broader constituency for pushing through needed policy reforms, as, for example, advocates for improved health care and action on climate change have done.

Similarly, meta-Rhinos, particularly involving governance and decision-making, should be at the top of the priorities list. Some other challenges may never be solved if we fail to improve the way we analyze and choose which problems to address.

Conundrums and Gordian Knots are the hardest Gray Rhinos to confront, as we have seen in Syria, with the Israel-Palestine conflict, or with inequality. We can shape our responses in several ways. With complicated issues like inequality, breaking down the problem into specific,

Gray Rhino Taxonomy

Rhino Type	Characteristics	Examples	Strategies
Inconvenient Truth	Widely recognized yet significant resistance may remain to acting; manufactured denial; high costs to fix; vocal stakeholders; no single "silver bullet"; unequal distribution of impact	Climate change, budget deficits, obesity; unsafe industrial conditions; infrastructure; cork taint	Reframe as opportunities; develop cost and benefit sharing strategies
Charging Rhino	Fast-developing challenge; often a smoldering issue that flares up	Arab Spring, Syria, subprime collapse, humanitarian, natural disasters	Use advantage of urgency to act
Recurring Rhino	Familiar recurrence (may become a Charging Rhino)	Financial crisis, pandemics, weather events, earthquakes, cyber threats	Use checklists and drills to form habits; create automatic triggers; build resilience; avoid complacency
Meta-Rhino	Structural issue that creates/worsens other challenges	Governance, Inequality, rule of law, gender exclusion	Prioritize these and tie them to related rhinos
Domino and Chimera-Rhinos	A danger that affects other issues; combined they may become many-headed chimeras (Chimera-Rhinos)	Water scarcity, food price volatility, health, inequality	Prioritize these and address related rhinos jointly
Conundrum or Gordian Knot	No obvious answer, often with deeply embedded obstacles to resolution	Syria, Israel-Palestine, inequality	Reframe; treat symptoms
Creative Destruction	Inevitable obsolescence or situation where required effort is greater than the benefit	Kodachrome, water mills	Embrace the new; orchestrate orderly unwinding
Unidentified Rhino	Uncertainty over the nature of the danger and/or the solution	Artificial intelligence, digital impact on media (a conundrum or creative destruction)	Test scenarios and identify the most likely; be flexible and alert

achievable goals is important: rule of law, tax policy, education, housing policy are all elements of the challenge. Use the widespread concern over inequality to draw attention to how your specific strategy can solve the bigger problem. In conflict situations, often change is nearly impossible to carry out until there is a precipitating event—that is, a Charging Rhino. Prioritizing threats within a Gordian Knot also can help to frame responses; in Syria, for example, policymakers have been caught for some time between the Scylla and Charybdis of the Assad regime and ISIS, with competing geopolitical interests of other nations complicating the picture. As I write, it appears that policymakers have decided that ISIS is the bigger of the two threats, a shift in the balance of priorities that may change the course of events even as a surge of refugees has created a newfound sense of urgency.

Welcome the urgency that comes from a Charging Rhino. Where possible, use the momentum responding to these in order to draw attention to any related rhinos. Also, for Charging Rhinos that are similar to threats that have happened before and from which we have recovered, we can create systems and drills to create readily available tools and habits that will allow a better informed response. We have much to learn from Recurring Rhinos, which might be the easiest to prepare for if it were not for the complacency that arises when people escape one occurrence unscathed. Nevertheless, the systems that have emerged for containing the spread of the annual flu virus, or for warning of approaching tornadoes and hurricanes, can be applied to a wide range of threats in economic policy or organizations.

The best way to tackle Inconvenient Truths is to reframe them as opportunities. (We'll learn more about how companies have done this in Chapter 7.) It's also important to analyze which stakeholders feel most threatened by the changes that these challenges make necessary, and to find ways to create benefits to ease the pain.

Nearly every Gray Rhino also is an opportunity for those who have the foresight to recognize how to provide a solution to a problem. We need to recognize and treat them as such in order to not just get out of the way but also to profit. Even Creative Destruction, perhaps the most painful Gray Rhino to acknowledge, is a chance to build something new and better.

CHAPTER 5 TAKEAWAYS:

- **Size up your rhino.** Different kinds of threats require distinct strategies.
- **Define the crisis.** An approaching Gray Rhino may be a threat for one group but not for another. If the people with the power to act are not acting, reframe the threat in terms that matter to them. Reframe threats as opportunities.
- **Information creates a powerful incentive for change.** Use radical transparency to frame problems and raise the cost of being a laggard.
- **Don't rest on your laurels.** Some of the companies that have solved one problem become complacent and thus vulnerable to a later threat.
- **You won't always get the answer right at first.** Every error is a step toward the right answer. Sometimes what seems to be a misstep is actually a path to the solution.

6

PANIC: DECISION-MAKING FACING A CHARGING RHINO

As a French major in college, I read Eugène Ionesco's surrealist play *Rhinoceros*, which was inspired by Ionesco's efforts to understand Fascism in the lead-up to World War II. When I reread the play recently, I found it uncanny how closely it mapped to the Gray Rhino theory: denial reinforced by groupthink, muddling and dithering over what to do or not to do, and panic as the townspeople began turning into rhinoceroses.

The play begins with the residents of a small provincial French town gathered at an outdoor café in the town square, where they notice a couple of rhinos running through the streets. Their first obsession is whether the rhinos they saw are one-horned or two-horned, Asian or African (White Swans? Black Swans?), and whether they are seeing one one-horned and one two-horned rhino or two of either kind.

Berenger, the alcoholic Everyman who is the play's protagonist, at first pays little attention, in keeping with his generally passive nature. When Daisy, a young blond receptionist, tries to raise the alarm, others make fun of her. But then the townspeople start transforming into rhinos, throwing the social order into chaos.

The next day their colleague, the irascible Botard, argues loudly that there are no rhinos in France and blames journalists for making up the story so that they can sell more papers. When a rhinoceros destroys the staircase of the office, however, it becomes impossible to ignore the growing herd. Berenger tries to persuade his colleagues and neighbors not to succumb to the savage animal nature that is taking them over, but to no avail. One by one, the characters, from the skeptical Botard to their boss, succumb to rhinoceritis, transforming into giant beasts. Another colleague, Dudard, tries to convince Berenger that this is a normal and rational occurrence.

As the play draws to an end, only Berenger, Dudard, and Daisy remain in their human form. It appears that some make the choice actively, and others simply succumb. "It's hard to know the real reasons for people's decisions," says Dudard, reflecting on the fate of another man who turned himself into a rhinoceros. But Dudard, too, ultimately gives in and rushes off to become a rhino himself: "I feel it's my duty to stick by my employers and my friends, through thick and thin."

Daisy and Berenger, the only humans left at this point, wonder what they could have, should have, done differently instead of unintentionally doing harm or allowing it to advance unchecked. Berenger begs Daisy to join him in having children in order to regenerate the human race. But by now Daisy has given up on saving the world. "Why bother to save it?" she asks, then joins the herd.

Berenger is left alone. "People who try to hang on to their individuality always come to a bad end," he concludes. He is the last of his kind; torn between joining his friends and staying himself, he vacillates. He tries to become a rhino but cannot. Finally, he takes a firm stand: "Now I'll never become a rhinoceros—never, never!" But of course it is too late: the human race is doomed.

As the cartoonist Walt Kelly's alter ego, Pogo, might have said, we have seen the rhino, and he is us. When faced with a problem we don't want to deal with, we embrace all manner of ways of avoiding it. When we wait too long to head off a Gray Rhino threat, we're all too likely to end up in a panic state.

We are unlikely to act unless the Rhino is up close and personal; yet the closer it gets the smaller the menu of options, the faster we need to make decisions, and the less likely it is that our choices will resemble what we think they might be.

The decisions we make with foresight, at the height of euphoria, and with crisis imminent all create very different results. The psychologist Daniel Ariely has shown that our emotional state determines how our inhibitions and our prejudices kick in. "Our ability to understand ourselves in a different emotional state does not seem to improve with experience," Ariely has written.

The solution is to avoid getting to the panic state by quickly moving from recognition to diagnosis to action. That's easier said than done, however.

Buy Low

Hans Humes, the chairman and CEO of Greylock Capital, an investment firm that specializes in debt issued by countries in distress, met me at his Madison Avenue office in a Cameroon soccer jersey. He'd ridden a bicycle to work through Manhattan during a chilly, early spring downpour. Not only did he not complain about the rain; he actually seemed energized by it. That's the kind of person he is.

I've known Humes since he traded emerging-markets loans and bonds for Lehman Brothers in the early 1990s, long before the firm's name came to represent the domino effect after its spectacular 2008 meltdown. In a market where twenty-something-year-old traders who traded hundreds of millions of dollars' worth of Latin American debt every day bragged about the fact that they didn't speak a word of Spanish or Portuguese, Humes was someone who knew the countries in and out. He'd lived all over the world, spoke fluent Spanish, and had a genuine intellectual curiosity, not to mention a keen understanding of policy and a knack for making good market calls. He always knew exactly who in each country had their finger on what was really going on. One of my early memories is of meeting him and a colleague on the day that Peru and Ecuador went to war. He definitely needed a drink that day, but was considerably less rattled than you'd think someone would be considering that two of the countries in which he'd made big investment bets had declared war—on each other, no less.

Humes has made a career of identifying opportunities when everyone else is panicking; he makes money while, at the same time, helping
to solve some sizable financial problems. Over the years, he's been one of
the first people I've turned to for insights into financial crises in some
of the world's most overlooked locations. Iceland in 2008? He was thinking about buying Glitnir bank bonds as the country crumbled. Liberia?
During the country's civil war, he was quietly buying up its debt dirt
cheap—so cheap, in fact, that as Liberia's largest creditor he would later
make a tidy profit accepting just three cents on the dollar while also helping to wipe out much of what the war-torn nation owed its creditors. He
was a co-chair of the global advisory committee negotiating with Argentina after the country's spectacular collapse in 2001. And, as the Greek
crisis unfolded in 2010, he was a key part of the negotiations that helped
Greece and its creditors step back from the brink of disaster early in 2012.

There is nobody I can think of who has a better sense of how to keep
his cool—and his sense of humor—through the most bone-jarring market roller coasters. Where the panic stage of a Gray Rhino fells so many
others, he's made a living out of staying cool, rational, and proactive. So
I asked him to sit down to talk about what others might learn about how
to prepare for and navigate the panic stage of impending financial disasters, and how he reads market signals when the sky seems to be falling. I Ie pulled in his co-president, AJ Mediratta, a Bear Stearns veteran
who joined Greylock as a portfolio manager after J. P. Morgan bought
his former company. Mediratta is also a veteran of debt restructurings
in Latin America, Asia, and the Middle East.

We started with the question that few people are better placed to
answer, and the question that led to the Gray Rhino concept: What made
the difference between Argentina and Greece? Why did Argentina and
its creditors miss an opportunity to head off an obvious danger by writing down some of its debt, while Greece's private creditors did manage
to fend off disaster at least for the moment? "Engagement," Humes said
quickly. He believes that if Argentina had gotten together with its creditors and talked seriously about what needed to happen to avoid a default,
they could have done a deal that would have reduced how much creditors

lost and would have prevented at least some of the pain that followed the country's collapse.

But at that time there was no real mechanism for countries to easily acknowledge that they simply couldn't pay what they owed. As Walter Wriston famously said as chairman of Citicorp shortly before Mexico opened Latin America's "lost decade" in 1982 by declaring a moratorium on its debt payments, "Countries do not go bankrupt." But of course they had gone bust many times over the centuries and would continue to do so. Sovereign defaults have long been classic cases of denial and refusal to act that have led to panics and collapse.

A big part of the problem was that during market panics the inflection point from boom to bust, when countries in debt and their creditors most needed to be talking with each other about solutions, they weren't. So there was no way to respond quickly to keep things from getting worse. That is what happened in Argentina when both Argentina and its creditors refused to consider a 30-percent write-down nine months before everything fell apart, creditors lost more than 70 percent of their investments, and Argentina went into an economic tailspin that created misery for millions.

Yet Argentina kick-started a learning process that proved the old saw: A crisis is a terrible thing to waste. When Uruguay, hobbled by the woes of its next-door neighbor, lost its investment-grade status shortly after Argentina's collapse, the government began to worry that it, too, might run into problems repaying its debt. In March 2003, Uruguay went to its creditors to propose a restructuring that would delay maturities of bonds over the next several years, pushing them out into the future. Though an element that would be critical for Greece—a reduction of the amount owed—was missing, Uruguay was instrumental in showing that a voluntary restructuring could work, at least on a small scale, where liquidity, not solvency, was the main issue.

Countries and creditors began inserting collective-action clauses into borrowing agreements to make it easier to come together to find ways to prevent messy defaults if they ran into problems in the future. By the time Greece's problems became apparent in 2010–11, the precedents established by Argentina and Uruguay, combined with a willingness by investors and policy decision-makers not only to talk about what had been the unspeakable a decade earlier but to get together to do something about it, made all the difference.

"The market has evolved," Mediratta said. "Creditors now come together quickly and form committees before countries default." A few minutes later, Humes popped out to take a call from an investor concerned about the latest developments in talks between Greece and its European creditors—would Greece get the next round of its bailout funds or end up defaulting? The media were full of headlines warning of default looming as the next payment due date rapidly advanced, but Humes and Mediratta remained calm. They had noticed a subtle shift in European rhetoric about Greece, which they read as an effort to recast the problem as less dire than in earlier messaging: the discussion had moved away from the total amount of debt to a new focus on interest costs, which were eminently manageable. This kind of roller-coaster emotion was what they dealt with every day. Like firefighters or emergency-room surgeons, they worked from experience, knowing how to look beyond the chaos for the signals that would guide them to either buy or sell. They had been through similar swings many times before.

"In the summer of 2011, every week Greece was going down a couple of points. Investors were calling, asking should we buy or should we short?" Mediratta recalled. "We said, 'Do nothing. It's too orderly.' Before you move, you need to see a capitulation: a cleansing moment. We wait for that, and that's when we go in and establish a position, when denial is over." In other words, they waited until others panicked, and then moved in. Of course, Mediratta noted, drawing attention to the fact that their business was not for the fainthearted, "When you're catching falling knives, you tend to lose a finger or two."

In May 2012, Humes gave an interview to *The New York Times*, which quoted him calling investing in Greece "a no-brainer." Just a few months earlier investors, including Greylock, had agreed to write off three-quarters of the value of the debt they held, shrinking the country's debt by 100 billion euros. But Greece's "official" creditors had no intention of writing down any of the remaining debt, and it was far from certain that Greece would be able to keep up with the payments it owed bondholders. Over the summer, amid Greek elections and uncertainty, the price of the newly restructured bonds tumbled. The financial website Zero Hedge, whose motto is "On a long enough timeline the survival rate for everyone drops to zero," mocked Greylock and Humes all summer long.

But Greylock's logic was simple: that the European Union and the International Monetary Fund were unlikely to allow Greece to go under, given the probable cost to the taxpayers who ultimately held the debt; the new Syriza government had made clear that it would not ask for further sacrifice from private investors who had stepped up early on, and who now held relatively little debt compared with the European Union and the International Monetary Fund; and that Greece's problem was mainly one of rolling over debt when it needed to, since its annual payments were quite modest. Besides, North Korean debt was trading at fourteen cents on the dollar—roughly the same price as Greece, when Greece was light-years ahead in infrastructure, education, and many other measures.

Ultimately, the bet paid off: Greylock ended up quadrupling its money at a time when everyone was saying go the other way. There are two lessons to be learned here. First, having systems in place to help deal with a crisis makes it much easier to turn around a problem that has progressed to the panic state. Second, it pays to understand the nature of pack behavior and to be able to read the signals amid the turmoil.

The Best and the Worst

Decision-making at times of high stress brings out the best and the worst in leaders. Memory improves, senses sharpen, adrenaline rushes as we go into overdrive. But we lose the opportunity to consider unintended consequences, costs, and benefits—and to reason through. The preparation we've done ahead of time makes all the difference.

Facing a threat head on, the decisions we make are distinct from the ones we make from a distance, given the luxury of time that allows us to reason through responses and solutions. This is the difference between the kind of thinking that the behavioral economist Daniel Kahneman calls System 1 (the intuitive, subconscious, snap decisions we make on the turn of a dime) and System 2 (the reasoned, logical processing we do when we have the luxury of time). Using Kahneman's framework, in situations of imminent threat we need to find ways to override System 1 and put in place structures that (ideally) we've employed System 2 to create ahead of time.

How well we deal with an imminent threat depends on the organizational strategies we set up in advance. While breaking up group-think is the key to recognizing Gray Rhinos early on, there is evidence that in responding to crises it helps to have a tight, centralized decision-making structure.

Researchers at the Moynihan Institute of Global Affairs at the Maxwell School of Public Service at Syracuse University have assembled a database of past crises that crossed borders, and look in greater depth at eighty-one such crises around the world. They further grouped these events into those with more or less of an element of surprise, and the amount of time leaders had to deal with them. The 1997 Thailand currency crisis, the Waco Branch Davidian disaster, and NATO's response to the Kosovo crisis were among the thirty-nine cases judged to have been anticipated, to some extent, with an extended decision-making frame; the Exxon Valdez and the 1975 attack on the SS *Mayaguez*, off the coast of Cambodia, were among the seven decision-making frames that were short, but still anticipated crises. Among the thirty-one "surprise" events were things like the fall of Alberto Fujimori in Peru and the 1990 Gulf War over an extended time period; the DC anthrax attacks, the Madrid Bombing, and the Federal Aviation Administration's response to 9/11 were short-term surprise events.

The Moynihan Institute team found that in hindsight decision-makers were more satisfied with their choices when they faced a time-urgent crisis than when they had more time to consider various options. In the "anticipated" situations, 64 percent of policymakers with relatively more time to prepare and 55 percent with less time judged themselves to have been unsuccessful. In the "surprise" situations, 53 percent of policymakers viewed themselves as moderately or highly successful.

Why would this be? The Moynihan Institute political scientists Margaret Hermann and Bruce W. Dayton suggest that decision-makers are happier with choices they made themselves. "The data suggest transboundary crises that are anticipated by policymakers are generally unlikely to also be viewed as time urgent," they concluded in a paper summarizing the crisis research. "Indeed, the very fact that such an event has been anticipated may provide policymakers with some sense of comfort and, as a result, less need to act quickly." Committee dynamics can take over, turning plans for horses into camels, when leaders incorrectly believe that they have more time to deal with an impending crisis than in reality they do. Complacency is also an issue. The Bush administration correctly perceived Hurricane Katrina as urgent, Hermann and Dayton suggest, but incorrectly assumed that plans were in place, since it was not the first, nor would it be the last, hurricane to strike the coast. In less common "surprise"-triggering events, they argue that leaders have more control over which stakeholders and constituencies should be part of a decision and can thus act more assertively.

These insights help explain why the danger is so high that leaders inadvertently fall into the panic zone with Gray Rhino threats: we believe we are better at dealing with anticipated threats than we really are. The problem with Katrina was that although there was a plan in place, it wasn't followed. Clearly, if we did not have road maps ahead of time for things like hurricanes and tornadoes we would be in bad shape. But we also seem to need better mechanisms for judging whether the steps outlined ahead of time work. So there is a paradox: extra lead time affords us the opportunity to make reasoned, rational System 2 decisions, but it can dull our sense of urgency when we need to turn to System 1 to make decisions.

The timing of a Gray Rhino also plays a big part in whether we slip into the crack between thinking ahead and turning on a dime. Consider Dornbusch's rule, named for the late MIT economist Rüdiger Dornbusch, an expert on financial crisis. "The crisis takes a much longer time coming than you think, and then it happens much faster than you would have thought," he said of the 1994–95 Tequila Crisis collapse of the Mexican peso and the shock waves that resulted. "That's sort of exactly the Mexican story. It took forever and then it took a night." The forever lulls us into complacency, so that we are less likely to put in place the safeguards we need to be able to snap into action quickly, and to be able to pivot if the plans we made don't work out. It's not even enough to have a plan in place. As Mike Tyson famously said, "Everyone has a plan till they get hit. Then, like a rat, they stop and freeze."

Committee to Save the World

In fact, fear motivates many of the decisions that lead to crises getting worse. John Lipsky, a former acting head of the International Monetary Fund, sees fear as the reason so many financial problems end up being dealt with in crisis mode—above all, the 2008 financial meltdown. "There is still no organization for crisis prevention or resolution despite what should have been a wake-up call," he said in an interview. "Why did it take a committee being formed on an emergency basis to save the world?"

We had plenty of warning of the danger of future financial crises, which have recurred for as long as finance has existed. The emerging-markets financial meltdowns of 1995 and 1997 and 2001 should have triggered better response systems, but the IMF and other financial institutions failed to activate these systems.

"The lack of political commitments reflects a fear of failure. If you create no expectations of success, then there is no failure. You make a choice to let it ride lest you be accused of having failed," said Lipsky. "Are you trying to solve a problem? Or are you trying to avoid being told, in four or five years, 'You screwed up,'" he asked.

"Taking emotion out is damaging," said Denise Shull, the founder of the risk and performance advisory consulting firm ReThink Group, which combines insights from neuroeconomics, psychodynamic psychology, and markets. "It's not enough to know what is to be done: one has to *feel* it." Speaking at a conference in New York, she argued that the core emotion behind financial crises is not greed but fear: the fear of missing out.

How We Rate Ourselves

If we are to prepare ourselves better to handle future crises, we need to have an accurate understanding of our actions—both how they change under stress and how they appear in retrospect. This is harder than you might think.

Therese Huston, a cognitive psychologist at Seattle University, has compiled evidence that decision-making strategies change when we're under stress. Interestingly, both men and women change the way they make decisions, but they do so in very different ways. A study by Mara Mather of the University of Southern California and Nichole Lighthall of Duke University, for example, awarded subjects points for inflating digital balloons but subtracted the points if the balloons popped. The team compared the decisions made both before and after the subjects had to submerge their hands in painfully cold water. Before the icy water, men and women made about the same number of pumps to inflate the balloons. Afterward, however, women stopped pumping sooner and men increased the number of pumps by as much as 50 percent more than women, showing that women respond to stress by becoming more conservative and men make riskier decisions. Nor, Huston warns, are we always aware when stress skews our decisions. Again, men and women differ in their self-awareness. She cites a 2007 study by Stephanie Preston of the University of Michigan in which women made better decisions as a stressful event approached than did men and, in retrospect, were more likely to rate their bad decisions as risky. "If we want our organizations to make the best decisions, we need to notice who is deciding and how tightly they're gritting their teeth," Huston wrote in a *New York Times* article about her research.

These findings become especially important in the context of the groupthink risks discussed in Chapter 2. Not only does having women as part of the decision-making process help in flagging and recognizing risks; the higher risks rise, the more essential it becomes to fill leadership roles with people other than the usual suspects.

The Columbia University neuropsychologist Heather Berlin wants us to realize the power of unconscious brain activity in shaping our motives and decisions. "People are often not aware of the countless different things that affect their decisions about what they do and say," she has written. Unconscious changes happen hundreds of milliseconds before we are conscious of them. She also warns that we can respond unconsciously to stressed, angry, or fearful faces around us, which trigger reactions in the amygdala—the part of the brain that's responsible for emotions and motivation.

Thus, once members of a decision-making group enter the panic mode, the people around them are likely to become panicked as well without necessarily recognizing that this is what is happening. In addition, as we evaluate our decisions we may create defense mechanisms to avoid feelings like guilt and anxiety. Part of counteracting the danger of making decisions in panic mode is to be aware of the important role emotion plays in the choices we make when faced with an imminent crisis. We are far more capable of engaging reason and logic when we're not in the grip of panic and fear.

Forcing the Crisis

While panic and fear do warp our decision-making, they can also play an important role in forcing action. It's always darkest before the dawn, we're told. That's often true when fighting inertia and trying to make change happen. Sometimes panic is the only way we can get leaders to pay attention, at least in the short term. In the early 1990s, I was a financial reporter at Dow Jones, writing about the restructuring of emerging markets, around the time that bankers were starting to use that term instead of "less developed countries."

My colleagues and I used to marvel at traders' seeming infatuation with the gallows. The worse things seemed in—pick your country: Venezuela, Russia, Ecuador, Brazil—the more traders seemed to be jumping in, betting that the more dire the situation seemed, the more likely things were to get better quickly. As Boris Yeltsin faced down Russian police in front of Parliament in 1993, traders in New York and London were buying every piece of Russian paper they could get. Why? Because investors and traders were counting on a crisis to force changes.

In financial markets, wily investors have made even more money than usual by accelerating a crisis when they see it coming. George Soros reportedly claims to get a backache whenever it's time to sell. In 1992, he saw that differences among the French, German, and British currencies were creating tensions that were likely to destroy the currency arrangement that was the precursor to the euro. He not only bet on that outcome but sped it up through a short-selling attack on the pound, which forced it out of the European monetary system. Soros, of course, wasn't trying to fix the problem, only to make money on it. But the case of the pound sterling shows that there are opportunities in spotting a problem early and directing the herd the way you want it to go.

The more acute the crisis, the more likely it is that the people who can make decisions will do so, though it may still be too late. On the popular television show *Grey's Anatomy*, the surgical intern Isobel "Izzie" Stevens faced this dilemma after she fell in love with one of her patients, Denny Duquette. Denny's heart was failing, but his condition was not severe enough to get him placed higher on the transplant list. She risked her career by cutting his LVAD wire so that his heart would get bad enough for him to receive a transplant. Unfortunately, he died, and the hospital suspended her.

The episode provides real food for thought. Is it justified to make a situation worse in order to increase the chances of saving it? Is it possible to make a crisis bad enough to force the people who have the power to do something—but not so bad that it kills the patient? How soon is soon enough? And, once you force decisions, how do you make sure they are the right ones?

The Paradox of Familiarity

Traders and physicians condition themselves to avoid acting emotionally in situations that raise their stress response but require them to stay calm. We run through endless building fire drills and airplane-safety announcements in the hope that the knowledge of what to do in the event of a fire or a crash landing will be firmly embedded. Police and firemen train in advance to embed in their subconscious the implicit knowledge that allows them to respond in crises using as much of their subconscious as possible without having to pause and "actively" think through their response. Yet even that training fails, as happened in 2014, when police responded to a call saying that a man was on a neighbor's porch with a "gun"; they thought they saw him point it at them and shot him dead, with a garden-hose nozzle in his hand. As for traders . . . they make millions of decisions daily, acting rationally so much of the time, but when it comes to bubbles they fail.

At the World Economic Forum Summer Davos meeting in Dalian in 2008, just after Lehman Brothers failed, a friend of mine spoke with the vice-chairman of a major U.S. bank and realized two things. First, the banker did not at all understand what was going on in the markets. Second, he was terrified. My friend called the chairman of the board of the company he ran and said that they immediately needed to prepare for the worst. They got a jump on companies that remained in denial. Sales fell in October, November, and December; other companies came up with reasons for this. But business didn't recover in January, and fell off the cliff in February. By the time other companies started to react, my friend's company had already acted. My friend avoided panic mode because he recognized panic elsewhere and made a plan ahead of time.

The successful decisions we make both on a regular basis and in situations that are out of the ordinary show that it's possible to keep panic from overtaking us. But to protect ourselves from times when we know that our emotions will trump our reason we need something more. We need to create systems that bypass human decisions both on the final ascent of the roller coaster and as the descent begins and accelerates.

These systems work in two ways: by creating habits and systems so strong that responding in time becomes second nature, and by creating automatic triggers that make it harder to run over the edge of the cliff.

Do I Have Ebola?

We panic easily and make terrible decisions about relative risks, paradoxically putting ourselves at greater risk. Take, for example, the Ebola outbreak of 2014. It captured the imaginations and tapped into the deepest fears of people in places far from the countries where the virus was running rampant. Because of the epidemic's high emotional value, Americans' risk perception was exponentially higher than the chances of most people getting the disease. These perceptions, unfortunately, were driven by incomplete and inaccurate information and by a barrage of media coverage. Yet this reaction stood in stark contrast to the reactions of many of the agencies that had been tasked with watching out for such an epidemic, and that downplayed the risk at hand.

In the fall of 2014, the United States was in the middle of silly season, with overreactions verging on utter panic. When a doctor returned to New York City from Liberia, where he had been treating Ebola patients, hysteria ensued despite the fact that the disease is not transmitted by casual contact, or by anyone who is not yet showing symptoms. Even Thomas Eric Duncan, the patient who died in Dallas, Texas, did not infect his girlfriend, family members living with him, or the more than fifty people who came into contact with him after he began to show symptoms. (Two nurses who cared for him during the worst of it, with projectile vomiting and diarrhea, did get infected.) As a helpful graphic put it, "Quiz: Have you touched the vomit, blood, sweat, saliva, urine, or feces of someone who might have Ebola? Answer: NO. You do not have Ebola." (Tongue in cheek, it added: "Do you watch the news? YES. You have Ebola.")

A day after returning from a short trip to Morocco, I ended up in the emergency room because of flashes and floaters in my eyes—hemorrhages, it turned out, likely caused by the frequent pressure changes of too much air travel. The staff at the front desk had been instructed to ask if any-one had been to Africa recently. My sister, who drove me to the hospital, said afterward that the best part of an unpleasant evening was seeing the alarm on their faces when I said that, yes, I'd just come back from Africa the day before, even though the symptoms I'd described to them were nothing like those for Ebola. It seemed to help a little bit only when I reminded them that Morocco was more than three thousand miles away from the countries suffering from the epidemic. (To be fair, about a month later an Ebola victim arrived in the United Kingdom via the Casablanca airport, into and out of which I'd flown. But, still, even that was a far cry from what must have been crossing the hospital staff's minds.)

More than 9,000 deaths occured, about a third of the people confirmed to have the virus, largely in Sierra Leone, Liberia, and Guinea. *The New England Journal of Medicine* excoriated the World Health Organization for not having acted more quickly. "Not only did it take more than three months to diagnose Ebola as the cause of the epidemic (in contrast to the recent outbreak in the Democratic Republic of Congo, where it took a matter of days), but it was not until five months and 1,000 deaths later that a public health emergency was declared, and it was nearly another two months before a humanitarian response began to be put in place," Jeremy J. Farrar and Peter Piot wrote in October 2014. "It is not that the world did not know: Médecins Sans Frontières, which has been spear-heading the response and care for patients with Ebola, has been advocating for a far greater response for many months. This epidemic, in other words, was an avoidable crisis."

Ella Watson-Stryker traveled to Guinea, Sierra Leone, Monrovia, and Liberia as part of MSF's Ebola response team. "The virus had been spreading for months and it wasn't reported till a doctor died," she re-called in a conversation at Columbia's School of International and Pub-lic Affairs, where we are both alumnae. The MSF team had the gruesome task of helping to persuade terrified people to follow heart-wrenching safety measures. "We had to explain that this was not a man-made virus, not a government plot to kill you, not a way for NGOs to make money," she said. "And then we had to tell them, 'Don't take care of the sick, don't bury the dead.' The things you would normally do to honor people you love, you can't do. It's a horrible message that people didn't want to hear, but that was our job."

Time magazine featured Watson-Stryker, representing "The Ebola Fighters" on the cover of its 2014 "Person of the Year" issue. No matter how hard they worked, it got worse. The more beds they built, the faster, it seemed, the facilities were overwhelmed by new cases. But regional health ministers didn't want to hear it. The World Health Organization didn't want to hear it—and even turned away the CDC. "We called for help in April. We called for help again in June. When we said we had an unprecedented situation, we were told we were exaggerating. We were told not to exaggerate the situation," Watson-Stryker said. "People denied they had the disease. Governments hid the number of deaths. They denied it for months."

The Ebola crisis started out like so many Gray Rhinos: with denial and muddling. The diagnosing of the responses was more complicated. The problems went far beyond the immediate situation: they were rooted in the fact that there was no functioning health-care system in Africa. Ebola was rooted in a crisis that was much larger than the medical challenges that arose: a problem of governance; perverse incentives; misdirected resources; failure of disease surveillance and response; a decision-making process that was warped first by inertia and then by the emotional intensity of the moment; a lack of ownership and agency from the most grassroots levels to the sterile halls of multinational organizations. The people with the resources that could have helped didn't notice until Ebola threatened their own. America really engaged fully only after an American doctor, Kent Brantly, was flown back to the United States for treatment after contracting Ebola while treating patients in West Africa; and when Thomas Eric Duncan who was diagnosed shortly after arriving in Dallas died several days later.

An imminent crisis is far more likely than a slowly unfolding threat to push us into action. But the opposite can happen, too: people can regress to the denial stage. That is what happened with Ebola, in part because the underlying problems had gone unaddressed for so long. The lack of resources to treat even the most basic health problems had created a state of learned helplessness that turned an infection into an epidemic. When there are no hospitals, no doctors, no medicines, even in the face of chronic malaria, cholera, and other diseases, why would anything be different with this illness?

Learned helplessness can lead to an even worse outcome: a reaction against efforts to solve a problem. In Guinea, when panic set in mere passive denial would have been a blessing compared with some of the reactions: people who associated the virus with the arrival of foreign doctors attacked and threatened medical personnel. The costs of allowing a situation to reach the panic stage can escalate, sucking resources away from longer-lasting and far more productive uses, and thereby perpetuating a vicious cycle in which lack of funds leads to other crises that then siphon off more resources.

At the end of 2014, the World Health Organization estimated that Ebola would cost West Africa roughly $32 billion, much of it from lost trade and economic activity, alongside a human cost that the mere number of more than ten thousand deaths doesn't begin to describe. Building a system ahead of time, by some estimates, would have required less than one-half of a percent of the cost of dealing with the epidemic ex post facto. In December 2014, the U.S. Congress approved $5.4 billion to fight the virus, nearly as much as the CDC's entire budget, which is around $6.8 billion. This is the cost of waiting for panic to make change happen. The choice should not be between paying for a pound of cure and doing nothing at all, but that's what it amounts to most of the time, because our decision-making systems are bad at creating action when we're not in a pickle. It doesn't have to be that way.

Yet waiting for panic is the status quo. The CDC estimates that only 16 percent of countries are fully prepared to address health threats. What we need to fight pandemics is, more often than not, the same thing we need to fight everyday health-care issues: a solid system that quickly gets care to the people who need it—or gets people to the care.

In many cases, treating Ebola turns out to be shockingly easy when it's caught quickly enough: antibiotics (Cipro), over-the-counter painkillers, and oral rehydration salts, combined with systematic disinfection practices and isolating those who are sick to avoid contagion. In rich countries, that's a simple set of remedies to provide. But when the resources for doing something so seemingly reasonable aren't available, the results are tragic. That's why in Liberia, Sierra Leone, and Guinea, between 50 percent and 70 percent of those infected by the virus died, while in the United States eight of the ten people who were infected survived.

The building that houses the Centers for Disease Control is modern and filled with light, with a view of downtown Atlanta in the distance past treetops and parkland. In normal times, the situation room is relatively quiet, with giant screens rotating maps and charts displaying the latest disease statistics: domestic clinical inquiries, cumulative cases and deaths, trends in surveillance indicators, weather, logistics support activities, monitored events, and more. On the day that I visited, the threat level had been downgraded to 1, the lowest intensity, reflecting confidence that the United States was succeeding in keeping Ebola from infiltrating its border. Yet a less emotionally jarring but far more dangerous threat was imminent.

Between 3,000 and 49,000 Americans die each flu season, a number that fluctuates dramatically. To be sure, even the higher number is a much smaller percentage of all flu cases than died from the latest Ebola epidemic. But while Americans were expending untold angst over Ebola, they weren't getting their flu vaccinations; the CDC estimates that only 40 percent of Americans were vaccinated against the flu. By the end of December 2014, while Ebola hysteria continued even though there had been only two U.S. deaths and ten cases (only two of which had been contracted in this country), the CDC had declared a flu epidemic, with fifteen children dead.

The 2014 Ebola and flu epidemics are good examples of how our emotions drive the decisions we make. Because Ebola was new in the United States, it attracted a lot of attention. In turn, media saturation generated hysteria. Social media, much of it driven by incomplete and inaccurate information, made Ebola panic go viral (so to speak). Yet, in terms of real threat to Americans, it didn't compare to a typical flu season. The unwinding of the epidemic in Africa was a different story. While the number of deaths paled next to that of, say, malaria, the rapid spread of the virus was a real cause for concern in places where the most basic medical care and prevention were not in place. Had the virus continued to double at rapid rates the situation could have become catastrophic. Despite the initial delay in response in early 2014, the ramping up of aid and medical staff in the region made sense, if a day late and a dollar short. The tragedy was that had the money spent on responding to Ebola instead been spent ahead of time on building basic medical infrastructure, it could not only have kept Ebola from spreading as much as it did but also have provided needed medical care to prevent and treat many other maladies. It also could have prevented the wasting of resources on hastily built facilities that turned out not to have been useful, like the eleven treatment units built by the U.S. military, of which nine never treated a single Ebola patient. The two that treated people together helped a total of twenty-eight Ebola patients.

The great irony was that 2014 was one of the years in which the annual flu vaccine fell short. Each year, 141 national flu centers in 111 countries study the virus strains that circulate and send information to the World Health Organization in order to help predict what the most prevalent strains will be the following flu season. Months before the next October to May flu season begins, the WHO makes a recommendation and each country decides which strains to license. Because the vaccine takes months to manufacture and viruses mutate over time, a lot of guesswork is involved. Nevertheless, typically the vaccine is 60- to 70-percent effective. In 2014–15, however, the circulating virus strains mutated rapidly, and the vaccine was estimated to be only about 23-percent effective. By the end of January, 69 children had died in the flu season and nearly 12,000 people had been hospitalized. Flu and pneumonia (to which the flu often progresses) were close to 9 percent of all deaths, significantly above the 7.2 percent rate, which is considered an epidemic.

Meanwhile, measles, which had been all but eradicated from the United States, was coming back. Not only had Americans become complacent, as happens all too often after a problem has been addressed; many parents were outright hostile to vaccinations. A report, which since has been widely discredited and its author's medical license revoked, had linked autism to vaccines, creating panic among parents and catalyzing an anti-vaccination movement. The measles cases in 2014, as in past years, had occurred largely in unvaccinated children. "Patient Zero" was an unvaccinated child at Disneyland; soon there were more than 150 cases in sixteen states.

We don't always move forward, alas; sometimes Gray Rhinos grow larger when we reverse course from action backward to denial.

Creating Habits

When it snows, we shovel sidewalks and driveways and put down salt as a matter of habit. When a tornado approaches and sirens go off, we go into the basement. When flu season begins, some of us—but, alas, not nearly enough of us—get shots to protect ourselves.

The annual flu vaccine is an example of a regular process that, even with all its flaws, shows the kind of thinking that could prevent so many other Gray Rhinos. Financial crises, for example, have much in common with viruses. We could benefit from applying the same principles that epidemiologists apply to the annual flu virus. They systematically look at warning signs, and have well-rehearsed road maps for how to respond.

Gaining confidence in our ability to predict the escalation of threats to full blown crises will help us spend less time in the denial stage and to take the kind of action that allows us to move forward. Given what we know about human nature, we won't always succeed. That's why we also need ways to override our natural resistance to what we don't want to hear or see. New systems on self-driving cars can "see" things humans can't. More important, they are not vulnerable to the kinds of things that humans do even when we know we shouldn't. They don't text while driving. They aren't teenagers whose elevated testosterone gives them a sense of invincibility that leads them to make bad decisions. They don't accidentally take the wrong medication and fall asleep at the wheel. Self-driving systems in other areas of life and decision-making can help us to prioritize threats and override our failure to see and act.

A growing number of regular tests sound warning signals and require action when those signals flash red. The now commonly used Apgar score for infant health, developed in 1952 by Dr. Virginia Apgar to quickly decide whether a newborn needs immediate specialized medical attention, is a good example. At one minute and five minutes after birth, obstetric staff check the baby's APGAR: Appearance, Pulse, Grimace, Activity, and Respiration. They hope for scores above 7, which indicates that a baby is in good health; babies with scores between 4 and 6 sometimes need help breathing; below 3 often requires immediate urgent care to save a baby's life.

What about something similar for the economy: scores that go beyond the regular economic indicators we now use, and trigger action? We need measures that are concrete and hard to deny and ignore. After the 2008 crisis, policymakers began applying what might be considered Apgar scores for the economy.

The stress tests designed for banks after the 2008 meltdown are another example. Each year, the Federal Reserve Board requires thirty banks with $50 million or more in assets to go through the Comprehensive Capital Analysis and Review (CCAR)—the fancy name for stress tests—to be sure they have enough capital on hand in case of a crisis; exercize proper internal processes for assessing capital adequacy; and can analyze their plans to pay dividends or buy back stock. Only the banks that pass are allowed to pay dividends or carry out buybacks. After the first round of tests, in 2009, the Federal Reserve ordered the ten banks that failed (out of nineteen) to raise a total of $75 billion in capital.

Europe, slower to adopt its own stress tests, eventually did so in 2013, with a warning that banks that failed the tests would have to prepare "specific and ambitious strategies" for responding, such as selling assets, merging with another bank, or forcing private creditors to reduce what they are owed.

In 2013, the Bank of England switched from targeting nominal GDP to targeting inflation, and later the jobless rate, as a trigger for when it would consider raising interest rates. With inflation consistently low and confronting worries about deflation, the U.S. Federal Reserve Bank similarly began to use the unemployment rate as the signal for when it would ease off its monetary stimulus.

These policymakers all looked in new places for information that could help them make better decisions based on what was likely to happen next. When it was first created in 1934, the concept of Gross Domestic Product was a new way to guide policymakers, who before then had been driving blind. Matthew Bishop and Michael Green have called the development of the GDP concept "one of the least heralded, but most important, lessons from the Great Depression." GDP took us a long way toward better planning, but we've outgrown it. A 2009 report by the Commission on the Measurement of Economic Performance and Social Progress, chaired by Joseph Stiglitz, warned that GDP leaves out important changes in the quality of goods and services, living standards, and sustainability. In his book *Brave New Math*, Peter Marber contends that part of the reason policymakers did not react to other warning signals more quickly in 2007–08 was that GDP looked strong, so they didn't look further.

An example of another system that "drives" for us: balanced mutual funds that automatically rebalance. They track when a better-performing part of our portfolio grows bigger than the allocation we want, and sell securities to shift funds elsewhere.

There are plenty of good early-warning systems, particularly for weather. Though there are always a few holdouts who rashly ignore them, the vast majority of people pay attention to tornado warnings throughout the Midwest or to hurricane warnings on the East Coast. Tsunami warning systems were set up in the Pacific in the 1920s and in the Atlantic in the 1940s and 1960s. Not unlike the recently created bank stress tests, these systems all followed disasters: the Aleutian Island earthquake and tsunami in 1946, and the Valdivia earthquake in 1960. After the 2004 tsunami, an Indian Ocean warning system was set up as well. As long as the earthquake that generates the tsunami is far enough from shore, the system can save many lives. False alarms for tsunamis are an inconvenience, but they don't lose people money; false alarms in financial crises, by contrast, can become self-fulfilling prophecies. What both share is that if people don't heed a true warning they pay a price.

Self-Adjusting Systems

We need to do more to create systems to protect us from the poor decisions we make as a crisis unfolds, whether in finance, health, weather, or anywhere in life, policy, and business.

John Cochrane of the University of Chicago's Booth School of Business has proposed a "narrow banking" system, harking back to a proposal made by a group of economists at the university, who suggested that banks' deposit-taking and loan-making functions be separated. The idea was to better control credit cycles, prevent bank runs, save interest burden on the government and thus dramatically reduce federal debt, and reduce private debt, as a 2014 study by two IMF economists concluded the proposal would do.

Under Cochrane's updated version of the Chicago Plan, banks and money-market funds would be allowed to invest only in short-term debt with the lowest possible risk; that is, Treasury bonds. Any other bank business would have to be financed via equity. In addition, to offset the risks to society created by lending, banks would pay a Pigovian tax, named for the English economist Arthur Pigou (who also gave his name to a club of economists supporting a carbon tax), on outstanding debts. *The Economist*, in reporting on the proposal, pointed out that switching from the existing system to the proposed one would be difficult. It also raised the question of whether new fragilities might emerge as other institutions replaced banks in making loans. Yet it noted that the merits of the proposal deserved serious consideration.

For Cochrane, the Gray Rhino is bank runs. "[C]urrent regulation guarantees run-prone bank liabilities and instead tries to regulate bank assets and their values," he writes. "[A] much simpler, rule-based, liability regulation could eliminate runs and crises, while allowing inevitable booms and busts." What is appealing about the modern version of the Chicago Plan is that it makes bank runs impossible, canceling some of the panic behaviors that essentially throw us right into the path of the Rhino.

Other countries have experimented with self-adjusting systems. Germany and Sweden put in place automatic stabilizing measures, which kicked in during the 2008–09 depths of the financial crisis. Chile, which depends heavily on commodities prices, has a copper-stabilization fund that puts money into a rainy-day fund when prices are high so that the government can draw on it when times are tough. (Venezuela tried this with an oil fund, but much of the money disappeared, a casualty of the country's widespread corruption.)

The people who are good at recognizing financial Gray Rhinos and thrive on volatility will not be the biggest fans of such a system, but they can take comfort in the fact that no system is able to completely remove risk; the need to improve rapid-response systems for pandemics is its own Gray Rhino.

To get leaders to act sooner, we can up the ante, as some investors have done, by manipulating markets, forcing change sooner rather than later. The rise of social media has created other ways of creating a sense of urgency, as evidenced both by the Arab Spring and by the Ebola viral social-media panic. We can apply lessons from epidemiology and hurricane, tornado, and tsunami warnings: inoculating and setting out road maps for responding. Recent efforts to improve financial supervision and safety nets have attempted to do so—not coincidentally, right after a financial tsunami. Still, we could do a lot better through a combination of better signals and having an auto-pilot kick in when we just don't see the signs.

The best way to get out of the way of a Gray Rhino is to find a way to skip the panic stage entirely, and to move from diagnosing to action as quickly as possible.

CHAPTER 6 TAKEAWAYS:

- **Herd behavior in times of panic throws us right into the path of a Gray Rhino.** Panic can magnify the original problems and turn a single rhino into a crash. It can catapult us backward, past denial to outright hostility and aggression, getting in the way of any progress that has been made toward solutions.
- **Create trip wires** against irrational exuberance. Set into motion **"auto-pilot" threat responses** that our denial reflex might keep us from doing on our own.
- **Raise the stakes earlier.** A stitch in time saves nine, so to speak—and the sooner you can create a sense of urgency, the lower will be the cost of solving a problem.
- Learn from epidemiology and hurricane, tornado, and tsunami warnings: **inoculate; set out road maps for responding; and train people to act automatically**—like midwesterners taking cover in the basement when the tornado sirens sound, or schoolteachers getting an annual flu shot.
- **Beware the rhino's horn.** Alleged (wrongly) to be an aphrodisiac, the horn is something to be used with caution. Forcing a crisis can reduce the total cost and speed a resolution, but it also can wreak havoc.

7

ACTION: THE "AHA" MOMENT

The air around Milwaukee's MillerCoors brewery is rich with the smell of hops and malt. The aroma wafts down to Interstate 94, where it is still so strong that you don't need to read the signs to know that you're near the Thirty-fifth Street exit. The brewery harks back to the German immigrants who shaped Milwaukee in the nineteenth century. Though its founding is an important part of the city's history, today this brewery is also an example of how a company has looked into the future, seen a clear danger, and acted to address the problem before it gets worse.

The brewery is just a few minutes' drive from Lake Michigan—one of the Great Lakes, which together hold six quadrillion gallons of water, or 20 percent of the world's fresh water. That abundance of water is one of the reasons that breweries proliferated in the Midwest. But even a resource that bountiful isn't limitless, and the eight U.S. Great Lakes states don't take this for granted. In 2008, Congress approved and President George W. Bush signed into law an accord initiated by those states in partnership with the Canadian provinces of Ontario and Quebec, to limit their ability to divert additional water from the lakes beyond the existing farming and industrial uses, which already had begun to take a toll, and which climate change has worsened. In the 1990s, average water levels in the lakes began to fall dramatically as changing weather patterns raised water and air temperatures and increased evaporation. In 2013, average water levels in Lakes Michigan and Huron fell to the lowest level since the National Oceanic and Atmospheric Administration began keeping records in 1918.

The reality of water scarcity influenced the way the Milwaukee brewery thinks about how it uses water. The same year the Great Lakes Compact was signed, 2008, MillerCoors started a companywide initiative to reduce its water use. SABMiller, a multinational beverage company, had formed a joint venture, in the fall of 2007, with the Colorado-based Molson Coors, the world's seventh-largest brewer. Both companies had independently been concerned about responsible water stewardship, and the joint venture reflected that.

They had recognized a stark reality: if they and their peers failed to respond to growing indications that water scarcity was a major threat, it was highly likely that they would miss major market opportunities. As Kim Marotta, MillerCoors director of sustainability, often says, the core of the strategy boiled down to a simple concept: "No water, no beer."

A former public defender with a business degree in marketing, Marotta had always cared deeply about the impact her work had on the lives of others. Water has been a central focus of her work at MillerCoors, where she has overseen projects on water stewardship with barley farmers and, within the breweries, projects that run the gamut from waste reduction to sustainable farming to reducing water use at every stage of manufacturing and distribution. "It's so core to everything," she told me in her Milwaukee office on the brewery campus, where water is used in every step of the process, from cleaning to infusing to boiling and fermenting.

MillerCoors sent a companywide water-efficiency team on a learning mission to South America, where some of SABMiller's most water-efficient breweries were located, and were surprised by what they learned. "It wasn't technology. It's not capital projects," Marotta told me. "It's people. That was the biggest 'Aha' moment." The team brought those lessons back to individual MillerCoors breweries across the United States and started putting them into action. "We set up water war rooms and asked everyone within the breweries to contribute ideas on how we could reduce our water usage. We knew that if we changed the culture and empowered our people, we'd be able to create change. Almost immediately the next month, we started to see reductions in our water usage," she said.

Inside the Milwaukee brewery, the sweet smell is intoxicating as grain is converted into sugar and fermented. The first step of brewing takes place in giant copper lauter tuns. Hot water is added to barley mash to break starches down into fermentable sugars. When the sugar content is right, the mash is separated into liquid and solids to create malt extract. The spent mash goes for cattle feed, eliminating the need for water to grow additional grain to feed livestock. As I toured the plant, seven out of eight MillerCoors breweries were sending zero waste to landfills; by the time this book is printed, the final brewery should also have achieved zero waste.

The liquid then goes into brew kettles to be boiled, reduced, and infused with hops. It's then transferred to another tank, where yeast is added to ferment the mixture over eight to ten days in carefully controlled temperatures. The last step is transferring the beer into bottles or cans before they're shipped out.

In the past, the staff ramped up the heat in the kettles, then turned it down when the water boiled over, then turned it up and down again, without controlling how much water evaporated. This approach wasted water, wasted energy, and didn't even produce the best-tasting beer. In the new way of doing things, they installed calorific and steam meters in the kettles and tested how to hit the optimal temperatures. They studied how long it took to thoroughly clean equipment and were able to reduce the amount of water used for rinsing while still ensuring that things were clean. They switched from wet to dry lubrication methods. They switched from water to ionized air to clean cans. They found ways to reuse water (though not, of course, in the beer itself).

The biggest impact of the company's water-saving efforts was in saving energy used in water transport and heating. But the work that went on within the breweries only scratched the surface, because that wasn't the main source of most of the water used to make beer. More than ninety percent of the water in beer comes from the agricultural supply chain: the barley, hops, and other grains used.

While MillerCoors had examples of breweries that had dramatically reduced their water use, it also had a track record of working with barley growers to use less water. Some of its 850 growers had been selling barley to the company for half a century. They developed drought- and wind-resistant barley, bringing yields per acre up from about 100 tons to between 140 and 160 tons per acre. Growers in southeastern Idaho evaluated how their use of pivots and nozzles affected the watershed, and experimented with new strategies. They evaluated when they needed to irrigate and when they didn't. They changed out parts in the system, lowering nozzles to reduce evaporation. They experimented with variable-rate irrigation, speeding up or slowing down the rate of water based on the needs of the crops and turning the water off when it rained. They tested different companion crops to improve soil health. When they estimated peak yield times, they discovered that they had been irrigating for a week too long. That week made a huge difference, since each rotation of the sprinklers used two million gallons of water. They shut off the end guns that had watered barley around the edges of the field. MillerCoors hadn't been buying the barley that the end guns had been irrigating, anyway, because the quality wasn't consistent.

With these relatively simple changes, MillerCoors' farmers in Silver Creek Valley, Idaho, reduced water usage by 550 million gallons in 2014. "There's a lot of low-hanging fruit," Marotta said. The company then asked if there was an opportunity to take one-off practices and help other farms to learn from them and scale up. MillerCoors created two model barley farms to teach other farmers how to learn from the practices it had tested, and is building a database to help measure how different techniques succeed in reducing water use.

Bringing Change to Scale

Andy Wales, who leads sustainable development at SABMiller, helped the company become a leader in identifying the costs and risks associated with water use, in reducing its own impact, and in setting even more ambitious goals.

Wales grew up in Birmingham, England, in a religious family and in a community where many of the adults spent much of their lives trying to help others. As a student at the University of Sussex trying to decide what to do with his life, he embraced the same ethos, assuming he'd end up working for Oxfam or Greenpeace or another nongovernmental organization out to save the world. After he graduated and spent stints working for aid organizations in Mozambique and Mumbai, he developed nagging concerns about how efficient the whole aid-for-development model was. So he decided to try business to see if there was another way to change the world more efficiently and on a bigger scale. He signed up for Forum for the Future, a fellowship program that chose just a dozen people a year and cycled them through a series of one-month placements with a wide variety of organizations. Wales spent time at *The Economist* magazine; with the Glasgow City Council on urban policy; and with the Liberal Democrats in Parliament, working on environmentally friendly transport.

And then came the stint that became a job and a career: Interface-FLOR, the billion-dollar carpet-tile company whose founder, Ray Anderson, had a profound "Aha" moment and led it through a radical sustainability transformation from 1994 until he died in 2011. When Anderson read Paul Hawken's 1993 book, *The Ecology of Commerce*, the effect was powerful. "I wasn't halfway through it before the vision I sought became clear, along with a powerful sense of urgency to do something," he has said. "Hawken's message was a spear in my chest." By 2009, InterfaceFLOR had switched to 100 percent renewable energy in its European operations. It reduced its water use by 75 percent, greenhouse-gas emissions by 44 percent, and energy use by 43 percent. The company once used recycled materials for just 0.5 percent of its products. Its tiles now use 51 percent of recycled materials and its textiles a full 100 percent. Working in business, Wales quickly concluded, was "the most efficient, dynamic way of making change at scale."

When Wales arrived at SABMiller in 2007, he had a mandate to help the company dramatically reduce its water use. Measurement was the most important tool in making the case for investing in what the company needed to reduce its water use. "Until you cost it out, it's really hard to make a clear decision," he said.

SABMiller started by measuring the water footprint of the beers it made, which varied dramatically from country to country. In Peru, for example, Backus used 61 liters of water to make each liter of beer. Of those, 4.3 liters were used within the brewery; the remainder came from the crops that went into the beer. While Ukraine's Sarmat also used 61 liters of water to make each liter of beer, 6.9 of those liters came from within the brewery. Tanzania, by contrast, used nearly three times as much water overall to make beer. And South Africa also showed heavy water use overall, at 155 liters per liter of beer, but had the best efficiency within the brewery, at just 4.1:1 liters of water per beer. The company quickly saw that there were opportunities to significantly reduce water use by learning from the most efficient breweries. In 2008, SABMiller set targets to reduce its brewery water use by 25 percent for each liter of beer by 2015. It met that goal a year early, then promptly set a new, more ambitious goal for 2020.

Although the company had already headed on a path to increase its water efficiency, the "Aha" moment for catalyzing large-scale change came in 2009. "The company knew water was important," Wales said. But the key moment came with the publication by the 2030 Water Resources Group of the 2009 "Charting Our Water Future" report, which predicted that by 2030 some 40 percent of the world would be facing water stress. "That was when SABMiller realized the scale of the economic opportunities that would be jeopardized if we didn't tackle the problem," Wales said. "Water changed from being a relatively geeky—and I'm one of those geeks—specialist issue to being a mainstream growth issue."

Coca-Cola CEO Muhtar Kent, Nestlé CEO Peter Brabeck-Letmathe,

SABMiller head Graham Mackay, and other CEOs all rallied behind the report's message and established partnerships with governments and nongovernmental organizations. The CEO buy-in was a key moment for making water into a global issue. Because national governments look primarily at national and regional risks, they often miss seeing the global scale and interconnectedness of the problem, Wales pointed out. "But CEOs see the same medium-term risks popping up around the world, and they can aggregate it across the business globally," he said. And, unlike climate change, where NGOs led the way, the business and NGO communities seemed to catch on at the same time when it came to the urgency of the water issue. It soon dawned on people just how connected brewing, heating, and cooling are to the company's environmental footprint, but, even more so, to its efficiency. In 2013 alone, Wales estimated, SABMiller saved $90 million by becoming more efficient in its use of water and energy.

It made every line manager accountable for utility use. It also looked at bigger systems. Working with the Nature Conservancy in Bogotá, SABMiller noticed that water prices were going up significantly, because as dairy ranching expanded upstream on the Paraná River it created more sediment. To fix the problem, the company set up payments for ecological services—in this case, controlling the sediment—to give the ranches an incentive to move cattle to flatter areas, away from steep slopes, in order to reduce runoff into the river. This relatively simple solution came from the company's willingness to work across sectors, since it was the Nature Conservancy that identified the problem and the solution. "Nobody would have thought of it without that systems approach," said Wales. The idea worked so well that the partners began introducing similar payments for environmental services in Quito, Lima, and elsewhere in Bogotá. "It's a linked challenge. If you do it in isolation from agriculture and energy, planning falls short," he said. "You can't do it within a fence. We've got to be part of a shared solution that the community accepts."

SABMiller expanded its work to eight countries, much of it through the Water Futures Partnership, joining with World Wildlife Federation's

U.K. office, and the German foundation Deutsche Gesellschaft für Internationale Zusammenarbeit (GIZ). SABMiller had concluded early on that water sustainability wasn't just a nice thing to do; it was essential. It saw just how many companies depend on water to manufacture their products, from beverages to technology to textiles to energy and consumer-goods firms. For the clearheaded in those companies, it soon became obvious that when it comes to water the biggest risk is not cost or regulation or slower growth but survival itself.

Why don't more companies recognize the issue? First, there was a communication problem, Wales believes. Until recently, water issues were not often presented in a clear, recognizable way that companies could understand and trust. Because of work by organizations and individuals to identify and quantify the risks associated with water scarcity in the face of rising demand, more and more firms are now recognizing that water scarcity poses a risk to their investments. Second, the shared nature of water resources creates a "tragedy of the commons" problem: a classic political-science dilemma in which people's perceived best interests as individuals appear to contradict the best interests of the group as a whole. This prevents cooperation and promotes selfish yet ultimately self-destructive behavior. Third, many people who are attracted to the corporate world are not likely to want to work in a complex environment with very different stakeholders. Building the capacity to have those conversations is important. Finally, it's too easy for people to assume that it's not their job to "fix" the water problem.

Water and climate change are clear examples of Gray Rhino challenges where we are seeing some action—in some cases, significant and dramatic action. Yet it's not at all clear that what's being done so far is anywhere near enough. Nor is there a consensus on the best approach. While it's obvious to me and many others that businesses, which make products from, process, and distribute water, have to be involved in using our water more responsibly, there are people who criticize corporate efforts to promote water efficiency as a thinly veiled attempt to privatize water. Ironically, many of these critics likely would share the goals of reducing water waste and pollution, whether corporate or otherwise.

And, if anything, water stress is more likely to lead to restrictions on the industrial use of water. That gives the companies at the forefront of the water-sustainability discussion a strong incentive to make changes on their own, so that they aren't forced to do so by circumstances that are out of their control.

Criticism notwithstanding, water is an important example of how a few leaders recognized a clear danger and moved through the stages of denial, muddling, and diagnosing; started to put in place systems to measure water risk and raise the appropriate red flags; and arrived at a sense of urgency that spurred them to action. But if the rest of us are to get out of the way these leaders have to inspire billions of people to join them, and there's a long way to go.

For many people, water shortage is a threat far away on the horizon. But for many parts of the world it is not far away but ever-present—and a reminder that the rest of us will be bumping up against that horizon awfully quickly if we don't do something. People are most likely to respond to a threat when it's practically on top of them, and when their options are limited. While this is better than waiting until after they get trampled, it's a risky strategy that is, in effect, a race against time.

Praying for Rain

More than four billion people around the globe already live in water-stressed or water-scarce areas. The world now consumes more than six times as much water each year as it did in 1900, as the population has grown and as water consumption per capita has increased. By 2030, by some estimates, the world will need 50 percent more food and energy. Within the next decade and a half, according to the 2030 Water Resources Group, demand for fresh water will be 40 percent more than supply.

Already, acute crises have erupted around the world. In 2007, amid one of the worst droughts in the history of the Southeast, water ran so short in Atlanta that Georgia governor Sonny Perdue organized a multi-faith prayer service on the steps of the state capitol in November. "Oh

Father, we acknowledge our wastefulness," he said. With only ninety days of water estimated to be left in October, the state had already banned virtually all lawn watering in the northern half and asked residents and businesses for a series of other conservation measures, including taking shorter showers. It had begged the federal government to stop allowing the diversion of water to Florida and Alabama. The near-miss prompted the state to pass a water-conservation plan early in 2008.

A year later, the state issued water-conservation guidelines with conflicting messages, including a press release with a statement from Dr. Carol Couch, the director of the Environmental Protection Department: "The ultimate goal of water conservation is not to discourage water use, but to maximize the benefit from each gallon used"—a decidedly confusing definition of *conservation*. The guidelines themselves started out with the declaration that "conservation must be foundational to plan," and included initiatives like toilet upgrades, "conservation kits," rain sensors, and, most important, tracking of water use. The plan marked the beginning of steps toward modest increases in efficiency use, though bigger parts of Georgia's plan involved suing to keep its water from going to Florida and Alabama, and beginning a "water grab" in Tennessee. In April 2013, Georgia authorized its state attorney general to sue Tennessee in an attempt to move the Georgia border with Tennessee a mile north so that a lake could be brought into its jurisdiction. For its part, Florida sued Georgia in October 2013 over water rights involving Lake Lanier.

Brazil's two biggest cities, São Paulo and Rio de Janeiro, have been facing dire water shortages, with the astronomical growth of the populations colliding with the worst drought in eight decades. Early in 2015, São Paulo had tapped the second of its three reserves and still had enough water only for a matter of weeks.

The water crisis that Californians have long known was looming became impossible to ignore in 2014, when a three-year drought, the worst in a millennium, left the Sacramento and San Joaquin river basins 11 trillion gallons below normal levels. The governor declared a state of emergency. The loss of crops and livestock and additional water-pumping costs topped $2 billion and cost more than 17,000 jobs. Even without the drought, however, California was already in dire straits. It received less than a third of the annual rainfall of Chicago and less than a quarter of that of New York City, yet the state was the fruit and vegetable capital of the country. The decisions it had made about water provided a cautionary tale of trade-offs between agriculture and cities. California had invested heavily in bringing in water across great distances to create and sustain its cities and farms. To compensate for the higher cost of water, many farmers had switched to higher-margin crops like almonds. But, in a classic example of unintended consequences, those crops were also more water-intensive and thus added to the problem. The bigger question remains: Why is half of the produce in the United States grown in one of the most arid regions?

Measure It, Change It

Peter Brabeck-Letmathe, the chairman of Nestlé, has expressed what businesses, governments, and NGOs are increasingly beginning to recognize as a major risk: "Under present conditions and with the way water is being managed, we will run out of water long before we run out of fuel." The environmental solutions firm Veolia Water has estimated that if businesses do not change the way they manage water an astonishing $63 trillion in investments—half the size of the entire global economy—could be at risk. Other businesses and policymakers are finally catching on. In 2013, 2014, and 2015, CEOs and thought leaders interviewed by the World Economic Forum identified water as a top global risk. How did leading companies come to the conclusion that they had to invest in water sustainability? Part of the reason was the emergence of major crises around the world, where businesses could not function because of water shortages; part of it was the fact that increasing awareness hit a tipping point.

In the mid-2000s, Coca-Cola and Pepsi both lost their operating licenses in parts of India suffering major water shortages. In 2012, some

53 percent of Fortune 500 companies reported that they had experienced business disruptions because of water-related issues.

The key for all of them, both in realizing what needed to be done and in taking initial steps to solve the water problem, was measurement.

The Carbon Disclosure Project, which was started to encourage companies to track and reduce their greenhouse-gas emissions, in 2008 launched a Water Disclosure Project to help track what companies were doing to better manage their water use. Nearly 600 investors controlling more than $60 billion in assets now use the project's annual report to monitor what companies are doing to recognize and respond to water risk. That's a strong start, but still only a fraction of the world's investors. In 2014, the Carbon Disclosure Project asked more than 2,000 companies to report how much water they used. About half answered. It analyzed a smaller subset of the largest companies within that group. Of these 174 Global 500 companies, only 38 percent reported that they track their water use. Of the companies surveyed, 68 percent reported that water scarcity was a major risk; interestingly, 75 percent saw opportunities in water conservation.

In 2007, the U.N. secretary-general established the CEO Water Mandate to create an international movement of committed companies to address the global water crisis. Members reduce their own water usage, encourage their suppliers and partners to improve their water management as well, join together with civil-society and intergovernmental organizations to promote water sustainability, and push for fair and coherent public policies and regulatory frameworks. Crucial to all of this work is transparency, particularly in reporting water activities and use.

The CEO Water Mandate is evidence that some companies have recognized the extent of the problem. Yet the actions of the companies leading the charge make clear how much further there is to go in responding to the challenge of water scarcity. As of this writing, only 120 companies had endorsed the CEO Water Mandate. There are more than 45,000 companies listed on stock exchanges around the world, a number that doesn't even include the many more that are not listed.

The European Union has moved to require more than six thousand companies to disclose their environmental impacts. But still, this is a very modest start. Where drought has hit hard, the absence of good data makes it even harder to fairly allocate scarce water. In California, for example, farmers have resisted efforts to compel reporting of water use, with the result that nobody knows for sure where all the water goes. Estimates that agriculture uses 80 percent of the state's water remain estimates, nothing more. "Perhaps the most important characteristic of California's agricultural water-use information is how poor it is," the Pacific Institute concluded in a 2015 report. "There are large uncertainties regarding agricultural water use due to a lack of consistent measurement and reporting, time lags in releasing information, and confusion about definitions." Even at the epicenter of an epic drought, we don't yet have the information that policymakers and business leaders need to make good decisions and to address a threat that is not just approaching but has arrived.

The Moment the Penny Dropped

General Mills, the Minneapolis-based global food company, looked at seventy-five critical agriculture locations and identified the fifteen that were at the highest risk. Of those, the company began to develop stewardship plans for the eight locations with the biggest potential impact on their business. The "Aha" moment came with fields in El Bajío, in Mexico. The team was astonished to learn that the underground aquifer was dropping by more than six feet every year. In other words, within two decades there would no longer be enough water to grow crops.

"That was the moment when the penny dropped for me," General Mills CEO Ken Powell said of learning about how dire the situation in El Bajío was. It wasn't a matter of corporate social responsibility; it was one of survival. "Our business simply cannot prosper without it," he told a group of business, government, and not-for-profit leaders assembled by the Nature Conservancy. "We know that this is a big issue which requires a big response."

El Bajío's plight was what convinced General Mills to pledge to reduce its water use by 20 percent by 2015. In 2006, the company set specific goals to reduce water usage wherever it could. It began reporting its water usage through the Carbon Disclosure Project's database.

Working with the FEMSA Foundation, General Mills helped El Bajío farmers switch from furrow to ditch irrigation, which cut their water use by nearly half. That was an important start, but it represented only two-tenths of a percent of the water use in the area. What's more, General Mills recognized that because most of its inputs come from agriculture, 99 percent of the water it uses annually—an amount equivalent to submerging the entire state of Illinois under twenty-two feet of water—comes from sources outside its own processing plants. Thus, if it wants to conserve water it needs to be involved with making sure that its suppliers use the water responsibly as well. It is experimenting with other initiatives, like using poultry compost instead of fertilizer and encouraging other suppliers to convert to drip irrigation, in an effort to reduce their water usage and increase crop yields.

SABMiller and General Mills aren't alone. Other companies have invested in water security, making a wager that will pay off in the medium term and risking the wrath of investors focused on short-term paybacks. The Coca-Cola Company and its bottlers together have spent nearly $2 billion on water efficiency and quality. Levi's has introduced "water-less" jeans, a bit of a misnomer, since they merely use *less* water, rather than being water-free, but this is a good start, nevertheless, in the water-intensive cotton industry.

What else can companies, cities, and nations do? They can invest in infrastructure, reclaim nature, reduce use, share data, come to agreements on how to more efficiently and fairly use water. Then they need to persuade others to do so as well, which is the bigger challenge.

Getting water on the global agenda has been a challenge despite the pressing nature of the issue, said Dominic Waughray, the head of Public-Private Partnerships and a member of the Management Committee of the World Economic Forum. Waughray has worked to bring public and private advocates together on its platforms to raise awareness and inspire action in using water more wisely. "It's a classic common property resource dilemma. The difficulty, therefore, is to get everyone to get together to create a commonly agreed solution," Waughray said. "There needs to be some kind of catalyst to bring public, private, and civil society sectors together to solve these common property problems." The solution is not a technical fix; it involves engineering a profound change in attitude on a global scale.

Waughray reflected on how awareness of water scarcity has evolved over the past decade. "It used to be you had a talk or meeting on water at the Forum and nobody would show up," he said. Now, however, discussions on water security regularly draw large crowds. How did this happen? "The best advice I ever got was from a Brazilian professor I told I was working on a water project. He looked at me with wise eyes and said, 'The only advice I can offer is words from President Lula: "The art of politics is to create the conditions for success when those conditions don't exist. This advice is rather stunning, I've found." To start addressing Gray Rhino issues, you have to first change the conditions keeping the status quo in place.

Within companies that have made water efficiency a priority, he's found, change always starts with individuals. "The rhino spotters are the people often acting at the edge of their own institutions, or leaders who can sense the horizon risks," Waughray said. "They have to have enough personal capital within the organization and emotional intelligence to encourage people to collaborate and do something about it." These leaders build and maintain networks of fellow influencers across institutions. "The conditions for change can often take shape from the influence of an increasingly connected group of individuals and how they start to move together. It's influential when you can get your peers together, CEO to CEO, and create an informal network or club."

Once the network for change emerges, where do they go from there? The most successful influencers have a commitment to stick with an issue and a long-term game plan for judging success. They use research to create a case for why an issue is a problem, how it puts investment, jobs, and the economy at risk, and then figure out what to do about it. They find a way to translate possible solutions from technical wonk-speak so that they appeal to broader audiences—for example, getting people you might not associate with an issue to express a concern, and use an international event to stimulate concern. They get important information to governments and encourage friendly competition among them to use that information. "It's only in a pre-competitive state that you can get surprising coalitions of interest, say, Pepsi-Cola and Coca-Cola to be working together, or the minister of energy and ministry of agriculture, since governments are as competitive as anyone," Waughray said. When you bring competitors together as peers and collaborators in finding solutions, you can then turn them loose to compete in putting those solutions into action. "No minister wants to stand in front of their peers and have nothing much to say about a problem, because it was too difficult to tackle, despite everyone knowing there was a problem."

Water Conflict

The late Illinois senator Paul Simon, known for his bow ties and his midwestern can-do attitude, identified water as an emerging threat in his 1998 book *Tapped Out*, a classic in its account of the early stages of recognition of a Gray Rhino.

Rachel Carson's book *Silent Spring*, originally published as a *New Yorker* magazine series in 1962, is still recognized as the clarion call that helped launch the environmental movement. "In an age when man has forgotten his origins and is blind even to his most essential needs for survival, water along with other resources has become the victim of his indifference," she wrote in a very early warning.

As late as the 1980s, environmentalists gave scant recognition to water shortage. By the early 1990s, *National Geographic*, Rotary International, the Worldwatch Institute, *Time*, the World Bank, and the World Economic Forum were beginning to draw attention to a looming threat.

Leaders of parched Middle Eastern nations—with 5 percent of the world's population but just 1 percent of its fresh water—recognized the danger early, following a series of water skirmishes in the mid-twentieth century. Israel and Syria clashed over the Sea of Galilee, the draining of the Hialeah swamp, the diversion of the Jordan River, and the role of water in precipitating the Six-Day War in 1967. Anwar Sadat and King Hussein of Jordan warned that water had the power to cause war. Boutros Boutros-Ghali, the foreign minister of Egypt at the time, issued a warning that has now become almost trite: that the wars of the future would be fought over water, not oil. The phrase is so common, in fact, that it has generated a miniwar of its own, with water experts challenging the statement.

More than 200 river basins in 148 countries cross national borders; many more cross state borders within nations. Between 1950 and 2000, they generated more than 1,800 conflicts. The Pacific Institute's Water Conflict Chronology Timeline continues to tabulate many conflicts each year within and among countries. In short, the potential for conflict, the opportunity cost of not using water as a way to cooperate, is huge.

Paul Simon applied a simple yet elegant risk-reward calculation to the benefits of finding ways to head off a global water crisis. "If we spent 5 percent as much each year on desalination research as we spend on weapons research, in a short time we could enrich the lives of all humanity far beyond anything that has been conceived," Simon wrote of the United States. He was proposing a way of calculating costs, benefits, and trade-offs driven not by politics but by common sense.

Similarly, *National Geographic* calculated that it would take less than $10 billion of investment to provide enough desalinated water to meet the needs of Israel, Jordan, and the West Bank. "By comparison, the gulf war to free Kuwait cost Arab countries $430 billion."

Embroidered Air Masks

Dynamics similar to water have come into play in broader environmental and climate-change conversations, business practices, and policies.

Trained as an engineer, the Chinese-American social entrepreneur

Peggy Liu worked as a McKinsey consultant, then moved to Silicon Valley as a product manager and then an entrepreneur. In 2004, she moved to Shanghai as a venture capitalist but soon became fascinated by the challenges China faced in meeting the needs of its rapidly growing economy, which was bumping up against the realities of finite resources.

In 2007, she organized the MIT Forum on the Future of Energy in China, the first public dialogue on clean energy between U.S. and Chinese government officials. Out of that grew the Joint U.S.–China Collaboration on Clean Energy, which she chairs, to help China go green faster. "China is at war with energy use," she says. "If in the next ten years China doesn't get it right, what we do anywhere else in the world doesn't matter. China's scale is giga-scale. The scale of the solutions has to be greater. We are bumping up against real planetary boundaries."

We sat down to chat at the Annual Meeting of the New Champions of the World Economic Forum in Tianjin, known informally as Summer Davos, after arriving a few days earlier for a retreat about an hour outside Beijing. When I left the airport, my eyes and nose stung from China's legendary urban air pollution. Even at the place where our group stayed, at the foot of the Great Wall, the air hung heavy and gray. That night, however, rain started falling and a strong breeze blew through. The next morning, we woke up to a brief respite from the pollution— and to a rare blue sky. Locals told us they hadn't seen the air so clear in years. But a day later the pollution from the power plants in the region had begun to descend again.

Liu checks her air-quality app every day. "Twice I've had to evacuate my kids from China because the pollution was so bad," she said. "It doesn't matter if you have air filters in every single room, or air-pollution masks— you shouldn't be exerting yourself or even breathing." She picked up her sons and left her home in Shanghai when the Air Quality Index went above 600; the government considers up to 50 to be "good" and 101 to be "unhealthy for sensitive groups." In January 2012, the AQI in Beijing hit 900 parts per million, prompting China to step up its efforts to try to clean up the problem by committing $275 billion over five years. The day we spoke, the AQI was about 220 in Tianjin. When Liu goes outside, she wears an embroidered face mask; her sons wear green masks. "Boy colors," she said with a grin.

"One of the questions I get asked is, Does China really want to go green? Or is it just greenwashing?" she went on. "People who ask that question have never visited China and don't understand the scale of the pollution—soil pollution, water pollution, air pollution, food-safety issues, drought, resiliency issues." And it's clear to her that China's leaders understand but that they are also racing against time. "There is no doubt in my mind that China leads all emerging countries and most developed nations," she said. "Every single leader talks about it in their State of the Union. It's baked into the Five-Year Plan. These are not small targets. History will look back at China and be amazed at the ferociousness with which they've handled this problem. . . . History will also look back and say this is too late."

That week, the World Meteorological Organization issued a new report warning that carbon-dioxide emissions had increased at a faster rate in the previous year than ever before. Carbon-dioxide concentrations in the atmosphere were 142 percent of pre-Industrial Revolution levels; methane was 253 percent higher. WMO secretary-general Michel Jarraud, echoing Liu's words, warned, "We are running out of time."

Abundance by Design

The next day, the Air Quality Index was flashing red at 157 in Tianjin when I moderated an inspiring session with the Stanford University professor William McDonough, whose life's work has been dedicated to using design not only to reduce waste but to repurpose it; and Mark Herrema of Newlight Technologies, which makes plastic out of not thin but *thick* air—fumes emitted from fossil fuels and methane sources that might otherwise be known as pollution but instead are extracted through carbon-capture technologies.

McDonough exudes an optimism so contagious that it's hard not to get excited, too, about his core message, the embodiment of the principle we saw in Chapter 5: that to inspire people to action you have to transform a problem into an opportunity. "A toxin is a material in the wrong place," McDonough says. As a child in Japan, he would listen to oxcarts taking a cargo of waste to farmers' fields. The clopping of the hooves and the rumble of the wheels stayed with him and became his ongoing inspiration for transforming "waste" into raw material that is, as he puts it, "cheaper than free."

McDonough's 2002 book with Michael Braungart, *Cradle to Cradle: Remaking the Way We Make Things*, shows how businesses can transform what was once seen merely as waste into cost-effective raw materials and design their products from the start to have a circular life. Instead of cradle to grave, McDonough envisions products that are reincarnated at the end of their life cycle. Cradle to cradle brings new meaning to the old saw "Waste not, want not."

"Nature has found a way to take CO_2 out of the atmosphere and put it into the soil," McDonough said. "What if we designed materials that can go back to nature safely?" He points out that cadmium and lead are put to good use when they're used to solder computers, yet when they leach into the biosphere they become neurotoxins and carcinogens. "Lead in a computer is solder; lead in a child's brain is death."

The same principle applies to carbon, which causes pollution and climate change but is also a source of life. "Can I bring carbon and nitrogen to the soil? Can we release oxygen by design?" McDonough asks. But he wants to take this principle a step further: "Let's not just reduce their badness; let's increase their goodness. We need to take the old paradigm of 'take, make, waste' and reverse it." In other words: waste, make, take.

Mark Herrema turns that idea into reality with a technology so breathtaking that the first time McDonough told me about it the essence of it didn't quite register, because it didn't seem possible: literally, making plastic out of not thin but thick air and preventing carbon from going into the atmosphere. Herrema had the "Aha" moment that became Newlight Technologies when he read a newspaper article about how much methane cows emit into the atmosphere when they belch and breathe. Until he read that article, he felt about the human contribution to climate change the way many people did: it seemed too abstract, and not "real." But when he read that each cow emitted 600 liters of methane into the air each day, a lightbulb went on. He multiplied one cow by a herd, and a herd by many herds, and then thought of all of those cow belches next to the sheer size of power plants, and all of a sudden the magnitude of the problem became clear.

"We have this massive amount of material going into the air," he said. But the real breakthrough came when he took the thought experiment further. "If all the things we're making in the world come from carbon yet we're emitting all of this carbon into the air, there's got to be some sort of connection here. What if instead of looking at carbon emissions as something bad . . . like fire . . . instead of being something that can destroy, what if instead we saw it as a source of light?" he asked. "If nature exists by sequestering carbon, why can't we do something similar?" He thought of the giant redwood forests created by photosynthesis; of the coral reefs created by pulling carbon out of water; and of the organisms living at the bottom of the ocean that feed on methane gases. Thus began many years of sleepless nights and a decade of frustration before the breakthrough moment at which his team took a big step toward making it cost-effective to create plastic out of harvested carbon.

Newlight creates biocatalysts: organisms that generate enzymes that interact with carbon-rich emissions to turn them into plastic. From a garage to a lab to a bigger lab, over a decade and after millions of dollars of research-and-development investment, the company finally found a way to turn carbon into plastic at a cost less than that for traditional, oil-based plastic. "All of a sudden, you have a paradigm where you don't even have to ask if you care about climate change," Herrema said. Because carbon-negative plastic costs less than the alternative, it completely changes the terms of the conversation over how to manufacture things. Newlight is now producing the first-ever carbon negative plastic chair to roughly half of the plastic used in Sprint cell-phone cases and the plastic bags used by Dell for its computer products. The company was doing exactly what McDonough was talking about—it was taking the "bad" and creating something good. It was just like the light filtering through the trees that Herrema loved to watch next door to his home: light hit the leaves and helped transform carbon into life.

Putting Assets in the Right Place

Desso, the Netherlands-based global carpets-and-sports turf company, is another example of turning waste into an opportunity for innovation. Its CEO, Alexander Collot d'Escury, was part of a team that set out in 2008 to transform all of Desso's products to conform to Cradle to Cradle standards. Since becoming CEO in 2012, Collot d'Escury and his team have continued to find new ways of incorporating unexpected materials, like the reengineered calcium carbonate—in other words, chalk—from local drinking water that Desso now uses in its carpets. More than half of Desso's carpets come from recycled sources as diverse as fishnets and old carpets. In arguing for a Europe-wide law that would require companies to increase package recycling and ban the practice of sending recyclables to landfills by 2025, he noted that just over a third of the 2.5 billion tons of waste generated in Europe each year is recycled. The proposed law met with stiff opposition from some trade groups, which would be at a disadvantage beside the nimbler companies that have already embraced "circular economy" thinking. The Dutch conglomerate Unilever dropped its membership in BusinessEurope over the trade organization's opposition to the worthy initiative.

McKinsey has estimated that the circular-economy approach could generate as much as $1 trillion in annual global cost savings by 2025. Among the examples it cited in a 2014 report: By manufacturing mobile phones that were easier to take apart and increasing incentives to return them, companies could cut manufacturing costs by half. Brewers could make nearly $2 per hectoliter of beer by selling used grains. And the United Kingdom could make $1,295 for each ton of recycled clothing. Many companies have embraced the circular economy.

Privahini Bradoo, a Young Global Leader of the World Economic Forum, co-founded BlueOak as a way to harvest electronic waste. In the United States alone, consumers throw out 3.2 million tons of e-waste each year, of which more than 80 percent ends up in landfills, where it is the source of more than 70 percent of toxic-metal concentrations. The world produces 50 million tons of e-waste each year. Businesses spend $12 billion a year in search of new ore deposits. Yet every twenty minutes U.S. users toss one ton of cell phones. The amount of e-waste abandoned each year contains copper that is equivalent to a third of global mine production. And as electronic device makers worry about how to procure enough rare earth metals, mainly from China (and called "rare" for a reason), the world does not recycle even 1 percent of rare earth metals contained in the electronic gadgets that we throw away. BlueOak is turning that problem into an opportunity by building mini-refineries to extract precious metals and rare earth elements from e-waste. The company's vision is "to revolutionize how we treat end of life electronics: converting the e-waste of today into a sustainable source of critical metals and rare earths for the technologies of tomorrow." The company has been recognized by Google and Harvard Business School, and has attracted some of the biggest names in venture capital.

This kind of thinking has shown success not only in start-ups but also in well-established multinational corporations. Unilever announced early in 2015 that it had achieved its goal of cutting to zero the amount of waste sent to landfills by its global network of more than 240 factories in 67 countries making products for brands that include Magnum, Knorr, Dove, and Domestos. Instead of sending industrial waste to landfills, Unilever turned it into low-cost building materials in Africa and Asia; in India, it turned organic waste into compost used for community vegetable gardens; in Indonesia, it used waste to provide energy to make cement. The initiative created hundreds of jobs and saved €200 million.

The announcement was part of a major initiative by Unilever's CEO, Paul Polman, who arrived at the company in 2009 with a plan to double the company's size and to dramatically reduce its environmental footprint. Until that point, the company had been muddling along. Polman came in with an ambitious plan to embed sustainability in all of its products, in order to both save costs and strengthen its brand. The company cut nearly one million tons from its manufacturing and logistics operations and saved nearly $400 million between 2008 and 2013. Thus, in addressing the environmental Gray Rhino, Polman also faced a corporate Gray Rhino head-on: he gave Unilever a new brand advantage while cutting its costs.

The Year We "Got It"?

We've come a long way from the publication of *Silent Spring* to the first Earth Day in 1974, when Pogo famously declared, "We have seen the enemy . . . and he is us." When I was a child in the 1970s, my parents kept the thermostat low, not only because of the environment but because they were raising a family on a teacher's salary and because my mother's parents had lived through scarcity in World War II and never let her forget it. It wasn't until I was older that I equated saving energy with saving the planet. But things have swung full circle: arguing that we need to save the planet takes us to a dead end. It's too abstract, too far out into the future, too little relevant to too many humans. But when it comes down to dollars and cents, to saving money and increasing profits by being efficient, or to avoiding obvious business risks, that's an entirely different story that can propel action.

The increasingly extreme weather events of recent years—from Hurricane Katrina and Superstorm Sandy to the persistent visits of the polar vortex, juxtaposed with the dramatic shrinking of Arctic sea-ice cover and historic droughts in California and Brazil—have helped wake us up to climate change. Slowly, the voices of people deeply concerned about the effects of climate change have overtaken those of the vocal climate-change deniers. Insurance companies have pushed their clients not just to take notice but to take measures to protect themselves, not because they are tree-huggers or baby-seal lovers but because there's a business interest.

One publication declared 2014 "the year big business embraced climate change action." The examples it cited were compelling. Members of the Rockefeller family, descendants of the oil and coal magnate John D.

Rockefeller, announced that they would divest from the fossil-fuel industry and reinvest in clean energy. (The decision would seem prescient, as
oil prices tumbled dramatically early in 2015.) Apple's CEO, Tim Cook,
told climate-change skeptics to take a hike if they didn't like the company's pledge to cut greenhouse-gas emissions.

Was 2014 the year the world finally "got" climate change?

After seeing video of Arctic ice cap melting and unlocking "new
oceans" from the ice, Ronald Reagan's secretary of state, George Schultz,
broke with Republican conventional wisdom and spoke out for government action to combat climate change.

Pope Francis prepared a call to the world's churches to combat climate change. In October, he told a meeting of Latin American and Asian
social activists, "The monopolizing of lands, deforestation, the appropriation of water, inadequate agrotoxics are some of the evils that tear man
from the land of his birth. Climate change, the loss of biodiversity and
deforestation are already showing their devastating effects in the great
cataclysms we witness." While initial news coverage ignored the elephant
in the room—the impact of population growth and the church's call to
be fruitful and multiply on the planet's ability to sustain them—the pope
later said it wasn't necessary to "breed like rabbits" to be a good Catholic.

The United States and China, which together account for more than
one-third of global greenhouse-gas emissions, in 2014 finally signed an
agreement to reduce greenhouse gases. The United States set a new target for cutting net greenhouse-gas emissions 26–28 percent below 2005
levels by 2025. China committed to targets to begin lowering CO_2 emissions as soon as possible before 2030 and to increasing the non-fossil
fuel share of all energy to around 20 percent by the same year.

At the same time, the percentage of Americans who believe that
global warming is real rose sharply. A study by Yale University and
George Mason University found that the percentage of those polled who
believed climate change was real rose to 64 percent in April 2014, from
57 percent in January 2010. President Obama made climate change a
major theme of his 2015 State of the Union address, noting that fourteen
of the fifteen hottest years on record have occurred in this century. Con-

gress soon declared climate change a reality, though it stopped short of acknowledging that humans are responsible.

On environmental issues ranging from water scarcity to pollution and waste to greenhouse gases, then, we are seeing some action even as the clock races forward. The closer disaster gets, the more likely we are to act, even as it becomes less likely that we can do enough to get out of the way. At the same time, the more we can frame the threats at hand as opportunities, the more likely we are to at least slow the rhino.

CHAPTER 7 TAKEAWAYS:

- By the time you act, **it may be too late.**
- **Measure.** Taking stock of the size of the problem can make a path to solving it clear.
- **Break it down.** If you cannot solve the whole problem, choose a manageable portion. Similarly, break the decision down into the smallest possible effective unit—a state versus a country, a city versus a state, a company versus an industry, a single unit of a company.
- **Turn a threat into an opportunity.** Our cognitive biases make us more likely to respond to the possibility of profit than to simply avoiding a problem.
- **It may take drama to get attention, but often surprisingly little drama to get results.** As MillerCoors found, simple behavioral changes led to big savings.

8

AFTER THE TRAMPLING:
A CRISIS IS A TERRIBLE THING
TO WASTE

On a clear, sunny late-June afternoon, earthmovers crawled the land alongside Calgary's Bow River next to a small residential street lined with high-end homes, their lawns perfectly landscaped and manicured on the other side of the chain-link fence blocking off the construction site. A stone's throw from the earthmovers, a paved pathway, its middle yellow line intended to keep pedestrians and bicycles on safe sides, dropped off into nothing where the bank below fell into the river during Calgary's epic 2013 floods.

This particular strip of land, along the end of Eighth Avenue SE in Inglewood, the city's oldest neighborhood, bore the brunt of forces of destruction that most of the time lie dormant. The area lies along a majestic bend in the river below where the Bow and Elbow Rivers, the lifestreams of Calgary, meet. Not so long ago, the bank stretched much farther into the river than it does now. But during the flood the force of the water—nearly 1,800 cubic meters per second—rammed straight into the banks instead of taking its normal leisurely meander around the curve. In less than twenty-four hours, close to 60 meters (over 150 feet) of earth disappeared into the water. Even more would have gone had city workers not moved quickly to dump 40 concrete Jersey barriers and 2,000 sandbags into the river to protect what was left of the shore and the homes alongside it.

Along the shore, piles of giant riprap boulders marked the city's efforts to keep more of the bank from washing away in the future. Across the city, teams had installed 10,700 tons of riprap in the Elbow River and 96,000 in the Bow—so much that they had to scramble to find enough boulders as the supply ran short. Two newly installed rock jetties extended into the water to divert the river's flow in future storms. Parts of the riverbank were dotted with orderly rows of plantings to help prevent future erosion. Dozens of new plants sat waiting for parks workers to dig holes for them. The standpipe near the end of the path was new; the old one had washed away. Just beyond, where the river curves in the direction of the nearby bird sanctuary, the bank looked like a slice of cake, with green grass on top and bare dirt below where the rest of the land had washed away. Bank swallows carried nest material to holes they had made in the newly exposed earth, making it impossible to fortify the bank because the birds had recently been designated as an endangered species.

It was almost exactly a year since record late-spring rains and snowmelt combined, rushing down the Elbow and Bow Rivers. The meeting of the two rivers was the reason Calgary sprang up from the prairie. As a result, much of the center city, an economic engine for Alberta Province and, indeed, for much of Canada, lies in a flood-plain. Calgary residents are as aware of their history as they are of the fact that the very source of their city's identity became its biggest threat. Canada's most expensive natural disaster ever, the 2013 storm cost around $6 billion, including $445 million in damage to public infrastructure. Nearly 100,000 people were evacuated. Telephones went silent, public transport stopped, and some 35,000 people were left without power. Roughly 4,000 homes and businesses were damaged. Miraculously, only one person, a woman who ignored the evacuation order, died.

As I toured Calgary and talked with city officials about their response to the 2013 flood, it was striking how fluent so many of them were in discussing the force of water pressure in the river. On the Bow River, several people tell me, the volume of water peaked at over 1,700 cubic meters per second—the highest in recorded history and thirteen times the average flow—above the Elbow. Downstream of where the two rivers meet, where I had witnessed the damage in Inglewood, the force rose to 2,400 cubic meters per second.

The 2013 flood was only the second state of emergency ever declared in Calgary. The first was a flood in 2005 that damaged 40,000 homes and forced evacuations of 1,500 people. Three people died. The waters left behind hundreds of millions of dollars' worth of damages, only $165 million of which was covered by federal programs. The two floods together provide an intriguing lens on how a city responds to a crisis in order to prevent similar damage in the future, and on where decision-makers are likely to trip up.

Google Maps on Steroids

After the 2005 flood, the province of Alberta convened a task force and commissioned a study on how to prevent damage from future floods. Known in shorthand as the Groeneveld Report, it recommended eighteen measures, costing $305 million, to mitigate future floods. Interestingly, many of the measures came from a 2002 draft report that followed smaller floods in 1997 and 1998. That paper had never progressed from draft form to become formal recommendations. Though the Groeneveld Report was indeed released, most of its recommendations, like the earlier draft, sat gathering dust.

Built on top of a hill and boring deep into a hillside, Calgary's Emergency Operations Center looks like something out of a James Bond movie. Though not formally part of the Groeneveld Report, the impetus for the center was the 2005 floods. The City Council approved the creation of the EOC, as officials call it, after the floods, and construction began in 2009. Chris Arthurs, the director of Recovery Operations for the city of Calgary, says the city got flak for the $47 million cost of the center when it was completed in 2012, less than a year before the flood. "But not any more!" she says as we pull up to the center.

The "diapered" building not only sits at a high elevation but is equipped with sump pumps to make sure it doesn't flood. It's out of the flight path and well away from transit routes where dangerous goods might pass by rail or truck. The structure, built on an old bunker site, has 40,000 feet per floor underground, thirty-two security cameras, three phone systems plus ham radio, a radio tower and digital trunk, a 50,000-liter tank, and a permanent supply of food to last sixty people seventy-two hours. Its generators—it has four, even though it needs only two—can power the place for a week to ten days. "But if you turn off the lights it can last three weeks," said Tom Sampson, the deputy chief of the Calgary Emergency Management Agency, who has since been promoted to chief of CEMA.

In the central operations hub, where responders gather for emergencies, the far wall is a mass of giant screens with news feeds and maps. Sampson brings up a map of the city with satellite images cross-referenced against 212 data points from tax and license data to utilities, incident calls, light-rail stations, hazardous-materials sites, schools, libraries . . . the list goes on. "It's like Google Maps on steroids," said Sampson. He pulls up a building from aerial view, zooms in, switches to a side view, spins it around, and uses a mouse to measure the height of one of the windows. He zooms back out, selects a five-foot rise in the river, and clicks the mouse. Large swaths of the neighborhood fill up, with a purple screen showing, down to the individual house on each block, what will be flooded. He then cross-references schools, libraries, and other possible community evacuation sites, showing which ones are out of danger and which ones would themselves be flooded. It's one of the few recommendations from the Groeneveld Report that became a reality in time to make a difference.

This modeling tool played a key role during the 2013 flood when it helped the EOC and the power company to identify a major risk: power substation 32, which the EOC identified as at clear risk in case of a flood. Enmax built a berm to protect the substation, with powerful results. Photos taken during the flood show angry brown waters lapping against the edges of a dry rectangle where the substation was located. If Enmax had not been so prepared, Sampson pointed out, "Not only would hundreds of millions of dollars have been lost, sixteen communities would have had to be uprooted." It was an example of preparations working as they should. "The last couple of years we practically didn't need exercises because there were so many real life events," Sampson said. The city had to deal with a train derailment, wind storms, three-alarm fires. . . . oh, right, and the flood.

Hell or High Water

Despite the flood's impact, Calgary struggled with the same forces that hampered efforts to respond to and prevent future disasters after the 2005 flood. When I visited the Mayor's Office, a copy of the *Calgary Herald* on the news rack reminded visitors of the size of the task still remaining. "Flood Aid to Fall by $1B," read the headline.

Elected in 2010, Mayor Naheed Nenshi never saw the Groeneveld Report until after the 2013 flood. "I didn't even know it existed," he told me. "Strangely enough, we opened the EOC—I had never been in the EOC until the flood, and I walked in for the first time." In fact, he told me somewhat ruefully, he had even voted against the final budget appropriation that created a third backup IT server in the center, because he didn't think the city needed a third one. "But of course the first two went down during the flood," he says, fully aware of the clarity that hindsight brings. He showed me photos on his smartphone of London's emergency-operations center, clearly proud that the United Kingdom's version looked quite retro by comparison with Calgary's.

As we talked about the challenges of responding to and planning appropriately for future disasters in the aftermath of the floods, he picked up a giant fuchsia squishy spiky stress ball, shifting it from one hand to the other. Born to immigrants from Tanzania, Nenshi is the first Muslim to become the mayor of a major North American city. A Harvard graduate, former McKinsey consultant, and business-school professor, he's an admitted policy wonk who doesn't take himself too seriously. I first met him nearly six months before the flood, at a workshop at the 2013 annual meeting of the World Economic Forum in Davos, where we teamed up to lead a workshop about the future of governance. Our group recommended transparency and connectivity as the hallmarks of successful governments of the future. Nenshi applies the same ethos to participatory budgeting and other "mega-engagement" strategies for getting feedback from Calgarians. Who knew that these ideas would come into play so dramatically just a few months later?

Nenshi's response to the Calgary floods earned him widespread recognition for his dedication and open, constant communication. His Twitter account has more than 250,000 followers and got him included in a 2013 BuzzFeed list of goofy world leaders "because he is the absolute best at Twitter . . . like, the king of Twitter . . . or maybe Mayor of Twitter is more appropriate." He embraced his status with characteristic good humor.

His administration helped bring Calgary back quickly with a can-do "Come Hell or High Water" slogan. The city pulled off its famed annual Stampede just two weeks after the flood, even though the stretch of the river running past the stampede grounds had overrun its banks and flooded stalls and the lower levels of stadium seating. When floods inundated Toronto not long after Calgary's disaster, a Twitter campaign requesting Nenshi's assistance heightened in volume after a *Toronto Sun* reporter tweeted that Toronto's mayor, Rob Ford, was in his SUV with his kids using the air-conditioning to keep cool after his home lost power. ("Just how much cash do Toronto citizens need to offer Calgary in order to trade Ford for Nenshi?" one poster asked tongue-in-cheek.) After the Calgary flood, Alberta province offered to buy all the homes in the flood zone at market value. Nenshi also made a very compelling proposal to residents whose homes were damaged by the flood: "If you apply for disaster relief, we will give you extra funds for resilience—but you must do resilience," he told them. (This could include moving utility appliances above flood level, sealing cracks, sealing windows below flood level, or, applying waterproof coatings.)

A year after the flood, the city faced a dilemma in planning to prevent future damage like that in 2013. The mayor and his team already had concluded that the $317 million plan to rebuild and fortify riverbanks wasn't going to be enough to protect the city. A few days earlier, the city's flood-mitigation team had presented a report to the City Council recommending close to $1 billion in projects to make the city less vulnerable to future disasters.

"A lot of folks in the community were very nervous this year: Are we going to see another flood? And, no matter what, even if you can say statistically it's a one-in-a-hundred chance it's not going to happen this year, you don't know that and people don't know that," Nenshi said. "We had a miserable, long, horrible winter here—everyone in North America did—and we were probably the only people in North America who did not unambiguously greet the coming of the spring. We were nervous. Every cloud in the sky, every time the temperature spiked really high, we worried about snowmelt. I get the flood forecasts multiple times a day. I know exactly what the river is flowing at. But I still look nervously at the sky, and every time I cross the river I still pause to take a look at what the level is looking like."

Still, the emotional impact of the floods had not yet translated into real investments in resilience, which would involve many years of construction and significant amounts of money. The three biggest-ticket items among which Calgary was trying to decide were major capital works: a conduit to divert water away from downtown; an off-stream diversion and storage site near Springbank that would help not only in floods but also in dry years, which are more common in Alberta; and a dry dam at McLean Creek, whose main effect would be to help drain floodwater but was unlikely to be of much help in a drought.

Nenshi grabbed a piece of paper and sketched a map of what the conduit would look like, rerouting water 5 kilometers from the Elbow through a tunnel 20 meters below downtown to a lower spot on the Bow. "In big-flow years when needed, we can take water from here to here," he said, drawing an arrow from one spot to the next, "protecting this portion of the Elbow River flow and basically protecting downtown Calgary."

Nenshi went on, "A lot of folks are happy to have the discussion. Some who weren't affected just say don't do it. And those of us who were affected by the floods say just do it, I don't care how much it costs; I never want to go through that again. All three are legitimate points of view. If you take those three mitigation measures together, they would cost up to one billon dollars. I am strapped for infrastructure: I need to do light rail, I need to do roads, I need water-treatment plants. I have twenty-five billion in unfunded needs already. For the province—to spend a billion dollars on infrastructure that we may never use . . ." he trailed off, letting the inevitable conclusion hang in the air. "If we're lucky, it will never be used. It is a really interesting public-policy question. We'd be spending a billion dollars against a one-in-a-hundred chance of five billion in damage."

Seen in those terms, the calculation doesn't make sense. But, as Nenshi is well aware, that might not be the right equation. Does the financial cost take into account the human cost? There are so many unknowns.

Is it really a one-in-a-hundred risk, given that Calgary has just had two hundred-year storms in a decade, with scientists predicting a further increase in violent storms? Indeed, the Canadian government would soon determine that building to a one-in-a-hundred-year standard wasn't good enough. Many of the comments from the public, as part of the feedback process Calgary undertook, called for more. "When The City grants approvals to build on or adjacent to the current [1:100] floodline, The City is asking for trouble," wrote one citizen. "The [1:100] flood is a statistical prediction that does not include the really large floods that could happen in the near or distant future." Other communities, in fact, had built to higher levels. Winnipeg's Red River Floodway diversion system protects up to 1:700. Alberta Province requires protection up to 1:1000. The Netherlands has fortified against a 1:1250 river flood, a level it reviews every fifty years.

The technical definition of a hundred-year flood is that there is a 1-percent chance of its happening in a year. But because each flood may carve out new river-basin boundaries, it can change the odds of future floods. Other factors come into play as well. The Intergovernmental Panel on Climate Change, which aggregates the views of leading scientists, predicts that extreme weather events will occur more frequently because of changes in the atmosphere caused by global warming. Along with more intense rainfall will come more frequent and stronger floods. In coastal areas, rising sea levels will make coastal damage more severe; in areas where rivers and lakes are fed by melting glaciers and snow, floods will similarly become more severe. The Insurance Bureau of Canada, in a 2012 report, has predicted that both droughts and floods will get worse. By another estimate, within three decades what is now a one-in-a-hundred-year flood could be one in thirty-five to fifty-five years. A 2013 AECOM study for the Federal Emergency Management Agency predicted a one-in-two chance of a significant increase in floods along coasts and rivers over the next ninety years.

The math gets even more complicated when you try to factor in savings from damage avoided, which is devilishly difficult. In 1968, despite protests that it was a boondoggle, Winnipeg's Red River Floodway was built to a 1:90-year level at a cost of $63 million. When the 1997 "Flood of a Century" hit, the floodway limited the damage in Winnipeg, even as the storms devastated nearby Grand Forks, North Dakota. Yet it was clear that the storm had stretched the floodway to the limits of its capacity, and that anything worse would overwhelm it. The largest flood in Manitoba history, in 1826, was 40 percent larger than the 1997 volume of water; if that were to happen again, the province would suffer $5 billion in damages. Thus, true to the stereotype of Canadian practicality, in 2005 the federal government, Manitoba Province, and Winnipeg together spent an additional $627 million to expand it to 1:700. Officials estimate that the floodway has prevented more than $32 billion in damages over its life, with $12 billion in costs avoided in a 2009 flood alone. Manitoba stood out because it had recognized the value of a stitch in time saving nine.

The province's experience exceeded the return that disaster experts have estimated such resilience work produces. The U.S. Federal Emergency Management Agency and the Multihazard Mitigation Council, for example, estimate that every dollar spent to make communities less vulnerable to natural disasters saves four dollars. And then there are the opportunity costs. According to Judith Rodin of the Rockefeller Foundation, who has made resilience a centerpiece of the foundation's work, 25 percent of small and medium businesses never reopen after disasters.

"Any entity can build resilience," Rodin wrote in her 2014 book, *The Resilience Dividend: Being Strong in a World Where Things Go Wrong.* "Too often, however, resilience thinking does not really take hold until a galvanizing event or a major shock—such as Superstorm Sandy—brings the need into high relief. But we should not need things to go terribly wrong for us to work to make them more right."

The math strongly favors averting disaster. Alas, the political calculus is far different. "We had the flood last June and the municipal election in October," Nenshi recalled. "It was right afterwards. I can count on one hand the number of people who asked, 'What are you going to do about flood prevention?' It was not an election issue in any way." Indeed, his press secretary had just given me a new article in *The Walrus* on Calgary's flood that even cites a 2009 study whose authors concluded that voters reward incumbents for disaster relief but not for disaster preparedness. "Now we're at the one-year anniversary and a lot of those emotions are back on the surface," he said. "If we don't make a decision to commit megamoney to flood resilience in the next—make up a number—twenty-four months, then it will be very difficult for the government to get that kind of money."

Just as problematic as the risk of letting a disaster go to waste, as it would turn out, was the risk of doing something for the sake of doing something but without enough foresight or coordination.

In late September, Alberta's premier, Jim Prentice, announced that the province would build the dry dam at Springbank, not at the McLean Creek site the City of Calgary had been considering. Astonishingly, he had not consulted city residents or flood experts. Nenshi issued a critical statement in response. "It represents a real departure from the previous plan, where the reservoir would have played a role in both flood and drought years," he wrote. "This dry dam would not be used except during a flood and would not allow for comprehensive water management, what the province had previously stated was their goal for this project."

Unintended Consequences

As I write, the final outcome remains to be seen. Yet the political interference in a thoughtful planning process is all too typical. The result of this dynamic is that the decisions we make after a crisis are more likely to range from nothing to the shortsighted to the ineffectual and the bizarre.

After the September 11 terrorist attacks, the Bush administration put in place many antiterrorism policies, including the now familiar (but no less cumbersome for being the norm) airport-security procedures that have cost untold billions in wasted time. We have come to take for granted the tedious and surreal ritual of taking off our shoes at the airport, despite—or perhaps because of—the fact that it's unlikely to be worth the aggravation and the lost time. Shaun Rein estimated in *Forbes* that the extra time travelers in American airports waste on the post-9/11 security measures costs between $20 billion and $30 billion each year. But people live with the inconvenience because it feels as if somebody did something, whether or not it was the best use of resources.

In other cases, decisions unintentionally have a beggar-thy-neighbor effect. Sachsen-Anhalt, in East Germany, did extensive work to rehabilitate dams and dikes along the Elbe River after catastrophic floods in August 2002 killed 20 people, caused over 11 billion euros' worth of damage, forced over 60,000 evacuations, and affected more than 300,000 people. Water breached dikes in 131 places. The response was to create a flood-forecasting system and a long-term plan, as well as repairs to many of the dikes.

When a new storm hit in June 2013, the Elbe rose to nearly four times its normal depth—even higher than in 2002. Many fewer dikes failed upriver, where there was much less flooding than there was in the past, even though the water level was higher. But that merely pushed the damages downstream. Just south of Magdeburg, in the center of the province and at a sharp curve where the Elbe met the Saale River, a dam burst.

Communities devastated by floods are littered with well thought-out, practical plans for preventing future floods. In many cases, only a fraction of what was proposed is ever done.

Galveston Island—dubbed the "Lone Star equivalent of the Hamptons"—is not even nine feet above sea level at its highest point. On a highschool field trip to Galveston, my class learned about a mainstay of Texas history: the Great Storm of 1900, a tropical cyclone that flattened the island and, with more than 6,000 people killed, is still by far the deadliest weather disaster in U.S history. Within two years, Galveston had built a 10-mile-long, 17-foot-high seawall to hold back the Gulf of Mexico from the east. Yet the sea continues to encroach on the island, with erosion of 10 to 15 feet a year. The island's wetlands, which help to reduce storm surges, have shrunk by a third since the 1950s. Hurricane Ike battered the island in 2008, resulting in more than $50 million in damage. More than 80 percent of its homes were affected by the storm.

Yet new developments keep going up and Galveston keeps seeking funds to protect the beach. A geohazards map of the island projected to 2062 is full of red swaths, mainly the current wetlands, beaches, tidal flats, and marshes indicating an imminent hazard potential. The city claims that its sewage system can withstand a Category 5 hurricane. By some estimates, it would cost more than $100 million to shore up Galveston. If you take a simple economics-of-probability approach, the math evens out if residents expect a hundred-year storm that costs $10 billion. For Galveston, the theory seems to be that it's worth rebuilding. Some communities make a rational decision not to prevent damage from happening but, instead, to be able to bounce back faster.

Wake-Up Calls

"Since the beginning of time, people have been calling disasters 'wake-up calls.' They're more like snooze alarms," Irwin Redlener, the founder of the National Center for Disaster Preparedness, told an audience at Columbia University's School of International and Public Affairs.

Was Sandy the wake-up call New York City needed?

New Yorkers had days of warning as radar tracked Hurricane

Sandy's march up the East Coast in October 2012, along with the weather system coming from the west that merged to create a "superstorm." The city was also well aware of the increased dangers of storm surges caused by rising sea levels and the increasingly violent storms caused by rising sea temperatures. Over the past century, the sea had risen by more than a foot; climate scientists predict that sea levels could rise another two and a half feet by 2050 or so. Urban planners and climate scientists had been predicting for years that New York City was increasingly vulnerable to a giant storm that could inundate low-lying areas and cause the widespread disruption and destruction that New Yorkers in low-lying areas would experience after Sandy—or that we might see in apocalyptic science-fiction movies. A 1995 Army Corps of Engineers report predicted that a Category 4 storm could create 30-foot storm surges, or more than twice the size of those driven ashore by Sandy. A 2006 study by the NASA Goddard Institute for Space Studies predicted that a Category 3 storm assuming only an 18-inch rise in sea levels would create destruction very much like what New York City experienced with Sandy, a "mere" Category 1 storm.

Weather maps gave weeks, then days, then hours worth of notice in high-resolution detail. But the real advance warning—the detailed studies on the rise of sea levels and the potential destruction of storms—went mostly unheeded. In 2007, the city did request that FEMA update its flood maps, which had not been revised since 1983 despite extensive development around the waterfront, for the area. The remapping process finally began in 2009. However, like so many obvious but not necessarily imminent threats, the bigger issue of the need to improve infrastructure to protect from storms was ignored.

Mayor Michael Bloomberg had been pilloried for mishandling a relatively minor snowstorm in December 2010, so he was particularly attuned to the need to be proactive in preparing as Hurricane Sandy moved up the eastern seaboard toward the city. Many people obeyed evacuation orders as Hurricane (later downgraded to Superstorm) Sandy approached, but others stayed put. That decision cost 110 people in the northeastern United States their lives. It had been so long since a hurricane made landfall—the most recent had been Agnes in 1972—and the previous year's evacuation order had seemed to be for naught. In August 2011, Hurricane Irene prompted the city to issue its first-ever mandatory-evacuation order, covering 375,000 people. The city later estimated that about 60 percent actually left. When Irene turned out to be anticlimactic at best, people took that to heart and paid even less attention to calls for evacuation; a city study reported that only 29 percent of respondents in evacuation zones had actually left. A third didn't believe the storm would be severe enough to cause damage or thought that their homes were safe. In other words, they were in denial—the first stage of a Gray Rhino.

After the storm, denial was not an option. The storm surge had flooded more than 50 square miles in New York City and damaged nearly 90,000 buildings, more than 300,000 housing units, and 23,400 businesses. Much of the city was all but shut down for close to a week, while other parts were crippled for months or even years. One acquaintance of mine had to close his once up-and-coming restaurant. A friend whose office was in the financial district had to work out of a temporary office for close to a year. Other friends had to find temporary housing for weeks and months; friends in the Rockaways nearly lost their home; another friend had to close his restaurant permanently. The cost of rebuilding and repairing New York's public infrastructure was estimated at $13 billion and the toll of lost economic activity at $6 billion. Private insurers were expected to have to cover $19 billion in losses and the federal government another $12–$15 billion.

In Sandy's aftermath, city officials reached out to the Netherlands, which set out after the 1953 North Sea Flood to protect itself from the kind of storm that occurs once every ten thousand years. Just over six months later, Mayor Bloomberg laid out a comprehensive $20 billion plan to make the city more resilient to storms. It remains to be seen how much of the plan becomes a reality or—like so many well-thought-out plans after a disaster—fades away into the land of good intentions. Detailed out in a 400-plus-page report, the first part of the plan included better mapping, forecasting, and efforts to communicate to the public. The second recommended coastal protections, including armor stone for exposed shorelines; bulkheads at water's edge; tide gates in Staten Island, the Rockaways, and other vulnerable locations; preservation of wetlands, reefs, living shorelines, and jetties; construction of floodwalls and levees, and local storm-surge barriers. More controversially, the mayor floated the idea of a giant seawall, which would cost between $20 and $25 billion and take decades to complete. The city also proposed tightening building-safety standards and replacing or retrofitting existing buildings. Finally, it planned to reform insurance, making it more affordable to low-income residents, working with FEMA to expand pricing options, spreading awareness about the importance of insurance.

Just over half of the roughly 36,000 buildings (or 163,000 homes and apartments) in New York's high-risk flood zone had federal flood insurance when Sandy struck, according to a RAND study. About two-thirds of those who were required to have flood insurance (generally because they had federally insured mortgages) actually did. Only about one in five who weren't required to have flood insurance did.

In June 2013, FEMA released a new map, covering a wider area at high risk from flooding, that essentially doubled the number of homes that would be required to have flood insurance. RAND estimated that nine of ten homes in the expanded area had not been built to floodplain standards, and that more than a third did not have insurance when Sandy hit. Not only will more buildings require insurance but the cost of that insurance will, in many cases, be between twelve and twenty-three times as much as it was before the flood.

Whether in flood- or fire-risk zones, people are set in their ways; sometimes it seems that the less an action serves their interests the more likely they are to insist on it. A 2013 study by CoreLogic identified 1.2 million homes across thirteen states in the western United States that were at high or very high risk of burning in one of the increasingly frequent and powerful wildfires. The business-analytics firm estimates that $189 billion in property values were at risk. The number was up nearly 50 percent from 2012. Disturbingly, the report also noted that from 1990 to 2008 Americans built 10 million new homes in zones at high risk of wildfires, or 58 percent of all new homes built during that time frame. In Ravalli County, in the Bitterroot Valley of western Montana, which suffered severe wildfires in 2000, voters gave the thumbs-down to safety-minded zoning measures. Their Board of Commissioners flat out rejected new maps that would have reflected the risks of living in areas where urban settlements meet the edges of wildlands and which are highly vulnerable to wildfires. More than three-quarters of the county's residents live in such dangerous territory, and worried that a new map would increase their insurance costs and, in turn, depress property values.

At times, drawing attention to the obvious is like screaming into a hurricane. After the 2010 Haiti and Chile earthquakes, in which the human and financial costs differed widely because of the steps each country took—or didn't take—to prepare, Donald Rubin, co-founder of the Rubin Museum of Art, started the Campaign for Safe Buildings to prevent future disasters like Haiti's. Recognizing the seeming futility of building codes in countries where there is little rule of law, he proposed codes and inspections supported and enforced contractually, in which only builders that comply get insurance and capital. He had hoped to see a large-scale movement for safe structures that could save billions of dollars and millions of lives. Instead, he was frustrated at just how hard it was for a good idea to gain traction.

In the digital environment rather than the natural one, the same reluctance to act after a crisis continues to have consequences.

Hackers from an offshoot of Anonymous attacked Sony's online gaming service, PlayStation Network, in spring 2011, affecting more than 100 million accounts. Yet when hackers attacked Sony again in December 2014, leading to an uproar over the movie *The Interview* and its plot, which involved the assassination of North Korea's leader, Sony still had not protected itself well against common attacks. It was vulnerable to phishing and Trojans. It had failed to train employees and to put in place proper data-storage and backup systems. Yet Sony was far from alone among companies. A partial list of some of the biggest names hit by hackers in 2014 alone includes Target, Neiman Marcus, Yahoo Mail, AT&T, eBay, UPS, Home Depot, Apple iCloud, Goodwill Industries, JPMorgan Chase, Dairy Queen, and several U.S. government agencies. Despite Sony's experience, other major companies, organizations, and even the government did not show clear signs of using the lessons of the digital crisis to make crucial changes.

Tough Decisions

The challenge, after a trampling, is to avoid overreacting and to keep from underreacting. It all comes down to how leaders and communities assess risk and value security, and whether leaders are willing to risk political capital to do the right thing when they know they're more than likely not to benefit. To be sure, the Manitoba premier Duff Roblin looks brilliant in hindsight for building the Red River Floodway in Winnipeg, but at the time it was pilloried as Duff's Ditch. Alberta's premier, should his plan for future Calgary resilience come to fruition, is unlikely to pay too dearly for a shortsighted decision; nor will he gain much from going along with Calgary's proposal.

CHAPTER 8 TAKEAWAYS:

- **Calibrate your response.** Weigh costs, benefits, and possible unintended consequences. Analyze alternatives from a big-picture point of view. Don't overreact or underreact, and be aware of the need to adjust as you go along. Beware of creating perverse incentives— "moral hazard"—by artificially lowering the cost of high-risk behavior.
- **A crisis is a terrible thing to waste.** Use the pressure created by a crisis to make changes that inertia or political expediency would otherwise make too difficult.

- **Be aware that you might seed the next crisis.** Sometimes the only way out of a crisis creates risks for the future; be prepared to reevaluate decisions once the heat of the crisis has passed.
- **Think resilience.** Sometimes it will be impossible to avoid being trampled; being able to bounce back then becomes essential.
- There's no better time than after a crisis has happened to put in place systems that can help prevent the next one. **But often even that isn't enough.**

9

RHINOS ON THE HORIZON: THINKING LONG-TERM

Once each quarter, the consulting firm the Future Hunters assembles clients and thinkers from government, academia, and business to spend the better part of a day thinking about the trends moving us toward the future. They pass around thoughtfully prepared analyses based on trend-related information gleaned from the news and transformed into about seventy-five abstracts each month that the Future Hunters team carefully annotates and cross-references to track how trends intersect. The group discusses and expands on the future scenarios in freewheeling, lively, and thought-provoking conversations that have tremendous implications for the way the world will work and what it means for businesses and for our daily life. The discussions are wide-ranging, extending from new technologies to demographics to cognitive analysis to social organization and risk management.

The CEO, Edie Weiner, trades off leading discussions with the vice-presidents Erica Orange and Jared Weiner and, before he passed away suddenly in 2014, Arnold Brown, the firm's co-founder. Brown had been a public relations executive at a life insurance company when the Institute of Life Insurance, an industry trade group in New York City, assigned Brown to analyze the potential impacts for the insurance business of some of the turbulent events of the 1960s: the war in Vietnam, the assassinations of Martin Luther King, Jr., and John F. Kennedy, antiwar protests, and the ongoing nuclear shadow of the Cold War. Brown later brought on Weiner, and together they began their systematic monitoring of relevant articles and condensing them into abstracts in a coherent approach to trend analysis. When the institute moved to Washington, DC, in 1977, Brown, Weiner, and Hal Edrich, their partner at the time, stayed in New York City and hung up their own shingle.

Their universe soon broadened from insurers to major corporations across a wide range of industries that have asked for their help in imagining which trends are most likely to affect business prospects and what they can do now to prepare. The majority of their clients are not startups or tech giants but more traditional industries that know that big parts of their professions could become obsolete if they don't think more creatively and plan for the future.

Their own company evolved as well. Orange went to college with Edie Weiner's son, Jared. Edie became a mentor to her and stayed in touch even after Orange moved to Washington, DC. After a few years, Orange hit what she now calls her "quarter life crisis." She called Edie for advice, and it occurred to the two of them that Orange's training in psychology and political science and her gift for pattern recognition perfectly suited her to a career as a futurist. So she joined the company and eventually became as invaluable to Edie as Edie herself had been to Arnold Brown decades earlier. Orange eventually married Jared, who joined the firm, too.

Futurism is much more widely recognized today than in the days when you could count the number of corporate futurists on the fingers of one hand. "Today, every company in the Fortune 1000 has some degree of future outlook," Edie Weiner told me. But many companies seem to be merely going through the motions. "Do boards take several hours a year at their meetings to take a look at the future seriously? The answer is pretty much no."

Companies' definitions of the future have changed as well. Above all, the time frame has compressed. "In the earlier years, companies felt they could do five- and ten-year plans and were confident they could look ahead," Weiner said. "Then they dropped strategic planning. Now it was all 'marketing' and two years became a long term. The markets rewarded that short-term thinking. Everything became shorter-term. A lot of companies didn't want to look beyond two or three years."

Weiner's main concern about the future is demographic change, which ties individuals to major economic and political trends and intersects with other changes, particularly the increasing role of technology and artificial intelligence. The baby-boomer generation is moving into a huge retirement bulge, which will send ripples across the entire economy as a large portion of the workforce exits and starts drawing on retirement and health-care infrastructures, neither of which has the capacity to handle the shift. "One of the things we have to consider is what is going to happen when the industrial world is significantly aging and doesn't have the youth to replace it in retirement," she said.

Demographic change also explains Japan's technological prowess. Japan's post–World War II baby bust pushed it to experiment with new technologies and lead the first wave of automation. "While we may look at that as a technological development, it's really a demographic trend," Weiner said. Today, Japan's aging and shrinking population is pressing it to explore robotics and artificial intelligence. Weiner envisions the next generation of artificial intelligence and robots as having enormous sensory capacity and the ability to emote. She is skeptical of the apocalyptic claims about the impact of artificial intelligence on the human race, but she recognizes that the next generation of technology will change our world dramatically. "It isn't the end of the world, but it's the end of the world that we know," she said. "The fact is that cell phones brought the end of the world as we know it."

This is part of what she calls the metaspace economy, the product of a long-term transformation as a result of disruptive technologies coming together and creating efficiencies. Unlike the agrarian economy, the industrial economy, or the post–industrial economy, the emerging metaspace economy is driven by intangibles tied to the digital economy. Future jobs will be created and disposable income will be spent in this new world. The sheer pace of change is making it difficult for the formal workforce to play catch-up, and whole new skills, competencies, and work processes are being adopted. And that circles back to demographics. "A lot of people are thrown out of work, but a lot of new businesses are created," Weiner said. "If you don't do anything about it, you end up with the situation we have—high young-male unemployment, overeducation and wrong education of young people, violence, terrorism, and an alienated young-male population."

One of my favorite parts of sitting in on the Future Hunters Trends Sessions has been seeing the words the team comes up with for new concepts like the metaspace economy. Over the years, they have coined more than a hundred words that help us envision and conceptualize new trends.

Within the metaspace economy, the rise of digital sports and gaming will generate new heroes: "e-thletes." We'll worry about e-doping; students will get e-thletic scholarships. Social robots will become a new market demographic. 3-D printing will evolve to "4-D printing" of things that can self-replicate and change shape over time.

The "precariat" is a mash-up of *precarious* and *proletariat*, representing the growing class of short-term contract workers who lack full-time benefits, including its millennial subset, the "milleniat." There is "risk in the white space": risk where it may not have been predictable before, or assignable to any liable individual or organization. And there's "templosion," or the implosion of everything into compressed time, as the way we experience time goes from something that was once linear and sequential to something multilayered and simultaneous, with multitasking of products and services and new career life cycles, and impatience with wasted time.

One of Orange's favorites is the Alien Eyes concept: seeing the world objectively as if you were experiencing it for the first time. "We accumulate all of this information, and it's our greatest asset but also our greatest liability," Orange said. "So we ask our clients to put on alien eyes, and ask what the future would look like if we were from another planet." Alien Eyes are an antidote to another Future Hunters concept: educated incapacity, or the baggage of accumulated knowledge that makes you incapable of change—a concept that should rightly take its place along-side the cognitive biases that keep us from responding to Gray Rhinos.

The whimsical way in which the Future Hunters use words belies just how crucial it is to have the right way to express a concept succinctly. "To really understand where the future is going, you can't get bogged down by the existing vocabulary," Orange said. She sees words as part of a set of thinking technologies that help us to see the future more clearly by helping us to create frameworks.

Words are important. They give you a way to get your head around concepts that are abstract, and focus on their implications in the real world, just as being able to articulate the Black Swan concept got people thinking more about how they and their businesses could become more resilient in the face of highly improbable, high-impact events; and just as the Gray Rhino now does in getting leaders to focus on highly probable, high-impact events.

Keeping the Rhinos on the Horizon

The best way to keep from getting trampled by a herd of Gray Rhinos is to keep a safe distance: when they are on the horizon, don't get too close. For businesses, organizations, companies, and each one of us, this means using times of relative calm—and even times of turbulence—to think about the future, consider possible scenarios, and lay out strategies for dealing with them.

The emergency room is the most expensive way of getting medical care; similarly, waiting until the last minute is the worst way to take care of our needs. As we have seen in early chapters, the cost of waiting too long can be staggering. Still, it's hard to think into the future when some-times it's a struggle just getting to the end of the week, or to payday, or to the end of the quarter. I wish I had a nickel for every time, while research-ing this book, I heard that people simply won't think long-term because there are too many short-term pressures that make it impossible to fo-cus on the future. It doesn't happen as often as it should, but some companies, organizations, governments, leaders, and individuals do think long-term. The rest of us can learn from them. So how do we move long-term thinking from a seeming luxury to a priority?

Sometimes it helps to play tricks on ourselves: to set short-term goals in order to get to the long term, and even to time the deadlines for those goals strategically. Yanping Tu and Dilip Soman of the Booth School of Business at the University of Chicago offered two groups of farmers in India payment if they saved a set amount of money by a deadline six months ahead. Those who were given a deadline in the same year set up accounts more quickly than those for whom the deadline was the following year, even though it was the same time period.

The late management guru Stephen Covey's insight in *The 7 Habits of Highly Effective People* is as important for companies and countries as it is for each one of us: separate tasks into urgent, important, and not. Important, urgent tasks should be at the top of the list, but we need to allocate time to important but *not urgent* tasks—over urgent but *not important*. Once I started to view work in this way, it changed my daily workflow and helped me do a better job of addressing what was most important—no matter what was clamoring for my attention day to day. And I found that as I addressed bigger-picture, systemic priorities I saved time and got more done. The same principle applies to organizations, companies, and governing bodies of all kinds.

The U.S. military carries out "war games" and other simulations of events and trends that have the potential for major impact, and this thinking has spread to other branches of government as well. Since 2003, the National Intelligence Priorities Framework has brought together State, Treasury, Defense, and Intelligence officials every eighteen months to look ahead at the top risks of the following three to five years.

Some companies—like the insurance firms that have worked with the Future Hunters—by their very nature depend on thinking long-term. Their actuarial tables and financial projections are designed for the future, yet executives must still remain alert to trends, like the increasing incidence of extreme weather, that can supercede the statistical projections that have been outlined over decades. The typical oil-and-gas company CEO thinks ahead by decades. He has to, given that it takes years to build the infrastructure necessary for drilling. Shell has a whole scenario planning group, which since the 1970s has used scenarios to explore plausible and predictable outcomes in geopolitics, geoeconomics and markets, energy, and other resource supply and demand trends. The projections are far from perfect and can be thrown off by unexpected short-term events, but these companies recognize long-term thinking as being essential to their strategies.

Still, as we have seen in earlier chapters, it's not enough just to recognize a trend; unless a company acts on an obvious danger, its foresight could be all for naught.

Elementary Thinking

Around the world, many of the oldest companies have redefined themselves as technologies have progressed, making some products obsolete and ushering in others. IBM, for example, celebrated a century after the founding of the Computing-Tabulating-Recording Company as a maker of scales, time clocks, and tabulating machines that would become IBM in 1924. Thomas Watson, Sr., upon taking over the company's leadership in 1914, had to pull together a group of companies that had been merged but had not yet coalesced. His message focused on purpose and values: themes that run through the strategies of many long-term thinkers. "We want you all to get together and everybody have their shoulder to the same wheel and push in the same direction," Watson said.

Watson made a gutsy decision in the depths of the Great Depression: instead of pulling back, he invested in a state-of-the-art lab. As we saw in Chapter 6, it's not easy to go against the tide, whether pulling the punch bowl away from the party during boom times or making a leap of faith. This kind of countercyclical thinking requires transcending the moment and looking to the future, using values and a strong sense of purpose as a compass.

Nearly a half century later, Thomas Watson, Jr., echoed his father's message in addressing a New York audience. "I firmly believe that any organization, in order to survive and achieve success, must have a sound set of beliefs on which it premises all its policies and actions," he said. "Next, I believe that the most important single factor in corporate success is faithful adherence to those beliefs. And finally, I believe that if an organization is to meet the challenges of a changing world, it must be prepared to change everything about itself except those beliefs as it moves through corporate life."

IBM itself would have to grapple with that concept many times over, particularly in the 1990s, as it saw its former dominance in the personal-computer market evaporate, and later, as new technologies like smartphones and tablets completely changed the way we think about computers.

"By 1984 we were the toast of Wall Street," Bridget van Kralingen, IBM's general manager for North America, wrote in a brutally honest reflection in *Forbes*. "Less than a decade later, we were toast." In 1993, the company set a new record—$8 billion—for corporate America's largest-ever loss. In a painful transformation, it switched from hardware to software and services. It spent more than $30 billion buying up two hundred companies to expand into analytics and other high-value business lines. For a couple of years, I wrote using one of the last ThinkPad laptops IBM made before it sold its laptop arm to the Chinese firm Lenovo.

Indeed, many long-standing companies, particularly in technology, look very different from when they started. Nokia was a wood-pulp mill and paper maker in 1871 and went into rubber, cable, and electronics before it entered the telecommunications world in 1963 with a radio telephone. It manufactured its first mobile phone in 1987, and in 1992 began its exit from its other lines of business. By 2014, well after it had peaked and fallen in the mobile-phone market, it had sold essentially all of its devices business to Microsoft and embarked on yet another transformation to mobile broadband networks, mapping and location intelligence, and new technologies.

Back to the Fundamentals

Dr. Kazuo Inamori is the founder of Kyocera, the manufacturer of ceramic electronic components, solar panels, and cell phones, which made him Japan's twenty-eighth richest man. He had suffered an adolescence of hardships that began with failing the entrance exam to junior high school, then escalated to being bedridden with tuberculosis and his family's losing their home in an air raid. After experimenting with new forms of ceramics, he founded Kyoto Ceramics as a twenty-seven-year-old in 1959 after quitting his previous job with another company over a disagreement with a manager. (The company would become Kyocera in 1982.)

So Inamori already had a history of dealing with challenges when, in the 1990s, Kyocera faced a set of crises: one of its biggest clients went bankrupt, another switched to a cheaper material, and its customer base was dangerously concentrated in Japan and needed diversification. He stepped aside to let a new generation of leaders run the company, assuming the title of founder and chairman emeritus in 1997. That year, a diagnosis of stomach cancer changed his life. He survived an operation to remove the tumor and went on to fulfill his dream of focusing solely on the study of Zen Buddhism. He was later ordained a priest.

He writes of the management philosophy that got him through tough times, an example of how turning to big-picture, long-term thinking can transcend the intense short-term pressures of crisis situations. "In those difficult circumstances, I would always go back to the fundamentals and ask myself, 'What is the right thing to do as a human being?' Everything I do in my work is based upon this fundamental principle," he wrote in his book, *Respect the Divine and Love People*. "Observing this rule, day in and day out, has brought me amazing results."

In February 2010, the government approached Inamori and asked him to come out of retirement to lead Japan Air Lines, which it had to bail out three times in less than a decade. In the previous year, the company had lost $3 billion; its shares were tumbling and it was about to be delisted, its debts had reached $29 billion, and it had just filed for bankruptcy. He agreed to do the job without pay. Things got much darker before the dawn, though the crisis, as is so often the case, opened the way for the company to make drastic changes. Inamori fired a third of the workforce and cut pay and benefits. Yet eventually the company turned around and was relisted in 2012, a milestone that led to his being able to step down in 2013.

Inamori is known for his business philosophy, which includes the need to treat employees and materials well and to jettison short-term thinking in favor of a long-term vision of its value. "A company can continue to exist over the long term only when it is needed by society," he has said.

In 2005, SoftBank, the Japanese Internet-services company, was facing a charging Gray Rhino: a $1 billion loss and a share price that had fallen to a tenth of its dot-com boom height. Like IBM during the Great Depression, SoftBank looked far into the future to ensure its survival. The company's founder and CEO, Masayoshi Son, thought ahead even as the company was being trampled, and made a long-term bet that not only pulled it out from under but catapulted it to one of the world's largest companies. He then announced a three-hundred-year business plan to emphasize the importance of thinking forward. To be sure, the three-hundred-year headline made the company's stated thirty-year plan, which was already beyond the scope of most people's thinking, sound practically like a short-term plan, which was probably the real goal. This is an example of a tried-and-true negotiating strategy: signal a much more ambitious goal to anchor people's thinking closer to your target.

SoftBank's emphasis on thinking far ahead is not uncommon in Asia, where companies have a particularly strong track record for thinking long-term. The world's oldest company, indeed, is said to be Kongō Gumi, a Japanese construction firm that dates back to the year 578. The Bank of Korea founded 5,576 large companies around the world that are more than a hundred years old: 3,146 of them in Japan, 837 in Germany, 222 in the Netherlands, and 196 in France. Japanese researchers have discovered still more of these long-lasting firms. In 2009, Tokyo Shoko Research counted more than 21,000 Japanese companies that were more than a hundred years old. Most of them were small, to be sure, including only 1,662 companies with annual revenues of more than $1 million and only 338 publicly listed companies that are over a hundred years old. Still, Japan has so many long-standing companies that there is even a word for them in Japanese: *shinise*.

While long-standing companies are common in Asia, Western companies are beginning to rethink the value of long-term strategy after a sharp decline in the past century. In the 1920s, the average life span of a U.S. company was sixty-seven years. Today, it is only fifteen years, according to Richard Foster of Yale University.

Yet there are exceptions. Berkshire Hathaway, along with its leader, Warren Buffett, the "Oracle of Omaha," is the American company perhaps best known for embracing the long term. Founded in 1839 in Rhode Island as Berkshire Fine Spinning Associates, bringing together two textile mills, it continued as a textile company until the 1960s, by which time Buffett had begun investing in it and then saw the writing on the wall for textiles. He took over the company and began to diversify it, beginning with insurance: appropriate for a company that would become so closely associated with long-term thinking. Like many other long-lasting companies Berkshire Hathaway now looks little like the textile mill of its origins; its holdings are widely diversified across finance, utilities, media, logistics, and retail.

Phil Libin, executive chairman of Evernote, a company that provides a convenient way to store and search both handwritten and digital notes and clips, has touted his plans to build "a hundred-year startup," meaning that the company will both still exist in a century and remain innovative and exciting a hundred years from now. Evernote could do worse than look to Berkshire Hathaway as a model.

A Hundred Years

Marc Mertens was born in the central Austrian village of Laakirchen, population 8,000. His first foray into business was a bar in his parents' garage. They were tolerant at first, preferring to know where he and his friends were. "Their generosity stopped when we wanted to bring bands in," he says. So instead he started an event-planning business. After moving to Los Angeles, in 2002 he launched an advertising agency. Very early in his career, he worked for many major commercial brands, but at some point he realized that he wanted to have more impact than simply to sell "a lot of sugar water."

So he relaunched his company as the creative consultancy A Hundred Years, which now has offices in both L.A. and Vienna. He has consulted with such companies as Boeing, Disney, One.org, NASA, and TED to help them develop long-term strategies that adapt to changing technological, economic, and social realities.

A Hundred Years offers a simple suggestion: take fifteen minutes each day to imagine what you would like the next hundred years to look like and what it takes to get there. A week after I met Mertens for the first time, a package arrived in my office with a fifteen-minute hourglass, an ingenious reminder of a simple but essential goal. I still keep it on my desk.

"A hundred years is bigger than blue-sky thinking," Mertens told me. "Rarely do we even think out ahead ten years from now. But a hundred years for us is a way to look at what is possible." Where others see what may be frightening, he sees opportunity. Thinking long-term meant that any ideas we have will eventually be out of our control. So thinking into the future forces us to think big, to think beyond ourselves.

"People are scared about the future. In a way, it's no surprise we're scared if we look at the news with all of the short-termism and the drama," Mertens said. "But it is crazy to be scared about the future if you think a hundred years back. Our office in L.A. is across from the Model T factory, where a hundred years earlier these cars started rolling off of the assembly line. Today, we're looking at electric cars. Wow, is that easier than what they had to do to fuel these oil-driven engines—all the research needed to pump oil out of the ground, ship it across the ocean, and have it available in every town," Mertens said. "How can we be scared of the future if we stay true to the advances we've made over the past century, even without the Internet? We didn't have the same amount of information." Today, we have different constraints but far more resources at our disposal.

"The biggest challenge for long-term thinking is that we look at the long-term problems instead of empowering ourselves to think about what we can achieve," Mertens said. He sees an existential tension between short-term existence and long-term purpose: the short term represents mere survival, but the long term represents passion and the very reason for existing. Thought about correctly, Mertens says, the short and the long term don't need to be separate. Companies can use a hundred-year lens, instead of the typical quarter-year yardstick, to identify new business opportunities and reduce their risks.

Bringing a long-term lens into a company's strategy forces it to focus on its purpose, which can benefit human resources and employee engagement. "People want to work for organizations that have meaning and purpose," Mertens said. This is also essential for marketing to millennials. "If your brand purpose is just to make more money, you're going to have a hard time doing that. It's going to be hard to develop evangelists and get people to rally around your brand." Long-term thinking, for Mertens, means stripping away the marketing language and focusing on the core of an organization: understanding its founding story, what it's really good at, and how the company can translate its strengths into long-term impact and competitive advantage.

Patient Capital

In keeping with the trends A Hundred Years has identified, an increasing number of companies and countries are seeking, with mixed success, to promote long-term thinking and acting. Their ideas range from incentive programs to encourage holding shares in companies longer, to incorporating long-term thinking in key performance indicators, to shunning quarterly-results reporting and creating a whole new set of indicators.

In a landmark 2011 *Harvard Business Review* article, Dominic Barton, the global managing director of McKinsey & Company, argued for a new form of "capitalism for the long term." The consulting firm has done research suggesting that it takes five to seven years to invest in and build a profitable new business. McKinsey analysts broke down the components of value embedded in the share prices of more established companies and found that between 70 and 90 percent of what the shares were worth was tied to cash flows the company did not expect for three or more years. His conclusion was clear and sobering: "If the vast majority of most firms' value depends on results more than three years from now, but management is preoccupied with what's reportable three months from now, then capitalism has a problem." He argues that companies need to change their incentives and structures to get their teams to focus on the long term; champion cultures in which the interests of all shareholders are essential to maximizing corporate value; and return governing power to boards so that they govern like owners instead of feeling beholden to hedge funds and market swings focused on the short term. Barton rightly points out that his proposals are not new, but he argues that the urgency of this challenge is both new and daunting. "Business leaders today face a choice: we can reform capitalism, or we can let capitalism be reformed for us, through political measures and the pressure of an angry public," he wrote.

The B Team—an alliance of business and civic leaders, including Richard Branson of Virgin Atlantic, Unilever CEO Paul Polman, *Huffington Post* founder Arianna Huffington, former prime minister of Norway Gro Harlem Brundtland, former president of Ireland Mary Robinson, Professor Muhammad Yunus of the Grameen Bank, Zhang Yue of China's Broad Group, Tata Group chairman emeritus Ratan Tata, and others—similarly pledge that they will "lead for the long run." One of their goals is to end, wherever they legally can, the default practice of companies reporting their results every quarter, and to replace it with new accounting and reporting measurements that better track social and environmental value.

The Acumen Fund, which raises charitable donations to invest in helping companies change the way the world tackles poverty, marshals what it calls "patient capital." As Acumen describes it on its website, "Patient capital has a high tolerance for risk, has long time horizons, is flexible to meet the needs of entrepreneurs, and is unwilling to sacrifice the needs of end customers for the sake of shareholders. At the same time, patient capital ultimately demands accountability in the form of a return of capital: proof that the underlying enterprise can grow sustainably in the long run."

The World Economic Forum and the Organization for Economic Cooperation and Development are similarly pursuing ways to encourage long-term investing. The size of the task is far from insignificant, as a recent major initiative showed. Over the past half century, the average time a stock is held has fallen from eight years to four months.

At the 2013 annual meeting of the World Economic Forum in Davos, about the need for long-term thinking, business and political leaders rallied behind the need to go beyond the short term. Italy's former prime minister Mario Monti blamed the European Union for short-term thinking in its tepid response to the euro crisis, remonstrating, "Leadership is the opposite of short termism." The IMF's managing director, Christine Lagarde, echoed his sentiment. "If we look beyond the short term, we would indeed move past the crisis," she said.

The consulting firm Mercer reached out to me after I blogged about these conversations and asked me to sit in on a meeting to discuss a study it was conducting on how to promote long-term thinking. The Generation Foundation, which is dedicated to strengthening the field of sustainable capitalism, commissioned Mercer and Stikeman Elliott to investigate how companies might issue loyalty-driven securities to encourage investors to hold shares for three years or more.

Patrick Bolton of Columbia University and Frédéric Samama of Crédit Agricole Group, proposed issuing L-Shares (short for "loyalty"), which would give investors who held on to shares a warrant that would give them the right to additional shares when the "loyalty period" expired. Bolton and Samama blame two things for adding to the pressure for companies to make their decisions based on what's good for the short term but not necessarily what's best for the business. First is the steady increase, over the past thirty years, of the component of CEO compensation based on stock prices. The second is the growing influence of independent directors and activist hedge funds and shareholder groups.

These short-term incentives, they argue, become particularly dangerous during speculative bubbles and busts by encouraging CEOs to "pump and dump" company stock; that is, for following strategies that inflate short-term earnings in order to build the speculative element of a stock's price but hurt its long-term value.

Adding to this problem is the shift in stock ownership from individual retail investors, who owned more than 75 percent of equities in 1951, to institutional investors, who by the beginning of this century controlled close to 70 percent of all traded shares. Some companies, particularly in Europe, have tried to create incentives to encourage shareholders to hold their stock longer. Michelin postponed a costly dividend in 1991. To soften the blow to investors, it issued a warrant that rewarded shareholders who continued to hold its shares.

Under a provision in French law, more than seventy French companies award twice the voting rights to shareholders who hold their shares for two years or longer. Under a similar principle, French companies, including Crédit Agricole, L'Oréal, and Lafarge, pay higher dividends to shareholders who hold certain classes of shares for two or more years, though French law limits them to providing these dividends to a select number of shares and paying no more than a 10-percent premium. Elsewhere in the world, companies—including British Telecom and Standard Life in the United Kingdom, Singapore Telecom, Deutsche Telekom, and Australia's Telstra have granted onetime bonus shares to longer-term shareholders. To be sure, two years is nothing compared with much longer-term thinking, but it is a big step beyond a single quarter.

Mercer concluded, however, that incentives in the form of stock "loyalty" warrants wouldn't work. Instead, it recommended longer time horizons for investment analysis, longer-term frameworks for measuring and rewarding performance, and stronger relationships between investors and companies.

Some of today's best business minds have joined together to push in the right direction. Just as the B Team seeks to do by inspiring other businesses, a few catalysts have sprung to action. The question is how quickly other businesses will follow their lead.

Tax Strategies

Governments can help this process along by leveling the playing field, which in the United States is weighted against true long-term investments. The capital-gains tax falls after just one year, hardly a true "long term" incentive. Rebalancing tax policy by increasing the length of time investors must hold shares to get a lower capital-gains tax, or even creating a set of tiers further lowering capital-gains taxes as the calendar stretches into the future, can send a strong message.

Making other changes to the tax code could reduce churning of stocks and encourage longer-term investing by some of the very organizations that receive tax breaks because their very nature is deemed to benefit society but which, paradoxically, add to short-term pressures. Tax-exempt pensions and endowments, like the giant Harvard and Yale endowments, paradoxically may push harder for returns, often selling stocks in a shorter time frame than other investors, because they don't pay taxes on profits when they sell the shares. Ending their preferential tax treatment would discourage some of the stock-churning. So would a pledge by the biggest universities and foundations to adopt a longer-term investment strategy, coupled with a commitment to transparency that would hold them to their promises.

Governments, companies, and individuals also could promote longer-term thinking and strategic capital investments by putting in place strategies for earmarking windfalls. During boom times, windfall revenue—whether from higher taxes or from royalties—would go to long-term rather than short-term goals. Chile has set a good example of such a practice with its copper stabilization fund, which squirrels away extra profits when commodity prices are high so that the government can use those funds for a rainy day.

To Measure or Not to Measure

In Chapter 8, we saw how important it is to measure results as a way of inspiring people to action. China's mastery of keeping an eye on important but not urgent tasks is impressive, from Deng Xiaoping's economic reforms to today's version of the Five-Year Plan, which incorporates modern strategy and metrics. By focusing its five-year plans on specific measurable results, instead of on heavy-handed actions, as the Soviet Union did, China transformed the five-year concept from the laughingstock created by the USSR to a recognized sophisticated management tool that has played an important role in China's rise to global economic powerhouse. It also has made steady progress on management of the 2008 financial crisis, the need to bring living standards up, and, most recently, in letting the air out of a property bubble. The constantly predicted coming "Chinese crisis" keeps getting pushed to the future. It would be folly to assume that China will be successful indefinitely, but there is much to learn from its approach to huge problems.

As used by the Soviet Union, the Five-Year Plan involved ham-handed micromanaging of the economy produced shortages and bread lines. But China redefined the concept, setting out targets and letting businesses figure out how to reach those targets, rather than setting out specific behaviors without any idea whether those decisions were good. Though not perfect, its five-year plans, in contrast to the old Soviet plans, have generated strong economic growth and significant respect, though it remains to be seen how they will weather the challenge of slowing growth and changing global dynamics.

We can also use reporting and key performance indicators to force people to track their behavior and get rewarded for it. When governments map out their annual budgets, they should report how much goes to long-term goals and estimate the return on those investments; and they should be required to earmark percentages for long-term goals.

To justify its research-and-development budget which it later would have to defend from activist investors with short-term priorities, DuPont in 2010 presciently set a goal for 30 percent of revenue to come from new innovations and began tracking how much revenue each year accrued from innovations developed in the past four years. In 2011, the number of new patents awarded to the company rose to 910, a record that boosted revenue by 10 percent over 2008–11. In 2014, it generated $9 billion in revenue or 32 percent of the total from products developed within that time frame.

Yet, as we saw above with the move to reduce quarterly reporting, sometimes *not* measuring can help direct attention toward the future. Though not without its own unintended consequences, the movement to eliminate quarterly reporting can help companies avoid change blindness and dangerous short-termism and make it easier to invest in needed changes that take time to show results.

CHAPTER 9 TAKEAWAYS:

- **Fresh eyes and fresh words can paint a picture of the future.** Just as escaping the clutches of groupthink requires an open mind and fresh voices, recognizing the dangers and opportunities of the future requires a new mind-set.
- **Recognize the value of purpose in the long term.** Companies around the world have become highly profitable by looking beyond the short term. In a rapidly changing metaspace economy increasingly shaped by millennials, the sense of purpose that drives long-term value is more important than ever.
- **Use "highly effective" strategy and long-term thinking** to save money and free up resources to create opportunities instead of merely patching holes. Bring short and long term into balance. Prioritize importance, not just urgency.

10

CONCLUSION: HOW TO KEEP FROM GETTING RUN OVER BY A RHINO

"The ride will be bumpy. We call it an African massage," said the guide who drove me up the mountain on Mthethomusha Game Reserve, at the southern edge of Kruger National Park in northern South Africa, near the border with Mozambique. We were on our way to the lodge where I'd be staying for a safari to see rhinos in the wild. South Africa is home to more than four of five rhinos left on the planet. It is ground zero of a war to save the rhino from extinction, fighting what feels like a losing battle, as poachers kill one rhino roughly every eight hours for its horn—the weapon that is supposed to help rhinos protect themselves and which, instead, has become the reason for their destruction.

As the Land Cruiser lurched and growled on its way up the steep slope, my driver stopped and pointed to a spot in the brush where, he said, there was a male kudu: a common striped African antelope. I squinted and tried to follow the line of sight from where his index finger was pointing but still couldn't make out the outline of the animal. My vision is terrible but even if it had not been quite so bad I would still have had a hard time seeing the antelope. As I soon learned, it takes practice to see many of the animals to whom Mother Nature gave the great gift of the ability to camouflage themselves.

On my first game drive a few hours later, as the sun slowly sank in the sky, my eyes gradually grew accustomed to following where our tracker pointed. Those dark dots on the hill were buffaloes. That rustling grass was an antelope. There, on the far edge of the valley to our right, was a herd of two dozen or so elephants. The family traveling with us saw the elephants even before our guide did, but it was several minutes before I saw them. Panicking slightly at not being able to notice a large group of multiton animals, I silently told myself that they had the benefit of having been on safari elsewhere before they arrived at this reserve, worried that my eyes were going from very bad to worse.

Even though I knew that my safari companions' eyes were simply better practiced than mine, I was still relieved when I finally saw the elephants. It was a large group of cows, calves, and young adult males and females. Our guide, Noel, eased the Land Cruiser off the road and turned off the engine. We sat and watched as some groomed and caressed each other, some played, and others pulled down tree branches and leaves to eat. Then, in the middle of the herd, a young male sauntered up to another, larger one and challenged him. They unfurled their trunks and grabbed on to each other, then pulled hard until the smaller one gave up and turned away. Then a giant bull, close to twice the size of the largest of the young bulls, took notice and headed toward the young troublemakers, and the whole herd started moving en masse.

We backed up to the road and continued on our way. Fifteen minutes or so later, our tracker, Aaron, signaled our guide to stop. He pointed down the hill, where another vehicle had gone off-road. Noel furrowed his brow and shook his head in concern; they were heading dangerously close to the large male, tempting fate. Human nature was coming into play in a dangerous way. Eventually, the bull turned away and Noel breathed a sigh of relief. Over dinner later in the week, I'd hear stories of an elephant bull in musth—the testosterone-saturated aggressive state at the height of the mating cycle—charging another safari vehicle, though the group escaped unscathed.

We kept our eyes out for rhinos. Aaron pointed out a rhino wallow: an indentation in the ground where rainwater had accumulated. Rhinos, which cannot sweat, dig wallows and lie down in the mud at the bottom in order to cool off and soothe their skin. Nearly an inch thick, a rhino's hide may appear tough, but it's not effective armor against the stinging insects of the bush, or against the ravages of the sun. Another sign that rhinos were near was a midden, a large patch of rhino dung trampled and spread around. Rhinos use these group-poop spots to mark territory and to communicate with one another. Dung beetles crawled all over the midden, rolling and pushing along tiny rhino-poop balls while fending off other dung beetles that were trying to steal the orbs. It was silly to think that each beetle couldn't just roll its own ball, since there was more than enough material to go around; rhinos produce as much as fifty pounds of dung a day. But, if I have learned anything while researching this book, it is that behaviors don't always make obvious sense. Apparently, that goes for dung beetles, too.

Just after sunset, when the light hadn't yet completely left the sky, we heard and saw rustling in the tall grasses off the road. We drove closer, and there they were amid the brush: three white rhinos, which are bigger, wider-lipped, more common, far less elusive, and more social among themselves than black rhinos, which tend to be solitary. These rhinos' horns were blunt, having been cut in order to discourage poachers. As our vehicle approached, the rhino trio ambled off into the dusk. Though brief and dim, this was my first sighting of rhinos in the wild.

The next day, I gained confidence in my ability to spot wildlife, as we saw giraffes, lions, kudu, nyala and impala antelope, many elephants, birds, snakes, an apparently suicidal turtle that tried to crawl under the wheel of our vehicle, and more rhino wallows. But we didn't see any more rhinos.

A group of us awoke at 4 AM the next day to drive to Kruger National Park, which abutted the Mthethomusha Game Reserve. Covering more than 7,500 square miles and six ecosystems, the park is larger than Israel and attracts tourists who generate 3 percent of South Africa's gross national product, conservatively estimated. It's also the home of the world's single largest rhino population, with more than 8,000 rhinos representing more than a third of all of the continent's rhinos.

Kruger, unlike the reserve where I stayed, does not dehorn its rhinos. With a dozen or so tour vehicles alongside the shoulder, a rhino bull ran across the road, his horns impressive in profile. Throughout the day, we saw hippos, lions, alligators, elephants and buffalo up close. But the male running quickly across the road was the closest a rhino came to us. All of our rhino sightings were fleeting: a pair of rhinos sunning themselves in the early fall air on a far-off rock; a rhino cow and calf feeding; a pair of rhinos browsing the trees on the side of the road but running off as soon as they saw us. My record as a rhino spotter was disappointing, though hardly a complete failure.

On my last evening back at Mthethomusha Game Reserve, the game drive yielded lots of zebras, which by some accounts are more closely related to the rhino than elephants are. Yet I still hadn't experienced what I had come to South Africa for: an opportunity to see rhinos up close. As the sun dropped behind the mountains and the darkness closed in, I resigned myself to the likely reality that what I'd seen so far was the best I could do. I was lucky to have seen as many rhinos as I had, even fleetingly and from afar. If the rhinos' situation did not reverse direction dramatically, soon people would no longer be able to see them in the wild at all.

And then Noel stopped the Land Cruiser and cut the engine. Aaron pointed ahead of us to our left. A crash of rhinos were gathered under some trees at the edge of the clearing. As our vehicle inched closer, a few of them turned around and disappeared under the trees. But three stayed and gazed at us as we watched back as much as we could in the deepening darkness.

A large cow was lying on the ground with her back to us. She didn't seem to be the least bit bothered by our presence or by the light that Aaron was shining on her back. Two rhinos watched from the background. Eventually, the cow stood up and shook off some debris, then turned around and ambled under a tree to the left. She stood there for a few moments. We could hear her shuffling but couldn't see her. One of the other rhinos had disappeared, but the remaining one, a large bull, approached the tree where the cow was hidden. With what we supposed were amorous intentions, he followed her as she disappeared into the dark behind the tree.

What struck me most was how peaceful the interaction was: a rhino cow so unperturbed by us that she didn't bother to immediately curtail her nap; a bull intent on courting her and utterly nonplussed by our presence. It was sobering to think that the next generation of humans might not have the chance to see these magnificent animals.

The staff at the lodge was acutely attuned to the dangers that faced the rhinos and, in turn, the local people who depend on wildlife to attract tourists and provide income. "People need to be taught how important rhinos are, not just for us but for the next generations," Noel said. "A lot of the people who come to South Africa are mostly interested in the rhinos. If rhinos are scratched off the planet, the dollars of the people visiting the country will drop off. This hurts everyone."

Despite dehorning its rhinos to deter poachers, the reserve still loses four or five rhinos a year. The horns grow back, though slowly, and poachers want every last bit of horn they can get. Weighing between two and five pounds, the horns are made of keratin—just like our finger and toe nails—which has no medicinal value but to which traditional Asian medicine has nevertheless ascribed healing powers. Contrary to myth, rhino horn is not known principally as an aphrodisiac but as an anti-fever agent.

Each loss strikes home. "One afternoon while driving, we suddenly realized that there were birds of prey—vultures—flying into an area," Noel told me, recalling the shock of a recent poacher attack. "There were a lot of them, so I wanted to go investigate. Usually it means there's a lion kill. As we drove in, we smelled a rotting animal. And then we saw the dead rhino. The first thing I did was check to see if the horns were still there, and they were. I called the manager of the reserve. It had been shot and continued running away, so they lost it and it fell in that area. We don't know if something scared them away."

Back at the lodge, Chris Edwards, the general manager, stopped by the table I was sharing with my safari mates. He's got a bone to pick with the media for making rhinos into the bad guys. "Look at Disney. In *Robin*

Hood, the rhinos were the villains," he said. So was Rocksteady, a Russian arms dealer turned humanoid rhino foe of the Teenage Mutant Ninja Turtles. Where would rhinos be, he wondered, if Disney had come up with a rhinoceros as cute as Dumbo? "A rhinoceros is a unicorn. It's just fat and gray," Chris said.

As I'd read widely and seen for myself in the past few days, rhinos tend to keep to themselves and are relatively docile when they do not feel threatened. The hippopotamus is considered to be far more dangerous than the rhino; the tiny mosquito is responsible for more deaths than any of the so-called Big Five most dangerous African animals.

A charging rhino is no doubt a fearsome sight, yet I feared I may have done the rhinoceros a disservice by using it as a metaphor for danger. I felt a twinge of guilt that when I was looking for an image to represent a giant, obvious threat, the rhino was what came to mind. The reality is that for endangered species, especially the rhinoceros, the human race is the Gray Rhino. Rhinos are in far more danger from us than we are from them. We need to turn our attention to saving a creature that has walked the earth for more than fifty million years, and whose fate will be an indicator of our ability to recognize and act on an important challenge. If the Gray Rhino framework gets people with the power to change the outcomes of a mortal threat to the very existence of the rhinoceros, then I can only hope that the poetic license I've taken will be worth it.

Fifty Million Years Old

The fight to save the rhinos themselves is a powerful example of how Gray Rhino thinking explains where we have failed but also where there is hope. The threat to the survival of a species shows how denial and willful ignorance can get in the way of solutions, and how easy it is to claim victory and forget how closely dangers still lurk. Governments have muddled in facing down the threat of poaching, often because of corruption and powerful entrenched interests. When they have been ready to move, the diagnosis—or, more accurately, the treatment protocol—has not always been clear. The fight to save the rhino cycles in and out of the panic and action stages. It provides a recurring example of a crisis being a terrible thing to waste.

People pay attention only when the situation appears to be critical, and by then it is too late for some of the remaining animals. Interventions earlier could have made a difference for some species that are now extinct or on the verge of extinction. Yet without the impetus of a looming disaster to galvanize us into action, we don't intervene. The power of imagination and opportunity hold the key to the future.

The ups and downs over the decades in the struggle to save the rhinoceros point to another lesson common to recurring Gray Rhino challenges: no matter how long you fight, you've never quite won.

At the beginning of the twentieth century, as many as half a million rhinos roamed Africa and Asia. Yet the need to conserve was already evident in the face of the big-game hunters who came for trophies, reducing the number of white rhinos to only a hundred. In March 1898, the South African Republic, recognizing the need to control hunting and to protect the rapidly falling number of wild animals, created a government wildlife park that in 1926 became Kruger National Park.

Shortly after his U.S. presidential term ended in 1909, Theodore Roosevelt went on safari, killing eleven black and—astonishingly, given how scarce they were at the time—nine white rhinos. At the time, black rhinos were so plentiful that Roosevelt complained that they were getting in the way of his group's finding other types of animals to kill.

Within seven decades, the number of living rhinos fell precipitously. Africa's civil wars of the 1960s brought with them a large influx of guns, many of them traded for ivory and rhino horn. By 1970, the number of black rhinos across Africa had fallen to 65,000. By 1993, there were only 2,300 black rhinos left.

Meanwhile, governments in the countries where rhinos lived devoted more resources to protecting them and to giving their people incentives to be part of the conservation effort. South Africa, Kenya, and other countries worked to build tourism industries around their wildlife so that local populations would have economic incentives to protect endangered species.

In South Africa, the apartheid government's security state proved to be effective in keeping out poachers, and the Southern white rhino population began to recover, even as other populations were falling. By 1960, there were 600 Southern white rhinos—six times the population at the turn of the century. In 1961, South Africa launched Operation Rhino, which transported rhinos from the Umfolozi and Hluhluwe reserves to other protected areas around the country, including, controversially, private reserves. In 1968, the country legalized a limited number of trophy-hunting licenses as a way of creating an economic incentive for reserves to care for them. Though hunting rhinos seemed counterintuitive to saving them, the scheme worked: the number of white rhinos had increased many times over since hunting was legalized.

Rhino conservation efforts merged with a wider movement to save threatened species, both in their habitats and in the countries that consumed their horn. In 1973, after ten years of preparation, eighty nations joined together to formally create the Convention on International Trade in Endangered Species, an international agreement to ensure that international trade in wild animals and plants does not threaten their survival. In 1977, CITES listed rhinos on its Appendix I, for species threatened with extinction, effectively ordering a ban on international rhino horn trade.

Several countries shut down the bulk of the legal rhino horn trade across and within their borders. Japan, a major consumer in the 1970s, gave in to international pressure and joined CITES in 1980. The country banned the importation of rhino horn and its Health Ministry required all medical providers to stop prescribing it and to designate substitutes. The focus then moved to Korea, which banned imports in 1983, removed rhino horn from its pharmacopeia, and joined CITES a decade later. Taiwan similarly banned imports in 1985 and, under pressure from the United States, banned sales. For a while, the renewed conservation efforts seemed to be making headway. Rhino populations in Africa increased significantly from the mid-1990s, to 20,405 white rhinos and around 5,055 black rhinos in 2012.

Yet as soon as one crisis is calmed another one arises, and the tide has turned the wrong way. Even after the relative successes in Japan, Korea, and Taiwan, the economic boom of the past two decades in Asia increased demand for rhino horn. Catering to newly minted megarich and to burgeoning middle classes in China and Vietnam, a $20 billion black market has arisen in Asia, with rhino horn selling for as much as cocaine. The market in Vietnam became significant only in 2005, sparked in part by rumors that a high-level official's cancer had been cured by rhino horn, despite medical science to the contrary. A much wider craze ensued as a new generation seized on rhino horn as a hangover preventive and cure, as a high-value gift item often used to close business deals instead of a Rolex, and as unscrupulous vendors began marketing it as a cancer cure to families of hospital patients.

Thus, after years of hard-won increases in rhino populations across Africa, a new, aggressive wave of poaching set in to meet the newfound demand from China and Vietnam. In 2009, the number of rhinos killed in South Africa rose to 122, from 13 in 2007 and an average of just 9 a year from 1980 through 2007. By 2014, the number of killings had increased yet another tenfold; poachers slaughtered 1,215 rhinos, with 827 of those killed in Kruger National Park alone. The number of poachers arrested trailed far behind. Poachers have adopted increasingly brutal techniques, such as anesthetizing rhinos and hacking their horns off to the bone while the animals are still alive, leaving them to awake to excruciating pain. They are now using increasingly sophisticated equipment, including military-grade helicopters and night-vision goggles. They've begun chopping off ears and tails to verify that the horns they sell came from real rhinos.

The South African government has become more aggressive in pursuing and prosecuting poachers. Yet it has still had to fight not only the criminals outside, many of them crossing in from Mozambique, but also those within its ranks—insiders who have earned the dubious distinction of "khaki-collar criminals." In 2014, thieves stole an entire collection of 120 horns from the Mpumalanga government tourism building in a crime widely assumed to have been an inside job. South Africans are particularly piqued at Mozambique, where international rhino-horn crime syndicates operate with impunity. Mozambican poachers have taken advantage of Kruger National Park rangers not being allowed to pursue poachers across the national border; when fleeing poachers crossed the border, they fired victory rounds to spite the rangers.

Luckily, the dramatic rise in rhino poaching has not gone unheeded. The world has begun to take notice, especially as news developments have brought worse and worse news. And people are taking up the challenge. "Rhinos have walked the earth for fifty million years, but three are killed every day. Every day by the time you have lunch one's gone; by the time you have dinner, one's gone; and while you're sleeping one's gone," Dr. Susie Ellis, the executive director of the International Rhino Foundation, told me. A group of zoo directors formed the organization in 1991 as the International Black Rhino Foundation but later expanded to all five rhino species in an effort to mobilize a response that would combat poaching and increase the number of rhinos. One of their first moves was to import twenty black rhinos into the United States and Australia as insurance populations. Today, the group is the biggest international organization fighting to save the rhino, along with the U.K.-based Save the Rhino and the World Wildlife Federation. "We want them to be there for our children," Ellis said.

Hoping to replicate the success of U.S. government pressure in the 1980s, the International Rhino Foundation has partnered with the Environmental Investigation Agency to petition the United States to impose trade sanctions against Mozambique for its support of criminal poaching and rhino horn–trading syndicates. "If these governments want to shut it down, they can shut it down," Ellis said. "It's a matter of political will."

We are at a crucial moment at which the very survival of the species depends on creating that political will, in a challenge that goes to the heart of the question behind this book. You could say that we are in the panic stage right now. Several new developments have heightened the sense of urgency, which may be a good thing for rhino subspecies that are still viable. But this awareness has come at great cost: we recently witnessed the extinction of one subspecies, another is imminent, and two more are highly likely.

In 2011, the International Union for the Conservation of Nature declared the Western black rhino extinct after it had not been seen alive for five years. At the close of 2014, Angalifu, a Northern white rhino at the San Diego zoo, died at the ripe old age of forty-four, leaving only five surviving members of the subspecies. The only remaining male, Sudan, had been dehorned and was under twenty-four-hour armed guard in Kenya in the hope of keeping him alive. Sudan's sperm count had fallen, since he's now forty-two, so conservationists weren't sure how much longer he'd be able to father a new calf, especially since the two females living on the reserve with him were also getting on in years. Global celebrities flocked to visit him and to promote an international Twitter campaign under the hashtag #LastMaleStanding to raise funds for his protection. Two other subspecies are likely to go extinct in our lifetime as well. There are fewer than 60 Javan rhinos and only about 100 Sumatran rhinos.

In response to the poachers, rhino keepers have been adding to their own arsenal high-tech tools like microchips, DNA testing and databases to track seized rhino horn to its source, and thermal cameras and artificial intelligence to alert park rangers to suspected poachers. They're also employing paramilitary training and canine antipoaching units to detect rhino horn and ivory contraband.

There have been efforts to dye the horns to make them less appealing, and to poison the horns so that anyone who ingests them will get sick. There is a certain delicious irony in the latter. Because horns do not have vascular systems to distribute the dye or poison throughout the horn, however, any injections remain localized and are therefore not as effective as they might be. And not all rhino horns are ingested; some are purely ornamental.

A few biotech companies have proposed using 3-D printers to create artificial horn to flood the market and lower the price enough to make it unattractive to crime syndicates. But conservationists have serious doubts. In a joint paper, the International Rhino Foundation and Save the Rhino International ask a series of questions. Would the substitute really reduce demand for rhino horn? Or would the fall in prices created by the cheaper alternative increase demand, provide a cover for illegal rhino horn, increase the profits of smugglers, and further endanger rhinos? The organizations concluded that the latter was the case, as did several other groups who issued later reports.

Perhaps the most controversial approach to rhino conservation is trophy hunting. Shortly before I arrived in South Africa, the United States had granted an import permit to a Texan game hunter who had paid $350,000, a new record, in an auction held by the Dallas Safari Club for the right to shoot an older black rhino bull in Namibia. My knee-jerk reaction, like that of many people, was revulsion. I will never understand why some people get a thrill out of killing anything for pure sport, especially an animal that may be one of the last of its kind. Yet, looking at the logic behind the transaction, I saw that the picture was more nuanced. By removing an older bull who was too old to reproduce and was reportedly preventing younger bulls from mating with females, in some people's view the hunt had the potential to increase the population. The proceeds were to go to support conservation efforts. And the example of the white rhinos in South Africa made it clear that allowing some legal hunting had the effect of increasing the value of living rhinos and thus in bringing them back from the edge.

"If an endangered species as charismatic as the black rhinoceros is under such extreme threat from poaching, then perhaps the message that the species needs saving has a larger problem to address than the relatively limited loss of animals to wealthy hunters," Jason Goldman wrote in *Conservation* magazine. Goldman cited a 2005 study published in the *Journal of International Wildlife Law & Policy* in which it was argued that trophy hunting could, in fact, save the rhinos. That paper recommends allowing permits to hunt only older, non-breeding males, or younger males who have spread their genetic material widely; any revenue would go straight to conservation efforts—in other words, exactly along the lines of the auction in question. "The real tragedy here is that the one rhino that will be killed as a result of Saturday's auction has received a disproportionate amount of media attention compared to the hundreds of rhinos lost to poaching each year, which remain largely invisible," Goldman concluded.

Conversely, it sounded like a good idea when South African Airlines announced, in April 2015, that it had banned the transport of endangered lion, elephant, and rhino trophies on its passenger and cargo flights, even if the hunter held a legal permit. Emirates and Lufthansa quickly followed suit. But if carefully managed trophy hunting can be successful in preserving endangered species, could that policy have unintended consequences?

The answers are not easy. Yet, overall, there is a broad consensus on strategies that do work: a combination of strict law enforcement, intelligence coordination to head off poachers before they have a chance to act, moving rhinos to safer areas with concentrated populations that can more easily be protected, engaging local communities and creating rhino-related sustainable income streams, and, above all, reducing demand.

What's Your Gray Rhino?

Today businesses, organizations, governments, and industries are dealing with many threats that are obvious, highly probable, and potentially devastating to those who are unprepared. Each of us faces at least one Gray Rhino, and often more: in your personal or family life, in your organization or business, and as a member of society and a citizen of the world. Our challenge, both collective and individual, is to recognize and head off the highly probable, highly obvious, high-impact dangers that are—or at least ought to be—treated as clear and present, yet all too often are neglected.

The Black Swan concept woke people up to the need to be open to the possibility of the unexpected. Behind every Black Swan is a crash of Gray Rhinos. You'd think we don't need to wake up to obvious crises; aren't we dealing with them already? Yet quite the opposite is true. We are terrible at paying attention to what should be anticipated. Sometimes the bigger the Gray Rhino is, the harder it is to see it and act in time to keep from getting trampled.

Once you know what a Gray Rhino is, they pop up everywhere. When Blue Bell Creamery recalled all of its ice cream in the spring of 2015 because of widespread listeria contamination, it followed a series of unheeded warnings. When an Amtrak train derailed tragically in May 2015, it turned out that plans to put in place safety systems had been delayed. Many people had to be aware that the rollout, in 2013, of the Affordable Care Act website, as riddled with bugs as an old house infested by termites, would be a disaster. Enron, Long-Term Capital, Kodak, BlackBerry . . . the list of companies that failed to confront their Gray Rhinos goes on.

We don't know exactly how, or when, every Gray Rhino will play out, but we would be unwise to ignore them. Will 3-D printing have the same impact on some manufactured goods that digital cameras had on old-fashioned photography and that the Internet and YouTube had on network television and traditional media? How will we deal with the enormous employment changes that artificial intelligence will usher in? In the face of widening income disparities with huge consequences for social and political stability, as well as for future human capital needs, how can leaders help globalization to lift everyone so that the dizzying wealth of a few does not collapse under its own weight? How will emerging megacities deal with the intense pressures their rapid growth is placing on their infrastructure and their resources? How will aging cities handle demographic change and the need to upgrade their infrastructure—and how will others counter an exodus of young people? How will the rise of the sharing economy affect traditional businesses, and what can these companies do to get ahead of the changes? How will Japan, Europe, and the United States deal with the economic, political, and social effects of the graying of their populations? How do leaders and citizens respond to the increasing scarcity of resources, including water, food, and key minerals, and the resulting potentially catastrophic effect on supply chains, social and political stability, and life itself? How will coastal populations handle the effect of the rising sea levels that make

Katrinas and Sandys and Phailins and Haiyans regular occurrences, as floods thought to occur only once every ten thousand years become "mere" hundred-year storms?

And how will we tackle the meta-Rhinos, the underlying problems with our decision-making and our political structures that make it harder for us to address the rest of the very obvious, high-impact threats facing the world? How do companies, families, and individuals face challenges that have profound impacts for those who experience them?

As you learn to recognize the stages, the pitfalls and opportunities of each step in the unraveling of a highly obvious threat become clear: changing denial to recognition, moving from muddling to coming up with a plan, avoiding the panic stage, moving to action as soon as possible, and picking up the pieces and building back better if you get trampled. In that spirit, I offer herewith a Gray Rhino Safari Guide: a set of principles for dealing with the five stages of future obvious, highly probable, high-impact threats; in other words, How to Not Get Run Over by a Gray Rhino.

1) Recognize the Rhino. Just as the Black Swan helped people focus on highly improbable crises, the Gray Rhino is a focal point for the highly probable, obvious crises that we take for granted, push aside, and otherwise ignore, at great cost. Simply recognizing that Gray Rhinos exist is a step toward not only getting out of the way but turning a problem into an opportunity. Everyone knows about the elephant in the room, which nobody talks about because it makes us uncomfortable. Gray Rhinos are similar to their pachyderm cousins but much more dangerous.

The first stage of a Gray Rhino, denial, is the one most often confused with Black Swans. Deeming a highly probable Gray Rhino to be a highly improbable Black Swan is merely a defense mechanism against recognizing an unpleasant reality. You can quibble over the definition of "highly probable" and what time frame it involves. Here it's important not to sweat the details. If there's a reasonable chance that something bad will happen in a reasonable time frame, it qualifies as a probable danger that you need to deal with.

To be able to acknowledge Gray Rhinos sooner, it helps to be aware of the odds stacked against seeing the obvious. Because our minds and our social dynamics set us up to avoid what we don't want to be true, we cling to questionable predictions and fail to heed the ones that are most likely to be true. We don't ask questions for which we don't really want to know the answers. The trio of monkeys who see-hear-and-speak no evil live within our organizations, our families, our governments, and our own heads. The strategies outlined in Chapters 2 and 3 can help us to recognize obvious dangers by better understanding the nature of our complicated relationship with predictions and by resisting our natural impulse toward denial and willful ignorance.

Don't be afraid to question what the usual suspects are saying, to go out on a limb, and to be wrong. Don't assume that everything will be okay because the powers that be say it will; they have a stake in the status quo, so they will resist the idea that anything could disrupt it. Keep probing and asking the tough questions. Be on the lookout for groupthink and stand firm against it. Make sure that there are different perspectives and voices around the table when your organization is making decisions, and be open to hearing them. As we saw with the Chabris and Simons experiment, it becomes easy to see the "invisible" gorilla when you're told it's there. Similarly, when you start looking for Gray Rhinos, you're more likely to see them.

2) **Define the Rhino.** Of course, once we start seeing Gray Rhinos it's quite possible to become overwhelmed. It's impossible to deal with every potential problem at once. That's where defining the scope comes in so that we can prioritize problems and frame them in a way that gets the attention of people who have the power to do something about them.

How you diagnose and frame a problem makes the difference in whether you get people to respond and whether or not that response will work. Is the problem the inconvenience of fixing a deficient fifty-seven-cent ignition switch that it will be inconvenient and costly to replace? Or is it that not fixing the switch will cost lives and billions of dollars and put the entire company at risk? Is the problem losing 30 percent of your investment now, or is it losing 75 percent not much farther down the road?

When companies operate on thinner margins, they have much more reason to address problems that don't seem worth their while when they're flush. For decades, the legendary motorcycle maker Harley-Davidson didn't pay much attention to its inefficiency, high absenteeism, and a workplace atmosphere where workers prided themselves on doing things their own way; the culture was very much in keeping with its maverick brand. "Before the great recession, Harley-Davidson didn't have to worry about counting the seconds," Adam Davidson wrote in a *New York Times Magazine* profile of the company. But in 2009, when people didn't have the money for a luxury item like a Harley, the company had no choice but to redefine inefficiency from being a part of its brand identity to being a threat to its very survival. That recognition led the company to make extensive changes, including painful job cuts and a pay freeze. But it also started looking for ways to be more efficient all across the plant. By adjusting the angle of a tiny plastic latch on a part that didn't fit quite right, it saved 1.2 extra seconds of manufacturing time per bike, which sounds small but made it possible for the company to make 2,200 more bikes each year, generating millions of dollars in revenue, with the same number of workers. The outside world redefined the problem for Harley-Davidson; the company responded just in time. But if management had recognized earlier that its inefficient ways were costing it so much and had the potential to wipe the company out, the company would not have come so close to having to close its doors.

Finding an emotionally resonant message that makes the threat real encourages people to pay attention. When Melbourne, Australia, put in a new tram system, it needed a way to get people—particularly those between eighteen and thirty, who were prone to walk and text at the same time—to watch out for the trams. The solution was an ad campaign featuring a series of yellow road signs with a black rhino on a skateboard. An accompanying video showed a crowd fleeing a large group of skateboarding rhinos careening down the street along the tramway and looking as if they're very much enjoying the ride, especially one rhino with a mischievous glint in his eye as he presses his giant foot to the pavement and pushes off to get the skateboard to speed up. "A tram weighs as much as thirty rhinos," the voice-over intones as a hapless teenager wearing headphones looks up to see a tram bearing down on him. Spike the Rhino, the campaign's mascot, has a twitter handle (@bewaretherhino) and his own Facebook page.

3) Don't stand still. If you can't make the big changes you need to make, think about what smaller steps are possible and how they might work with what doable actions others are pursuing. Muddle if you must, but, if you do, muddle strategically by preparing for the moment toward which procrastinating eventually leads.

Intuition and reason are especially likely to deceive us when we're euphoric or downbeat but also when we're static. If you can, make a plan ahead of time and use it. Think of the emergency responses people in hurricane and tornado zones learn in grade school. Even better, create automatic triggers that will force you to act at times when panic might otherwise cloud your judgment.

People take reasonable precautions all the time, even though they know it's not certain that they will face a danger that is nevertheless easily imagined: to wear a seat belt, buy insurance, switch from cheeseburgers to salads, get a flu shot, and exercise; even if we never have a car wreck, or suffer damage to our home, or face a medical crisis, or become exposed to the flu.

4) A crisis is a terrible thing to waste. Sometimes it's just not possible to get out of the way. And sometimes the biggest problem is not what we think it is. When facing creative destruction that brings in the new, is the threat the likelihood that we won't save a business—or that we won't let go soon enough? Sometimes the only time to keep future Gray Rhinos from charging is right after a disaster, when people are still afraid of the consequences of a future threat. If you get trampled, pick yourself up and see what new pathways the Gray Rhino's charge has opened up. Calamities can create unexpected opportunities.

Chicagoans often talk about the unexpected rebirth that followed the Great Chicago Fire of October 8, 1871. The fire destroyed more than three square miles of the city, killed 300 people, toppled 18,000 buildings, left 100,000 people homeless, and caused damages that would have amounted to over $4 billion in today's dollars. Catherine O'Leary and her cow were initially accused of having started the fire but were later revealed to have been framed for the sake of a good story. Mrs. O'Leary was soundly asleep in bed, and the cow was reportedly on the loose when the fire started. But to make up for the slander they suffered I'll give them credit for the dramatic transformation that resulted from the fire.

The fire catalyzed a building boom, replacing old wooden buildings with brick and stone, many of which are still standing today. It's credited by many with creating new block configurations with alleys, which keeps garbage off the streets, an innovation that my nostrils appreciate immensely after twenty-three years in New York City. Dumped into Lake Michigan, the millions of tons of rubble created by the fire extended the shoreline east into the lake, creating what is now the beautiful Grant Park. Many historians credit the fire with spurring the city to push to bring the 1893 World's Columbian Exposition to Chicago. As the tech incubator 1871, named for that fateful event, describes it, "The story of the Great Chicago Fire of 1871 isn't really about the fire. It's about what happened next: A remarkable moment when the most brilliant engineers, architects and inventors came together to build a new city. Their innovations—born of passion and practical ingenuity—shaped not just Chicago, but the modern world."

The fire had, in fact, been foreseeable. The exceptionally dry summer and early autumn had left Chicago's wooden buildings and bridges highly vulnerable. "The absence of rain for three weeks [has] left everything in so flammable a condition that a spark might set a fire which would seep from end to end of the city," reported the *Chicago Tribune* not long before the fateful night. The Fire Department had requested new hydrants, larger water mains, more men, two fireboats for the river, and a building inspection to bring the city's many firetraps up to code. Their pleas were all for naught.

5) Stay downwind. The best leaders act when the threat is still far away. We are least likely to respond to signs of danger when a Gray Rhino is easiest to fix, and most likely to act only when the cost of responding is high and the likelihood of succeeding is low—or even after we've paid the cost of going through a disaster, as Chicago did.

Staying downwind requires two strategies. First, keep your eye on the horizon. So that you can anticipate how seemingly far-away dangers might unfold. Second—and this is far more difficult—tackle the meta-rhinos that get in the way of making good decisions and acting on them: the decision-making processes that lead to groupthink and blind us; the perverse incentives that discourage policymakers and business leaders from doing the right thing; and the inefficient ways in which we allocate resources that waste money in the short term when, instead, we could be investing in significantly larger long-term gains.

Sometimes it's impossible to get others to agree to make changes when the sky is sunny and problems seem far away. In that case, make a plan so that when the inevitable happens you'll have steps to take.

6) Be a rhino spotter; become a rhino keeper. Heading off a crisis starts with a rhino spotter: one person who recognizes an obvious danger that others ignore and speaks up. Just as it takes practice to be able to see a rhino in the wild, learning to acknowledge Gray Rhinos is a skill.

Individuals matter in recognizing Gray Rhinos, recruiting others to recognize and devise solutions, and in turning ideas into action. "People may recognize a need, but it's the action piece that's the hardest part. The most difficult thing is figuring out what to do," said Erica Orange, whom we met in Chapter 9. "It comes down to that one person. If a company doesn't have that one champion, it's not going to happen." She's seen it again and again in the companies the Future Hunters advises. The companies that have been most successful in recognizing tectonic shifts are the ones with a passionate internal advocate, consistent with what we saw in Chapter 7 with organizations in which influencers drove change within companies and among peers and partners.

These are the rhino keepers: the people who are willing to go against the crowd, knock down the perverse incentives, and inspire others. They are the ones who might be a bit mad. It takes courage to put yourself out there and sacrifice to avoid a disaster, whether as part of a company or as an individual or as a citizen of a community, nation, or the world. That was the message I heard over and over while researching this book. It was what kept me writing in spite of all the people who told me that human nature was just too hardwired against us recognizing obvious dangers and acting in time to prevent calamity.

A Rhino Keeper

Mina Guli is a Gray Rhino spotter and keeper. Her cause is water. She grew up in Australia, where she lived with the reality that water was scarce. As a child, she learned to save water from washing her hands and from taking a shower; her family had buckets all over the house to catch and reuse every possible drop. She remembers when the shopping malls turned off their fountains. "We just used to watch the level of the dams go down and down. It was terribly sad," she recalled. That experience shaped her career in environmental law and finance, including the creation of the first carbon markets. Eventually, she moved to Beijing as a co-founder of Peony Capital, an environmental fund for Chinese companies.

Moderating a World Economic Forum panel with Nestlé chairman Peter Brabeck-Letmathe in 2011, she had a series of "Aha" moments. The first was the realization that 95 percent of our water consumption happens outside our homes: the 2,700 liters of water it takes to grow and process the cotton in a T-shirt; the 11,000 liters required to make a pair of jeans; and as much as 18,000 gallons to make a hamburger (not for Guli, though—she is a strict vegetarian). The second was that there were many organizations that viewed water as a sanitation and hygiene issue, but nobody from the demand side. But the biggest realization, which resonated with her childhood memories, was this: "We're running out of water, because we're using it faster than we can replenish it," she said.

Those realizations were so big and frightening and felt so urgent on a personal level that Guli knew water was her calling. She quit her job to found Thirst, an organization dedicated to engaging young people in changing the way the world uses water. She knew that she had to do something dramatic.

Thirst's first project was setting a Guinness World Record for the largest human water dragon, which roughly 2,000 students joined together to create in November 2013. Thirst has since partnered with more than 100 schools and 120 clubs in 18 of China's 20 provinces to create awareness of how what we consume affects the world's water supply. It started an innovation contest for students to develop technologies to reduce water use at home and at school.

In April 2013, she set out on a run across the Sahara to draw attention to water scarcity. Seven kilometers in, she felt a terrible pain in her hip. "I sat down on a rock and thought, I'm in a really bad place. I can give up and go home, and there's no shame in that. Something is seriously wrong. But then I thought about what message that would send: that it's okay to give up when things get hard, or that you have to stand up even when things go against you." So she went on and finished, 243 kilometers later. When she got back, a doctor found that she had two cracks in her hip.

But she wanted to do more to get the message out, and realized that if she was going to attract the media attention that water deserved, she had to do something completely nuts. She drew inspiration from the British-South African lawyer and advocate Lewis Pugh, sometimes called "the Sir Edmund Hillary of swimming," who swims long distances to draw attention to the urgency of protecting the oceans. She wanted to use her running the same way. So, still on crutches, Guli was soon planning her next effort: to run across seven deserts on seven continents in seven weeks, aiming for World Water Day in February 2016. "You need those people who are willing to be nuts enough to identify the problem but determined and persistent enough to do something," Guli said. "You need not only a rhino spotter but to make a commitment to pursue the rhino and to conserve it."

A Matter of Course

"It is amusing to realize how soon we got to accepting our difficulties with rhinos as a matter of course," Teddy Roosevelt wrote in the January 1911 *National Geographic*, recalling his experiences on safari. During the expedition, one of the African porters had been tossed into the air and injured by an angry rhino. "Here in civilization if you asked a man to kindly go down and scare off a rhinoceros for you, the man would look at you with a certain surprise: in Africa it was a matter-of-course incident," he wrote. "When near a rhino there is always a chance that he will charge, whether through stupidity, or fright, or anger. The trouble is that one never knows whether he will or will not charge him."

Roosevelt's description is as accurate in describing a long-standing struggle as it is as applied to the safari. Just because we recognize a Gray Rhino doesn't mean we'll be able to get to safety in time, or turn a threat into an opportunity and profit from it. But if we don't recognize the Gray Rhinos in front of us it's a near-certainty that we will be trampled. Gray Rhino thinking is a combination of realism and optimism. You have to be clear-minded and open to hearing and thinking of unpleasant things if you're going to be able to spring to action in time to steer clear of danger. But you also have to be optimistic enough to think you've got a decent chance of success, and be able to reframe a threat as an opportunity.

Without being Pollyanna, I am an optimist. There are enough examples in this book of leaders who do recognize and act on highly probable, high-impact threats that can bring down individuals, families, businesses, societies, and the world. They are the rhino spotters and keepers. With that in mind, I want to close with an image of hope.

On a wintry day, I visited Chicago's Lincoln Park Zoo to meet King, an Eastern black rhino born nearly two years earlier at the zoo. Stepping into the warm, humid air of the Regenstein African Journey and walking past the meerkats and klipspringers was like being temporarily transported to a far-away continent. Rachel Santymire, the director of the Davee Center for Epidemiology and Endocrinology, welcomed me. Santymire has researched genetics, social patterns, and environmental stressors among rhino populations in South Africa's Eastern Cape. By studying fecal samples and sleep patterns (using hidden cameras on latrines), she has helped to identify ways that zoos can reduce stresses on rhino populations. Most of that research took place before the recent escalation in poaching, which put additional studies on hold. She's deeply concerned about the future of the rhino. "My work matters in the long run, but you've got to have populations first," Santymire said. A recent study warning that the white rhino may be extinct in the wild as soon as 2026, left her in tears. "My son will be ten years old then. What am I going to tell him? That his mother used to work on rhinos but can't anymore because there are none left? And when you take them out, who's going to support the habitat?"

Those questions are why the Lincoln Park Zoo's star rhinoceros is so important: unless a wider public understands just how special rhinos are, it will be impossible to create the pressure needed to save them. Public education is an important part of the plan. If you've never seen a rhinoceros, why would you want to save it?

Baby King's mother, Kapuki, who is ten years old, weighs about 2,600 pounds. She likes to crush and push around giant plastic barrels, look at herself in the mirror, and spend as much time near humans as she can. The zoo brought Kapuki to Chicago in hopes that she and Maku, the zoo's male rhino, would breed. The Association of Zoos and Aquariums Species Survival Plan had chosen her through its matchmaker efforts across the zoo system, seeking to identify the greatest genetic diversity possible as a rhino yenta. Fourteen and a half months after Kapuki and Maku consummated their union, little King entered the world in 2013. The first rhino calf born at the zoo since 1989, King weighed only sixty pounds at birth and drew huge crowds for the first year or so of his life.

Now almost two years old, he was rapidly approaching his mother's size. This day, though, he was still very much a shy baby. As they munched on alfalfa and grass, King hid behind his mother and peeked out from time to time. Kapuki, who lived up to her reputation for being social, came right up to the bars separating her from me. She grabbed a bunch of alfalfa with her prehensile lip, which looks a bit like a parrot's beak or a giant pink thumb, and chewed away. In the wild, the lip acts much like a thumb, allowing black rhinos to browse bush and trees and grab sticks and shrubs, unlike their white rhino cousins, whose wide, flat lip limits them to grazing on grass.

Rhinos reach sexual maturity at about six years old. Once King turns four or so the zoo staff acknowledged that he may well be sent to another zoo to find a mate; under the terms of the Species Survival Plan agreement, it's not up to the Lincoln Park Zoo to decide. Or perhaps, as his father ages, another female might come to join him, they hope.

Eventually, King's curiosity at visitors overcame his shyness and he came closer to investigate. Rhinos generally stop nursing at about the age of two. The reason quickly became clear as King lay down as gently as a rhino can and nuzzled his already substantial horn under Kapuki's belly. Kapuki shifted her weight slightly and looked at us with what seemed to be a mixture of resignation and affection. She knew, and we did, too, that what was happening was magic. In that moment, despite the onslaught of sad news about rhinos around the world, it was possible to hope. This giant baby represented a new beginning and a story of dedicated conservationists who are trying to ensure that a prehistoric species will still walk the earth when their children are grown and their grandchildren are born.

Maybe we've taken the first step toward helping this magnificent animal avoid the Gray Rhino of its extinction. Perhaps this book will help you avoid your own.

ACKNOWLEDGMENTS

Heartfelt thanks go to my literary agent Andrew Stuart and to my editor George Witte, both of whom embraced the Gray Rhino concept from early on and gave thoughtful feedback throughout the process. Thanks also to Tom Neilssen, my speaking agent at BrightSight Group, who immediately "got it." The whole team at St. Martin's Press has been fantastic to work with, including Carol Anderson, Amelie Little, Kate Ottaviano, and Sara Thwaite.

Fellow Young Global Leaders of the World Economic Forum have provided inspiration, friendship, introductions, suggestions, encouragement, and thoughtful conversations and insights without which this book would not exist. Special thanks go to Analisa Balares, Georgie Benardete, Katharina Borchert, Binta Brown, Matthew Bishop, Dana Costache, Michael Drexler, Sophal Ear, Rossanna Figuera, Stephen Frost, James Gifford, Elissa Goldberg, Mina Guli, Hrund Gunnsteinsdottir, Avril Halstead, Dave Hanley, Noreena Hertz, Brian Herlihy, Brett House, Terri Kennedy, Sony Kapoor, Valerie Keller, Peter Lacy, Tan Le, Peggy Liu, Christopher Logan, Leslie Maasdorp, Butet Manurung, Felix Maradiaga, Greg McKeown, Erwan Michel-Kerjan, Akira Kirton, Kevin Lu, Jaime Nack, Naheed Nenshi, Oliver Niedermaier, Olivier Ouillier, Eric Parrado, Mitchell Pham, William Saito, Sonja Sebotsa, Lara Setrakian, Ben Skinner, Lorna Solis, Ray Sosa, Mark Turrell, and Andy Wales. My deepest respect and admiration goes to all the YGLs who have identified their Gray Rhinos and are out there collaborating to transform threats into opportunities.

Klaus and Hilde Schwab's support of the Forum of Young Global Leaders created a tremendous community of people determined to change the world for the better. Many thanks to them and to the Forum of Young Global Leaders staff, including David Aikman, Adrian Monck, John Dutton, Shun Nagao, Eric Roland, Jo Sparber, Miniya Chatterjee, Katherine Brown, Merid Berhe, Shareena Hatta, and Rosy Mondarini.

The realization that this was the next book I wanted to write and the decision to make it a priority came during the Global Leadership and Public Policy for the 21st Century module at the Harvard Kennedy School organized for the Forum of Young Global Leaders. My deepest gratitude goes to the dedicated professors who organized and taught the module, especially Iris Bohnet, Mahzarin Banaji, Max Bazerman, Dutch Leonard, and Bill George; to program director Leticia DeCastro; and to the members of my True North Leadership Circle. Many thanks to the World Economic Forum and to the program's generous supporters, David Rubenstein of the Carlyle Group, the Bill & Penny George Family Foundation, Marilyn Carlson Nelson, and Howard Cox, Jr.

Some of the ideas in this book benefited from discussion at the World Economic Roundtable organized by the World Policy Institute and New America, and to the Roundtable's founder, Sherle Schwenninger. Roundtable members contributed valuable questions, comments, and suggestions.

I am grateful to my World Policy Institute colleagues Ian Bremmer and Mira Kamdar for their enthusiastic support from the early days of the Gray Rhino; to all of the Institute's fellows for providing a community of incredibly smart, innovative thinkers; and to Annika Christensen, Amanda Dugan, Brendan Foo, Dara Gold, Michael Lumbers, and Alice Wang for their help. Special thanks to World Policy Institute adviser Bill Bohnett, who was there when I came up with the rhinoceros image, and whose Black Swan quip led me to realize that it doesn't matter if a rhino is black or white, because they're all gray. Many of the directors and advisers of the World Policy Institute provided encouragement, insights and ideas, as well as support and guidance of me and of the organization I was proud to have revived: Jim Abernathy, Peter Alderman, John Allen, Henry Arnhold, Jonathan Fanton, Diane Finnerty, Michael Fricklas, Diana Glassman, Sam Eberts, Nadine Hack, Hans Humes, Martin Kaplan, Elise Lelon, Peter Marber, Michael Patrick, Jack Rivkin, George Sampas, Mojgan Skelton, Mary Van Evera, John Watts, Rosemary Werrett, and Debbie Wiley. I deeply miss Dieter Zander's friendship, helpful questions, and feedback during our many conversations over afternoon tea.

Thanks to my colleagues at the Chicago Council on Global Affairs and to the Council's Young Professionals and Emerging Leaders groups for conversations that helped me to refine ideas and concepts. Emerging Leader Emma Belcher of the MacArthur Foundation told me about Sydney's skateboarding rhinos.

This book would not exist without the many people who agreed to be interviewed and who offered ideas, sources, and leads. Dan Alpert, Steve Blitz, Michelle Garcia, Robert Hardy, Constance Hunter, Bob Kopech, Orlyn Kringstad, Jeff Leonard, John Mauldin, Terry Mollner, Sam Natapoff, Yalman Onaran, Dan Sharp, Frank Spring, Devin Stewart, David Teten, Tom Vogel, Eric Weiner, and Worth Wray offered useful questions and comments. For their help in South Africa, thanks to Leigh-Ann Combrink of Rhino Expeditions, Dipak Patel, and the staff at Bongani Mountain Lodge. For all things rhino, many thanks to Cathy Dean. Susie Ellis, Jo Heindel, Ashli Sisk, and to the Lincoln Park Zoo.

For the sake of brevity, I've sought to mention here those who have most directly been involved with the book. Yet in reflecting on all of the people who made this book possible, I think of the conversations on Facebook and Twitter that provided me with sometimes small and sometimes larger ideas. Above all, I consider how profoundly my days and intuitions have been shaped by my neighbors back on West Ninety-fourth Street, the people and dogs I used to see daily in Riverside Park on the Upper West Side of New York City; my fellow volunteers in dog rescue and in the West Nineties community; and now my new neighbors and the new faces and interactions in Lincoln Park and on the streets and trains of Chicago, my new city. It took me too long to realize that moments away from my desk and professional life, the moments that are not directly focused on writing and thinking, nevertheless are a powerful source of inspiration and insight. So I would be remiss not to mention those who are not named specifically but whose cumulative positive influence is not something I take for granted.

The circle of my closest friends provided combinations of encouragement; logistical help; patience when I disappeared into my computer keyboard; and occasional indulging of cravings for injera, sushi, the Ninety-sixth Street taco truck, and key lime pie: Aaron and Randi Biller (and Trooper!), Mary D'Ambrosio, Joe Harkins, Deb Kayman, Anne Kornhauser, Jean Leong, Margarita Perez, Maria-Caroline Perignon, Leigh Sansone, and Carol Spomer. Dr. Daniel Grayson designed the rhino graphic for my Davos Gray Rhino talk. He and the lovely Flo Lyle went way above and beyond in giving my beloved boxer, Mitzi, a home downstairs from home when I traveled, and in always being there for me. Amy Waldman offered helpful editorial feedback alongside doing best friend duty.

Special thanks go to my family for their love and support, especially my parents, Danielle and Ed Wucker, and my niece Cassandra Pine-Wucker for researching what to do if you're about to get run over by a rhino. Finally, my "little red rhinoceros," Billie, took seriously her important job: to get me to take a walk in the park whenever I sat at my desk for too long. Good girl!

NOTES

PREFACE

viii   **In Spring 2011, I published a paper:** Michele Wucker. "Chronicle of a Debt Foretold." New America Foundation, May 2, 2011.

xi   **With that in mind, the commission proposed:** The New Climate Project. *Better Growth, Better Climate*. London: Global Commission on Climate and the Economy, 2014. http://newclimateeconomy.report.

xiv   **A 2008 traffic study:** Nelson Nygaard Consulting Associates. "Blueprint for the Upper West Side." November 2008.

xiv   **In November 2013:** http://transalt.org/sites/default/files/news/reports/UWS _Blueprint.pdf.

      Nelson Nygaard. "West 96th Street and Environs Pedestrian Safety and Circulation Study." November 2013. http://www.nyc.gov/html/mancb7 /downloads/pdf/Manh_CB7_West96_Study_complete.pdf.

xiv   **Total pedestrian deaths in New York:** Thomas Tracy and Tina Moore. "Pedestrian Deaths from Vehicle Strikes Are Quickly Rising in New York City." *New York Daily News*, January 13, 2014. http://www.nydailynews.com/new-york/pedestrian deaths-auto-strikes-rise-nyc-article-1.1577396.

1. MEET THE GRAY RHINO

3   **On November 28, as Enron's stock price:** Cathy Booth Thomas and Frank Pellegrini. "Why Dynegy Backed Out." *Time*, December 3, 2001. http://content.time .com/time/business/article/0,8599,186834,00.html.

8   **In 2013, forty-one weather-related disasters:** Brian Kahn. "Record Number of Billion-Dollar Disasters Globally in 2013." *Climate Central*, February 5, 2014. http://www.climatecentral.org/news/globe-saw-a-record-number-of-billion-dollar -disasters-in-2013-17037.

8   **Water shortages around the world:** WWAP (United Nations World Water Assessment Programme). *The United Nations World Water Development Report 2015: Water for a Sustainable World*. Paris, UNESCO 2015.

9   **By 2045, Africa will be home to:** Kingsley Oghobor. "Africa's Youth: Ticking Time

Bomb or Opportunity?" *Africa Renewal.* May 2013. http://www.un.org/africarenewal /magazine/may-2013/africa%E2%80%99s-youth-%E2%80%9Cticking-time -bomb%E2%80%9D-or-opportunity.

12 **When the United Nations Global Compact and Accenture:** Accenture and United Nations Global Compact. Study Lead, Peter Lacy. "Architects of a Better World." September 2013. http://www.accenture.com/Microsites/ungc-ceo-study /Documents/pdf/13-1739_UNGC%20report_Final_FSC3.pdf.

12 **As the typhoon approached:** "Typhoon of Historic Proportions Slams Philippines, Brings Worries of Catastrophic Damage." *Washington Post,* November 8, 2013.

16 **The International Monetary Fund and the Bank for International Settlements:** International Monetary Fund. *World Economic Outlook 2007.* Washington, DC: October 2007. See also Bank for International Settlements. "77th Annual Report: 1 April 2006–31 March 2007." Basel, June 2007. http://www.bis.org/publ/arpdf /ar2007e.pdf.

17 **Even former U.S Federal Reserve Chairman:** Alan Greenspan. "Never Saw It Coming: Why the Financial Crisis Took Economists by Surprise." *Foreign Affairs.* November/December 2013. http://www.foreignaffairs.com/articles/140161/alan -greenspan/never-saw-it-coming.

19 **A key lesson of a famous business school:** Jack W. Brittain, Sim Sitkin. "Carter Racing." Delta Leadership: 1986, revised 2006.

20 **If they had done so:** Max Bazerman. *The Power of Noticing: What the Best Leaders See.* New York: Simon & Schuster, 2014.

23 **As John Maynard Keynes reportedly said:** This quote has been attributed to A. Gary Shilling in a February 1993 *Forbes* article (page 236), though uncertainty remains over its origin. http://quoteinvestigator.com/2011/08/09/remain-solvent/.

24 **His story, brilliantly described:** Michael Lewis. *The Big Short: Inside the Doomsday Machine.* New York: Norton, 2010.

25 **Cities like New York and New Orleans:** Jeff Chu. "How the Netherlands Became the Biggest Exporter of Resilience." *Fast Company,* November 1, 2013. http://www .fastcoexist.com/3020918/how-the-netherlands-became-the-biggest-exporter-of -resilience#1.

2. THE PROBLEM WITH PREDICTIONS: UNLEASHING DENIAL

30 **In fact, the PunditTracker blog:** "Vote: Worst Financial Prediction of 2013." PunditTracker. http://blog.pundittracker.com/vote-worst-financial-prediction-of -2013/. Accessed 2014; dead link September 2015.

36 **The same day that Professor Wadhams spoke:** Joby Warrick and Chris Mooney. "Effects of Climate Change 'Irreversible,' U.N. Panel Warns in Report." *Washington Post,* November 2, 2014. http://www.washingtonpost.com/national/health-science /effects-of-climate-change-irreversible-un-panel-warns-in-report/2014/11/01 /2d49aeec-6142-11e4-8b9e-2ccdac31a031_story.html.

38 **The neuroscientist Tali Sharot:** Tali Sharot. *The Optimism Bias: A Tour of the Irrationally Positive Brain.* New York: Vintage, 2011.

41 **A *Science* study calculated:** David Lazer, Ryan Kennedy, Gary King, and Alessandro Vespignani. The Parable of Google Flu: Traps in Big Data Analysis. *Science.* March 14, 2014: Vol. 343 no. 6176 pp. 1203-1205.
    DOI:10.1126/science.1248506.

41   **Though individual predictions are erratic:** James Surowiecki. *The Wisdom of Crowds: Why the Many Are Smarter Than the Few and How Collective Wisdom Shapes Business, Economies, Societies, and Nations.* New York: Doubleday, 2004.

41   **Nate Silver has applied:** Nate Silver. *The Signal and the Noise: Why So Many Predictions Fail—But Some Don't.* New York: Penguin Press, 2012.

43   **In defending Rumsfeld:** Geoffrey K. Pullum. "No Foot in Mouth." University of Pennsylvania blog. December 2, 2003. http://itre.cis.upenn.edu/~myl/languagelog /archives/000182.html.

44   **That is where the danger lies:** Herodotus. *The Histories,* 409.

47   **She notes the tendency:** Herodotus. *The Histories,* xxvi.

47   **These decisions are biased:** Olivier Oullier. "Behavioral Finance and Beyond." *Perspectives* (special edition on asset allocation by risk factor), 2013. http://oullier .free.fr/files/2013_Oullier_Perspectives_Behavioral-Finance-Decision -Neuroeconomics-Bias-Neuroscience-Economics.pdf.

48   **It's especially scary:** Noreena Hertz. *Eyes Wide Open: How to Make Smart Choices in a Confusing World.* New York: HarperBusiness, 2013. The study she cites is by Jan Engelmann, C. Monia Capra, Charles Noussair, and Gregory S. Berns. "Expert Financial Advice Neurobiologically 'Offloads' Financial Decision-Making Under Risk."

50   **Finally, not surprisingly:** Barbara Mellers and Michael C. Horowitz. "Does Anyone Make Accurate Geopolitical Predictions?" *Washington Post Monkey Cage,* January 29, 2015. http://www.washingtonpost.com/blogs/monkey-cage/wp/2015/01 /29/does-anyone-make-accurate-geopolitical-predictions/. See also their 2015 scholarly study of the project, "The Psychology of Intelligence Analysis: Drivers of Prediction.

  "Accuracy in World Politics." *Journal of Experimental Psychology: Applied* 21, no. 1: 1–14. http://www.apa.org/pubs/journals/releases/xap-0000040 .pdf.

51   **It might induce them:** David Brooks. "Forecasting Fox." *The New York Times,* March 21, 2013. http://www.nytimes.com/2013/03/22/opinion/brooks-forecasting -fox.html?_r=0.

3. DENIAL: WHY WE MISS SEEING RHINOS AND DON'T GET OUT OF THEIR WAY

54   **The deal put Bjorgolfsson:** Luisa Kroll. "Crazy Comeback: The Man Many Blamed For The Economic Meltdown Is a Billionaire Again." *Forbes,* March 23, 2015. http://www.forbes.com/sites/luisakroll/2015/03/03/crazy-comeback-from-near -bankruptcy-back-to-icelands-only-billionaire/.

56   **But if a crisis is prolonged:** Robert M. Sapolsky. *Why Zebras Don't Get Ulcers: The Acclaimed Guide to Stress, Stress-Related Diseases, and Coping,* 3rd ed. New York: St. Martin's Press, 2004 (W. H. Freeman, 1994).

56   **Denial functions as a buffer:** Elisabeth Kübler-Ross. *On Death and Dying: What the Dying Have to Teach Doctors, Nurses, Clergy and Their Own Families.* 1969. Reprint, New York: Scribner, 1997.

57   **Team members downplayed:** Jeffrey Young. "Obamacare Launch Day Plagued by Website Glitches." *Huffington Post,* October 1, 2013. http://www.huffingtonpost .com/2013/10/01/obamacare-glitches_n_4023159.html.

Roberta Rampton. "Days Before Launch, Obamacare Website Failed to Handle Even 500 Users." Reuters, November 21, 2013. http://www.reuters.com/article/2013/11/22/us-usa-healthcare-website-idUSBRE9AL 03K20131122.

57 **But it now appears:** The New York Times Editorial Board. "Lessons of New York's Prison Escape." *The New York Times.* July 6, 2015. http://www.nytimes.com/2015 /07/06/opinion/lessons-of-new-yorks-prison-escape.html?action=click&pgtype =Homepage&module=opinion-c-col-left-region&region=opinion-c-col-left-region &WT.nav=opinion-c-col-left-region&_r=0.

Michael Winerip, Michael Schwirtz, and Vivian Yeejune. "Lapses at Prison May Have Aided Killers' Escape." *The New York Times*, June 21, 2015. http://www.nytimes.com/2015/06/22/nyregion/new-york-prison-escape -an-array-of-oversights-set-the-stage.html..

57 **Yet Interpol and many diplomats:** Eric Schmitt. "Use of Stolen Passports on Missing Jet Highlights Security Flaw." *The New York Times*, March 10, 2014. http:// www.nytimes.com/2014/03/11/world/asia/missing-malaysian-airliner-said-to -highlight-a-security-gap.html.

58 **After the rainiest:** Darryl Fears. "Before the Washington Mudslide, Warnings of the Unthinkable." *Washington Post*, March 29, 2014. http://www.washingtonpost .com/national/health-science/before-the-washington-mudslide-warnings-of-the -unthinkable/2014/03/29/0088b5f2-b769-11e3-b84e-897d3d12b816_story.html.

58 **It is human nature:** Timothy Egan. "A Mudslide, Foretold." *The New York Times*, March 29, 2014. http://www.nytimes.com/2014/03/30/opinion/sunday/egan-at -home-when-the-earth-moves.html.

59 **But nobody heard it:** Ian Mitroff with Gus Anagnos. *Managing Crises Before They Happen: What Every Executive Needs to Know About Crisis Management.* New York: American Management Association, 2002.

60 **Three years later:** Atul Gawande. "A Lifesaving Checklist." *The New York Times*, December 30, 2007. http://www.nytimes.com/2007/12/30/opinion/30gawande .html?_r=0.

60 **The surgeon and writer Atul Gawande:** Atul Gawande. *The Checklist Manifesto: How to Get Things Right.* New York: Picador, 2009.

61 **He argued that the answer:** Alan Greenspan. "Never Saw It Coming." *Foreign Affairs*, November/December 2013.

63 **As 2008 drew to a close:** "FOMC: Transcripts and Other Historical Materials, 2008." http://www.federalreserve.gov/monetarypolicy/fomchistorical2008.htm.

64 **As a corollary** Carolyn Kousky, John Pratt, and Richard Zeckhauser. "Virgin Versus Experienced Risks." In Erwann Michel-Kerjann and Paul Slovic, eds., *The Irrational Economist: Making Decisions in a Dangerous World.* New York: PublicAffairs, 2010.

64 **Financial crises are an example:** Carmen M. Reinhart and Kenneth S. Rogoff. *This Time Is Different: Eight Centuries of Financial Folly.* Princeton: Princeton University Press, 2009.

65 **Tomasdottir, who likes:** Sheelah Kolhatkar. "What If Women Ran Wall Street?" *New York*, March 21, 2010. http://nymag.com/news/businessfinance/64950/?imw =Y&f=most-viewed-24h5.

66 **A 2007 report:** Catalyst. "The Bottom Line: Corporate Performance and Women's

Representation on Boards." http://www.catalyst.org/media/companies-more -women-board-directors-experience-higher-financial-performance-according-latest.

66 **A 2013 Thomson Reuters study:** "Mining the Metrics of Board Diversity." Thomson Reuters, July 20, 2013. http://thomsonreuters.com/press-releases/072013 /Average-Stock-Price-of-Gender-Diverse-Corporate-Boards-Outperform-Those -with-No-Women.

67 **Paradoxically, given the high-profile women:** S. E. Asch. 1955. Opinions and Social Pressure. *Scientific American* 193: 31–35.

67 **In many cases boundaries:** Stanley Milgram. "Which Nations Conform Most?" *Scientific American*, December 1, 2011. http://www.scientificamerican.com/article /milgram-nationality-conformity/. Originally published in vol. 205, no. 6 of *Scientific American* in December 1961.

68 **Those ideas include everything:** Steven Liu. Wowprime Corporation Presentation, http://www.wowprime.com/investor/2013.3.11-HSBC%E7%94%A2%E6%A 5%AD%E8%AB%96%E5%A3%87-%E8%8B%B1%E6%96%87.pdf.

"Wowprime's Key to Success—People First!" April 1, 2012. Taiwan in Depth via Taiwan Panorama. http://taiwanindepth.tw/ct.asp?xItem=189601 &CtNode=1916.

See also Joyce Huang, "Taiwan's Wowprime Attracts Eaters and Eager Employees." *Forbes*, August 29, 2012. http://www.forbes.com/sites/forbesasia /2012/08/29/wowprime-restaurants-attract-eaters-and-eager-employees/.

68 **Countless studies and experiments:** Noreena Hertz. *Eyes Wide Open.* HarperBusiness, 2013.

70 **The Stanford professor:** Robert N. Proctor. "Agnotology: A Missing Term to Describe the Cultural Production of Ignorance (And Its Study)." In *Agnotology: The Making and Unmaking of Ignorance.* Stanford, CA: Stanford University Press, 2008.

http://scholar.princeton.edu/rccu/publications/agnotology-missing -term-describe-cultural-production-ignorance-and-its-study.

71 **And so the industry:** Naomi Oreskes and Michael Conway. *Merchants of Doubt: How a Handful of Scientists Obscured the Truth on Issues from Tobacco Smoke to Global Warming.* New York: Bloomsbury Press, 2010.

72 **Major fossil-fuel companies:** Peter C. Frumhoff and Naomi Oreskes. "Fossil Fuel Firms Are Still Bankrolling Climate Denial Lobby Groups." *Guardian*, March 25, 2015. http://www.theguardian.com/environment/2015/mar/25/fossil-fuel-firms -are-still-bankrolling-climate-denial-lobby-groups. See also Robert J. Brulle. "Institutionalizing Delay: Foundation Funding and the Creation of U.S. Climate Change Counter-Movement Organizations." *Climactic Change*, December 21, 2013.

More details are at: http://drexel.edu/now/archive/2013/December /Climate-Change/#sthash.DNqJYWJ9.dpufhttp://drexel.edu/now/archive /2013/December/Climate-Change/.

72 **A 2013 Pew Research survey:** Pew Research Center. "Climate Change and Financial Instability Seen as Top Global Threats." Survey Report. June 24, 2013. http:// www.pewglobal.org/2013/06/24/climate-change-and-financial-instability-seen-as -top-global-threats/.

72 **Another technique for manufacturing:** Beat Balzli. "Greek Debt Crisis: How Goldman Sachs Helped Greece to Mask Its True Debt." *Spiegel Online International*,

February 8, 2010. http://www.spiegel.de/international/europe/greek-debt-crisis
-how-goldman-sachs-helped-greece-to-mask-its-true-debt-a-676634.html.

74 **Bazerman makes a set of sensible recommendations:** Max H. Bazerman. *The Power of Noticing: What the Best Leaders See.* New York: Simon & Schuster, 2014. See also Max H. Bazerman and Michael D. Watkins. *Predictable Surprises: The Disasters You Should Have Seen Coming and How to Prevent Them.* Boston: Harvard Business School Press, 2004.

74 **Their pollution readings:** Michael Greenstone. "See Red Flags, Hear Red Flags." *The New York Times,* December 8, 2013. http://www.nytimes.com/2013/12/08 /opinion/sunday/see-red-flags-hear-red-flags.html.

76 **This was, of course, a variation:** Christopher Chabris and Daniel Simons. *The Invisible Gorilla: How Our Intuitions Deceive Us.* New York: Broadway Paperbacks, 2009.

4. MUDDLING: WHY WE DON'T ACT EVEN WHEN WE SEE THE RHINO

81 **By 2050, it estimates:** United Nations Department of Economic and Social Affairs, Population Division. *World Urbanization Prospects 2014.* http://www.un.org /en/development/desa/news/population/world-urbanization-prospects-2014.html.

81 **The price tag is steep:** McKinsey Global Institute: "Infrastructure Productivity: How to Save $1 Trillion a Year." January 2013.

81 **The United Nations estimates:** Charley Cameron. "UN Report Finds the Number of Megacities Has Tripled Since 1990." *Inhabitat,* October 8, 2014. http://inhabitat .com/un-report-finds-the-number-of-megacities-has-tripled-in-since-1990/.

83 **Yet John Husing, an economist:** "Not So Golden." *The Economist,* November 30, 2013.

83 **Diet is now the biggest risk factor:** Institute for Health Metrics and Evaluation. *The State of US Health: Innovations, Insights, and Recommendations from the Global Burden of Disease Study.* Seattle, WA: IHME, 2013. http://www.healthdata.org /policy-report/state-us-health-innovations-insights-and-recommendations-global -burden-disease-study.

84 **This phenomenon:** Robert Kegan and Lisa Lahey. *Immunity to Change: How to Overcome It and Unlock the Potential in Yourself and Your Organization.* Cambridge, MA: Harvard Business Review Press, 2009

84 **Yet obesity rates in children:** Centers for Disease Control and Prevention. "Prevalence of Childhood Obesity in the United States, 2011–2012." http://www.cdc.gov /obesity/data/childhood.html.

84 **The agricultural system offers:** Michael Moss. "The Dopest Vegetable." *The New York Times Magazine,* November 3, 2013. http://www.nytimes.com/2013/11/03 /magazine/broccolis-e.xtreme-makeover.html?_r=0.

86 **When cash-strapped states:** Erik Sofge. "The Minnesota Bridge Collapse, 5 Years Later." *Popular Mechanics,* August 1, 2012. http://www.popularmechanics.com /technology/engineering/rebuilding-america/the-minnesota-bridge-collapse-5 -years-later-11254114.

86 **The bridge collapse cost Minnesota:** Minnesota Department of Transportation and Economic Development. "Economic Impacts of the I-35W Bridge Collapse." http://www.dot.state.mn.us/i35wbridge/rebuild/pdfs/economic-impacts-from -deed.pdf.

http://www.minnpost.com/politics-policy/2008/09/officials-hail-new-i-35w-bridge-and-workers-who-made-it-happen.

86 **The ASCE estimates:** American Society of Civil Engineers. "2013 Report Card for America's Infrastructure." http://www.infrastructurereportcard.org/.

86 **The Goldman Sachs economist:** Myles Udland. "America's Old Bridges Are a Problem." *Business Insider,* January 18, 2015. http://www.businessinsider.com/goldman-on-american-infrastructure-2015-1.

87 **The World Bank estimates that Africa:** The World Bank. *World Development Report 1994: Infrastructure for Development.* Washington, DC: June 1994.

87 **He returned to the hospital:** Dan Ariely. *Predictably Irrational: The Hidden Forces That Shape Our Decisions.* 2008. Revised and expanded edition, New York: Harper Perennial, 2010.

88 **We cannot fully trust:** Daniel Kahneman. *Thinking, Fast and Slow.* New York: Farrar, Straus & Giroux, 2011.

90 **Two years after the bottom:** Vladimir Popov. "Shock Therapy Versus Gradualism: The End of the Debate." *Comparative Economic Studies* 42 (Spring 2000): 1.

90 **A wrong sequence may be worse:** Weiying Zhang. *The Logic of the Market: An Insider's View of Chinese Economic Reform.* Washington, DC. Cato Institute: 2014.

91 **The heat must stay within a tolerable range:** Ronald Heifetz and Marty Linsky. *Leadership on the Line: Staying Alive Through the Dangers of Leading.* Cambridge, MA: Harvard Business Press, 2009.

91 **Louis XVI in France in 1789:** Timur Kuran. "Sparks and Prairie Fires: A Theory of Unanticipated Political Revolution." *Public Choice,* Vol. 61, No. 1 (Apr., 1989), pp. 41-74.

97 **The Trust for America's Health has estimated:** J. Levi, L.M. Segal, and C. Juliano. "Prevention for a Healthier America: Investments in Disease Prevention Yield Significant Savings, Stronger Communities." Washington, DC: Trust for America's Health, 2008. http://healthyamericans.org/reports/prevention08/Prevention08.pdf.

97 **Reduced tobacco use:** C. Schoen, S. Guterman, S. A. Shih, J. Lau, S. Kasimow, A. Gauthier, and K. Davis. "Bending the Curve: Options for Achieving Savings and Improving Value in U.S. Health Spending." New York: Commonwealth Fund, December 2007.

Josh Cable. "NSC 2013: O'Neill Exemplifies Safety Leadership." *EHS Today.* http://ehstoday.com/safety/nsc-2013-oneill-exemplifies-safety-leadership?page=1.

98 **The things I've been talking about:** Mark Roth. "'Habitual Excellence': The Workplace According to Paul O'Neill." *Pittsburgh Post-Gazette,* May 13, 2012. http://www.post-gazette.com/business/businessnews/2012/05/13/Habitual-excellence-the-workplace-according-to-Paul-O-Neill/stories/201205130249.

98 **An internal audit found:** Tom Cohen. "Audit: More than 120,000 veterans waiting or never got care." CNN. June 10, 2014 http://www.cnn.com/2014/06/09/politics/va-audit/

99 **Fourth and last:** Richard P. Shannon, MD. "Eliminating Hospital-Acquired Infections: Is It Possible? Is It Sustainable? Is It Worth It?" *Transactions of the American Clinical and Climatological Association* 122 (2011): 103–14. http://www.ncbi.nlm.nih.gov/pmc/articles/PMC3116332/.

5. DIAGNOSING: RIGHT AND WRONG SOLUTIONS

105 **Scholars have debunked this explanation:** Kees Rookmaaker. "Why the Name of the White Rhinoceros Is Not Appropriate." *Pachyderm*, January-June 2003. http://www.rhinoresourcecenter.com/pdf_files/117/1175858144.pdf.

107 **CEOs clearly recognize:** Accenture and United Nations Global Compact. Study Lead, Peter Lacy. "Architects of a Better World." September 2013. http://www .accenture.com/Microsites/ungc-ceo-study/Documents/pdf/13-1739_UNGC%20 report_Final_FSC3.pdf.

109 **It's rarely a good idea:** Thomas Fox-Brewster. "195 Incidents in 10 Months: Leaked Emails Reveal Gaps in Sony Pictures Security." *Forbes*, December 12, 2014. http:// www.forbes.com/sites/thomasbrewster/2014/12/12/195-security-incidents -sony-pictures-hack/.

109 **Sony employees went to the media:** Hilary Lewis. "Sony Hack: Former Employees Claim Security Issues Were Ignored." *Hollywood Reporter*, December 5, 2014. http://www.hollywoodreporter.com/news/sony-hack-employees-claim-security -754168.

109 **Yet, a *Fortune* article pointed out:** John Gaudiosi. "Why Sony didn't Learn From Its 2011 Hack." *Fortune*, December 24, 2014. http://fortune.com/2014/12/24 /why-sony-didnt-learn-from-its-2011-hack/.

110 **When, by late December:** Richard Adhikari. "Security Firm Spills the Beans on Snapchat Vulnerabilities." *Tech News World*, December 28, 2013. http://www .technewsworld.com/story/79705.html. See also Violet Blue for Zero Day. "Researchers Publish Snapchat Code Allowing Phone Number Matching After Exploit Disclosures." *ZDNe*, December 25, 2013. http://www.zdnet.com/researchers -publish-snapchat-code-allowing-phone-number-matching-after-exploit -disclosures-ignored-7000024629/. See also Adam Caudill. "Snapchat: API & Security." Personal blog. June 16, 2012. http://adamcaudill.com/2012/06/16/snapchat -api-and-security/.

110 **Given that it's been around *four months*:** Gibson Security website. http://gibsonsec .org/snapchat/.

110 **When Snapchat finally responded:** Barbara Ortutay. "Snapchat Finally Responds to Hack, but Doesn't Apologize."*AP/ Huffington Post*, January 3, 2014. http://www.huffingtonpost.com/2014/01/03/snapchat-hack_n_4531636 .html.141

111 **The Belvedere Hotel:** Emily Young. "Davos 2014: Hosting the rich and famous." BBC News. January 24, 2014. http://www.bbc.com/news/business-25843923.

111 **An Oxfam report released:** Ricardo Fuentes-Nieva and Nicholas Galasso. "Working for the Few." Oxfam Briefing Paper, January 20, 2014. http://oxf.am/KHp.

112 **Inequality reduces economic growth:** *The Economist*. "Free Exchange: Inequality v Growth." March 1, 2014.

113 **Kodak invented the first digital camera:** Ernest Scheyder and Liana Baker. "As Kodak Struggles, Eastman Chemical Thrives." Reuters. December 24, 2011. http://www .reuters.com/article/2011/12/24/us-eastman-kodak-idUSTRE7BN06B20111224.

113 **He pointed out that the average life span:** Erik Sherman. "Kodak, Yahoo and RIM: Death Comes for Us All." CBS MoneyWatch, December 6, 2011. http://www.cbsnews.com/news/kodak-yahoo-and-rim-death-comes -for-us-all/.

114 **The company is now writing:** Kodak company website. http://www.kodak.com
/ek/US/en/Our_Company/History_of_Kodak/Milestones_-_chronology/1878
-1929.htm.

114 **Hawking, whose work in theoretical physics:** Rory Cellan-Jones. "Stephen Hawking Warns Artificial Intelligence Could End Mankind." *BBC News*, December 2,
2014. http://www.bbc.com/news/technology-30290540.

114 **Similarly, Tesla founder:** Justin Moyer. "Why Elon Musk Is Scared of Artificial
Intelligence—and Terminators." *Washington Post*, November 18, 2014.

115 **They recognize the danger:** "Elon Musk's Deleted Edge Comment from Yesterday
on the Threat of AI." *Reddit*. http://www.reddit.com/r/Futurology/comments
/2mh8tn/elon_musks_deleted_edge_comment_from_yesterday_on/.

115 **The World Economic Forum:** World Economic Forum, Global Risks 2015, 10th
edition. Geneva: January 2015. http://www.weforum.org/reports/global-risks-report
-2015.

116 **An Oxford University study:** Carl Benedikt Frey and Michael A. Osborne. "The
Future of Employment: How Susceptible Are Jobs to Computerization?" Oxford:
September 17, 2013. http://www.oxfordmartin.ox.ac.uk/downloads/academic/The
_Future_of_Employment.pdf.

120 **We avoid using the word:** "Still Waiting." Liana Foxvog, Judy Gearhart, Samantha
Maher, Liz Parker, Ben Vanpeperstraete, and Ineke Zeldenrust. Clean Clothes
Campaign and International Labor Rights Forum, 2013.

120 **Tuba Group, the owner of the Tazreen factory:** http://www.evb.ch/cm_data
/Fatal_Fashion.pdf citing the company's website, which had been taken down by
March 2014.
   http://s3.documentcloud.org/documents/524545/factory-profile-of
-tuba-group.txt.

125 **These new competitors:** Timothy Aeppel. "Show Stopper: How Plastic Popped the
Cork Monopoly." *Wall Street Journal*, May 1, 2010. http://www.wsj.com/articles/SB
10001424052702304172404575168120997013394.

126 **Amorim commissioned PricewaterhouseCoopers:** Chris Redman. "Portugal's
New Twist on the Cork Industry." *Time*, November 8, 2010. http://content.time
.com/time/magazine/article/0,9171,2027774,00.html.

127 **In the United States:** Chris Rauber. "Cork it: Many Bay Area Wine Producers Are
Switching Back to Natural Cork." *San Francisco Business Times*, May 29, 2015.

128 **Several wondered how:** Nicholas Carlson, "What Happened When Marissa Mayer
Tried to Be Steve Jobs," December 17, 2014. http://www.nytimes.com/2014/12/21
/magazine/what-happened-when-marissa-mayer-tried-to-be-steve-jobs.html?_r=0.

6. PANIC: DECISION-MAKING FACING A CHARGING RHINO

136 **Our ability to understand ourselves:** Daniel Ariely. *Predictably Irrational* (expanded
and revised edition). New York: HarperCollins, 2009.

138 **But at that time there was no real mechanism:** Michele Wucker. "Passing the Buck:
No Chapter 11 for Bankrupt Nations." *World Policy Journal* 18 (Summer 2001): 2.

139 **In May 2012, Humes gave:** Landon Thomas, Jr. "A Band of Contrarians, Bullish
on Greece." *The New York Times*, May 4, 2012. http://www.nytimes.com/2012/05
/05/business/global/bondholders-bullish-on-greece.html.

142 **Indeed, the very fact that such an event:** Margaret G. Hermann and Bruce W.

Dayton. "Transboundary Crises Through the Eyes of Policymakers: Sense Making and Crisis Management." Moynihan Institute of Global Affairs, Syracuse University. Undated paper. http://www.maxwell.syr.edu/uploadedFiles/Leadership_Institute/Journal%20of%20Contingencies%20and%20Crisis%20Management%20paper.pdf.

143 **It took forever and then it took a night:** PBS Frontline "Interview with Dr. Rudi Dornbusch." Supplementary material to "Murder Money & Mexico: The Rise and Fall of the Salinas Brothers." April 1997. http://www.pbs.org/wgbh/pages/frontline/shows/mexico/interviews/dornbusch.html.

143 **As Mike Tyson famously said:** Mike Berardino. "Mike Tyson Explains One of His Most Famous Quotes." *Sun Sentinel*, November 9, 2012. http://articles.sun-sentinel.com/2012-11-09/sports/sfl-mike-tyson-explains-one-of-his-most-famous-quotes-20121109_1_mike-tyson-undisputed-truth-famous-quotes.

144 **If we want our organizations:** Therese Huston. "Are Women Better Decision Makers?" *The New York Times*, October 17, 2014. http://www.nytimes.com/2014/10/19/opinion/sunday/are-women-better-decision-makers.html.

148 **Even Thomas Eric Duncan:** Maggie Fox. "Don't Panic: Why Ebola Won't Become an Epidemic in New York." NBC News. October 24, 2014. http://www.nbcnews.com/storyline/ebola-virus-outbreak/dont-panic-why-ebola-wont-become-epidemic-new-york-n232826.

148 **As a helpful graphic put it:** http://i.imgur.com/tFZV024.jpg.

149 **This epidemic, in other words, was an avoidable crisis:** Jeremy J. Farrar and Peter Piot. "The Ebola Emergency—Immediate Action, Ongoing Strategy." *New England Journal of Medicine*, October 6, 2014. http://www.nejm.org/doi/pdf/10.1056/NEJMe1411471.

150 **The World Health Organization didn't want to hear it:** David von Drehle and Aryn Baker. "The Ebola Fighters: The Ones Who Answered the Call." *Time*, December 10, 2014. http://time.com/time-person-of-the-year-ebola-fighters/.

151 **In many cases, treating Ebola:** Jeffrey Gettelman. "Ebola Should Be Easy to Treat." *The New York Times*, December 20, 2014. http://www.nytimes.com/2014/12/21/sunday-review/ebola-should-be-easy-to-treat.html?_r=0.

152 **By the end of December 2014:** Justin Ray. "Flu Deaths in U.S. Reach Epidemic Level: CDC." NBC News. http://www.nbcbayarea.com/news/health/CDC-Epidemic-Flu-H3N2-Virus-287118961.html#ixzz3R6Pk4hCi.

153 **The two that treated people:** Norimitsu Onishi, "Empty Ebola Clinics in Liberia Are Seen as Misstep in U.S. Relief Effort," *The New York Times*, April 11, 2015. http://www.nytimes.com/2015/04/12/world/africa/idle-ebola-clinics-in-liberia-are-seen-as-misstep-in-us-relief-effort.html?_r=0.

154 **A report, which since has been widely discredited:** CNN Wire Staff. "Retracted Autism Study an 'Elaborate Fraud,' British Journal Finds." January 5, 2011. http://www.cnn.com/2011/HEALTH/01/05/autism.vaccines/.

156 **Matthew Bishop and Michael Green:** Matthew Bishop and Michael Green. "We Are What We Measure." *World Policy Journal*, Spring 2011.

157 **The idea was to better control credit cycles:** Jaromir Benes and Michael Kumhof. "The Chicago Plan Revisited." IMF Working Paper, August 2012. https://www.imf.org/external/pubs/ft/wp/2012/wp12202.pdf.

157 **Under Cochrane's updated version:** John H. Cochrane. "Toward a Run-Free Finan-

cial System." Working paper, Booth School of Business at the University of Chicago, April 16, 2014. http://faculty.chicagobooth.edu/john.cochrane/research /papers/run_free.pdf.

157 **Yet it noted that the merits:** *The Economist.* "Free Exchange: Narrow-Minded—A Radical Proposal for Making Finance Safer Resurfaces." June 7, 2014.

7. ACTION: THE "AHA" MOMENT

164 **The company once used recycled materials:** Mark Peterson. *Sustainable Enterprise: A Macro Marketing Approach.* Thousand Oaks, CA: SAGE Publications, 2012.

165 **But the key moment came:** 2030 Water Resources Group. *Charting Our Water Future.* New York: 2009.

169 **Oh Father, we acknowledge our wastefulness:** Jenny Jarvie. "Georgia Governor Leads Prayer to End Drought." *Los Angeles Times,* November 14, 2007; Associated Press. "Ga. Governor Turns to Prayer to Ease Drought," *USA Today,* November 13, 2007.

169 **It had begged the federal government:** Greg Bluestein. "Atlanta May Go Dry in 90 Days." *Seattle Times,* October 20, 2007.

169 **A year later, the state issued:** Georgia Department of Natural Resources. "Georgia's Draft Water Conservation Implementation Plan Is Released." Press Release. Atlanta. December 18, 2008.

169 **In April 2013, Georgia authorized:** "Water wars: Tennessee, Georgia locked in battle over Waterway Access." CBS News. April 8, 2013. http://www.cbsnews.com /news/water-wars-tennessee-georgia-locked-in-battle-over-waterway-access/.

169 **For its part, Florida:** "Florida files water lawsuit against Georgia in U.S. Supreme Court." *Atlanta Journal Constitution.* October 1, 2013. http://www.ajc.com/news /news/state-regional-govt-politics/florida-files-water-lawsuit-against-georgia-in-us- /nbCKT/.

169 **The loss of crops and livestock:** Richard Howitt, Josué Medellín-Azuara, Duncan MacEwan, Jay Lund, and Daniel Sumner. "Economic Analysis of the 2014 Drought for California Agriculture." University of California, Davis. July 23, 2014. https:// watershed.ucdavis.edu/files/biblio/DroughtReport_23July2014_0.pdf.

171 **Of the companies surveyed:** Carbon Disclosure Project. "From Water Risk to Value Creation: CDP Global Water Report 2014." https://www.cdp.net /CDPResults/CDP-Global-Water-Report-2014.pdf.

172 **There are large uncertainties:** Heather Cooley. "California Water Use." Oakland, CA: Pacific Institute, April 2015. http://pacinst.org/wp-content/uploads/sites/21 /2015/04/CA-Ag-Water-Use.pdf.

175 **The late Illinois senator Paul Simon:** Paul Simon. *Tapped Out: The Coming World Crisis in Water and What We Can Do About It.* New York: Welcome Rain Publishers, 1996.

176 **The phrase is so common:** Cameron Harrington. *New Security Beat.* "Water Wars? Think Again: Conflict Over Freshwater Structural Rather Than Strategic." April 15, 2014. http://www.newsecuritybeat.org/2014/04/water-wars/.

176 **Between 1950 and 2000:** Aaron Wolf, S. Yoffe, and M. Giordano. *International Waters: Indicators for Identifying Basins at Risk.* UNESCO, 2003.

176 **By comparison, the gulf war:** Priit Vesilind. "The Middle East's Critical Resource: Water." *National Geographic* (May 1993). Cited in Simon, *Tapped Out.*

178 **WMO secretary general Michel Jarraud:** "Greenhouse Gas Emissions Rise at

Fastest Rate for 30 years." *Guardian*, September 9, 2014. http://www.theguardian .com/environment/2014/sep/09/carbon-dioxide-emissions-greenhouse-gases.

181 **The proposed law met with stiff opposition:** Oliver Balch. "European Commission to Decide Fate of Circular Economy Package." *Guardian*, December 12, 2014. http://www.theguardian.com/sustainable-business/2014/dec/12/european -commission-to-decide-fate-of-circular-economy-package.

181 **And the United Kingdom could make:** Ellen MacArthur Foundation in collabora- tion with the World Economic Forum and McKinsey & Company. "Towards the Circular Economy: Accelerating the Scale-Up Across Global Supply Chains." 2014.

182 **Unilever announced early in 2015:** http://www.unilever.com/mediacentre /pressreleases/2015/Unilever-achieves-zero-waste-to-landfill-across-global-factory -network.aspx.

183 **One publication declared 2014:** Jessica Shankleman. "2014, the Year . . . Big Busi- ness Embraced Climate Action." *BusinessGreen*. http://www.businessgreen.com /bg/feature/2387980/2014-the-year-big-business-embraced-climate-action.

184 **After seeing video of Arctic ice cap melting:** Alex Nussbaum, Mark Chediak, and Zain Shauk."George Shultz Defies GOP in Embrace of Climate Adaptation." *Bloomberg Business*, November 30, 2014. http://www.bloomberg.com/news/articles /2014-12-01/reagan-statesman-s-sunshine-power-hint-of-thaw-in-climate-debate.

184 **Climate change, the loss of biodiversity and deforestation:** John Vidal. "Pope Francis's Edict on Climate Change Will Anger Deniers and US Churches." *Guardian*, December 27, 2014. http://www.theguardian.com/world/2014/dec/27 /pope-francis-edict-climate-change-us-rightwing.

184 **A study by Yale University:** Anthony Leiserowitz, Edward Maibach, Connie Roser-Renouf, Geoff Feinberg, & Seth Rosenthal. "Climate change in the American mind: April, 2014." Yale University and George Mason University. New Haven, CT: Yale Project on Climate Change Communication. http://environment.yale.edu /climate-communication/files/Climate-Change-American-Mind-April-2014.pdf.

8. AFTER THE TRAMPLING: A CRISIS IS A TERRIBLE THING TO WASTE

194 **The Insurance Bureau of Canada:** Institute for Catastrophic Loss Reduction. "Telling the Weather Story." Insurance Bureau of Canada. June 2012. http://www .ibc.ca/nb/resources/studies/weather-story.

194 **A 2013 AECOM study:** AECOM. "The Impact of Climate Change and Population Growth on the National Flood Insurance Program Through 2100." Prepared for Federal Insurance & Mitigation Administration and Federal Emergency Manage- ment Agency. June 2013.

194 **Officials estimate that the floodway:** Jamie Komarnicki. "Winnipeg floodway has saved $32 billion in flood damages." *Calgary Herald*, October 3, 2013.

194 **The U.S. Federal Emergency Management Agency:** Federal Emergency Manage- ment Agency. (2007). *Fact Sheet: Mitigation's Value to Society* (electronic version). Washington, DC. Also see Multihazard Mitigation Council (2005). *Natural Hazard Mitigation Saves: An Independent Study to Assess the Future Savings from Mitigation Activities.* Washington, DC: Institute of Building Sciences.

195 **Indeed, his press secretary:** Chris Turner. "Owen's Ark: How Calgary Survived the Flood—And Why Other Cities Won't." *The Walrus*, June 2014. Citing *American Political Science Review*, 2009.

195 **In late September, Alberta's premier:** Sarah Offin. "Calgary's Mayor Critical of Prentice's Flood Announcement." Global News. September 26, 2014. http://globalnews.ca/news/1585968/calgarys-mayor-critical-of-prentices-flood-announcement/.

195 **This dry dam would not be used:** Trevor Howell. "Prentice Plan for Springbank Dry Reservoir Faces Fight from Landowners, Nenshi." *Calgary Herald*, September 25, 2014. http://www.calgaryherald.com/news/Prentice+plan+Springbank+reservoir+faces+fight+from+landowners+Nenshi/10239193/story.html.

196 **Shaun Rein estimated in *Forbes*:** Shaun Rein. "Airport Security: Bin Laden's Victory." *Forbes*, March 3, 2010. http://www.forbes.com/2010/03/03/airport-security-osama-leadership-managing-rein.html.

196 **Just south of Magdeburg:** "Thousands Flee as German Dam Bursts." *Al Jazeera*, June 10, 2013. http://www.aljazeera.com/news/europe/2013/06/201361051413232258.html.

197 **The island's wetlands:** Forrest Wilder. "That Sinking Feeling." *Texas Observer*, November 2, 2007.

197 **A geohazards map of the island:** Bureau of Economic Geology, University of Texas at Austin, adapted for the *Texas Observer*, November 2, 2007.

199 **Just over six months later:** A Stronger, More Resilient New York. http://www.nyc.gov/html/sirr/html/report/report.shtml.

200 **Just over half:** Lloyd Dixon, Noreen Clancy, Bruce Bender, Aaron Kofner, David Manheim, Laura Zakaras. "Flood Insurance in New York City Following Hurricane Sandy." Santa Monica, CA: RAND Corporation, 2013. http://www.rand.org/pubs/research_reports/RR328.

201 **Disturbingly, the report also noted:** CoreLogic. *2013 CoreLogic Wildfire Hazard Risk Report*. Irvine, CA: CoreLogic, 2013. http://www.corelogic.com/about-us/news/2013-corelogic-wildfire-hazard-risk-report-reveals-wildfires-pose-risk-to-more-than-1.2-million-western-u.s.-homes.aspx.

201 **More than three-quarters:** Felicity Barringer. "Homes Keep Rising in West Despite Growing Wildfire Threat." *The New York Times*, July 6, 2013. http://www.nytimes.com/2013/07/06/us/homes-keep-rising-in-west-despite-growing-wildfire-threat.html.

202 **It had failed to train employees:** John Gaudiosi. "Why Sony Didn't Learn from Its 2011 Hack." *Fortune*, December 24, 2014. http://fortune.com/2014/12/24/why-sony-didnt-learn-from-its-2011-hack/.

202 **A partial list:** Riley Walters. "Cyber Attacks on U.S. Companies in 2014." Washington, DC: Heritage Foundation, October 27, 2014. http://www.heritage.org/research/reports/2014/10/cyber-attacks-on-us-companies-in-2014.

9. RHINOS ON THE HORIZON: THINKING LONG-TERM

205 **When the institute moved:** http://www.wfs.org/futurist/july-august-2012-vol-46-no-4/futurists-and-their-ideas%E2%80%94change-masters-weiner-edrich-brown-i.

206 **Future jobs will be created:** http://www.futureofwork.com/article/details/metaspace-economy-predicting-disruption.

209 **Those who were given a deadline:** http://www.nytimes.com/2015/01/04/business/if-you-want-to-meet-that-deadline-play-a-trick-on-your-mind.html?hp&action=click&pgtype=Homepage&module=mini-moth&region=top-stories-below&WT.nav=top-stories-below&_r=0.

210 **Watson made a gutsy decision:** http://fortune.com/2011/06/16/5-lessons-from-ibms-100th-anniversary/.

211 **I firmly believe:** http://www-03.ibm.com/ibm/history/ibm100/us/en/icons/biz beliefs/.

211 **By 2014, well after it had peaked:** http://company.nokia.com/en/about-us/our-company/our-story.

212 **He stepped aside:** Hana R. Alberts. "Japan Airlines Meets Its Savior." Forbes.com, January 2010. http://www.forbes.com/2010/01/14/japan-airlines-kyocera-markets-face-kazuo-inamori.html; http://global.kyocera.com/inamori/profile/index.html.

212 **Observing this rule:** http://global.kyocera.com/inamori/profile/index.html.

213 **He then announced a three-hundred-year:** Dave McCombs and Pavel Alpeyev. "Softbank Founder Has 300-Year Plan in Wooing Sprint Nextel." *Bloomberg Business*, October 12, 2012. http://www.bloomberg.com/news/articles/2012-10-11/softbank-founder-has-300-year-plan-in-pursuit-of-sprint-nextel.

213 **The world's oldest company:** Kim Jae-kyoung. "Centennial Firms Dry Up in Korea." May 15, 2008. http://www.koreatimes.co.kr/www/news/biz/2008/05/123_24196.html.

213 **The Bank of Korea founded:** http://japanese.yonhapnews.co.kr/economy/2008/05/14/0500000000AJP20080514003900882.HTML.

214 **Most of them were small:** http://www.tsr-net.co.jp/news/analysis_before/2009/1199565_1623.html.

214 **Today, it is only fifteen years:** Alexandra Levit. "How to Stay in Business for 100 Years." *Business Insider*, January 7, 2014. http://www.businessinsider.com/how-to-stay-in-business-for-100-years-2013-1. See also: Kim Gitelson. "Can a Company Live Forever?" BBC News, January 19, 2012. http://www.bbc.com/news/business-16611040.

216 **Phil Libin, executive chairman of Evernote:** Alyson Shontell. "How Evernote's Phil Libin Plans to Build a '100-Year Startup.'" *Business Insider*, November 1, 2013. http://www.businessinsider.com/how-evernotes-phil-libin-plans-to-build-a-100-year-startup-2013-10.

217 **Business leaders today face a choice:** Dominic Barton. "Capitalism for the Long Term." *Harvard Business Review*, March 2011.

218 **Over the past half century:** Jesse Eisinger. "Challenging the Long-Held Belief in 'Shareholder Value.'" *The New York Times*: June 27, 2012. http://dealbook.nytimes.com/2012/06/27/challenging-the-long-held-belief-in-shareholder-value/?_r=0.

218 **If we look beyond the short term:** Michele Wucker. "Down with Short Termism; Long Live the Long Term." February 5, 2013. World Economic Forum Agenda. https://agenda.weforum.org/2013/02/down-with-short-termism-long-live-the-long-term/.

219 **These short-term incentives:** Patrick Bolton and Frédéric Samama. "Loyalty-Shares: Rewarding Long-term Investors." *Journal of Applied Corporate Finance*, Volume 25 (5) (Summer 2013).

219 **Instead, it recommended:** Jane Ambachtsheer, Ryan Pollice, Ed Waitzer and Sean Vanderpol. "Building a Long-Term Shareholder Base: Assessing the Potential of Loyalty-Driven Securities." Generation Foundation, Mercer, and Stikeman Elliott LP. December 2013. https://www.genfound.org/media/pdf-long-term-shareholder-base-17-12-13.pdf.

221 **To justify its research-and-development budget:** "DuPont CEO sees global growth, innovation and productivity in 2011 and beyond." RP Newswires. http://www .reliableplant.com/Read/27912/DuPont-CEO-growth-productivity.

222 **In 2011, the number of new patents:** "A Record Year for DuPont Innovation." DuPont News release, March 15, 2012. http://www2.dupont.com/media/en-us/news-events /march/record-year-innovation.html.

222 **In 2014, it generated $9 billion:** Bill George. "Peltz's Attacks on DuPont Threaten America's Research Edge." April 9, 2015. http://www.nytimes.com/2015/04/10 /business/dealbook/peltzs-attacks-on-dupont-threaten-americas-research-edge .html.

10. CONCLUSION: HOW TO KEEP FROM GETTING RUN OVER BY A RHINO

231 **By 2014, the number of killings:** Save the Rhino. "Poaching: The Statistics". https://www.savetherhino.org/rhino_info/poaching_statistics.

231 **The number of poachers arrested:** Wildlife and Environment Society of South Africa. "Current Rhino Poaching Stats." http://wessa.org.za/get-involved/rhino -initiative/current-rhino-poaching-stats.htm.

233 **Sudan's sperm count:** Beth Ethier. "Last Known Male Northern White Rhino Requires 24-Hour Protection." *Slate.* April 16, 2014. http://www.slate.com/blogs/the _slatest/2015/04/16/northern_white_rhino_last_known_male_sudan_protected _by_guards_as_efforts.html?wpsrc=sh_all_dt_tw_top.

233 **Two other subspecies:** Victoria Brown. "Saving the Sumatran Rhino—Too Little Too Late?" *The Star Online.* (Malaysia) May 1, 2015. http://www.thestar.com.my /Opinion/Online-Exclusive/Behind-The-Cage/Profile/Articles/2015/05/01/saving -the-sumatran-rhino/. See also Jeremy Hance. "Sumatran Rhino Is Extinct in the Wild in Malaysia," *The Epoch Times.* April 27, 2015 http://www.theepochtimes .com/n3/1335352-sumatran-rhino-is-extinct-in-the-wild-in-malaysia/. See also: Kevin Sieff. "A Species on the Brink," *The Washington Post.* June 16, 2015. http:// www.washingtonpost.com/sf/world/2015/06/16/how-the-fate-of-an-entire -subspecies-of-rhino-was-left-to-one-elderly-male/.

234 **In a joint paper:** Joint Statement by the International Rhino Foundation and Save the Rhino International. "Synthetic Rhino Horn: Will It Save the Rhino?" https://www.savetherhino.org/rhino_info/thorny_issues/synthetic_rhino_horn _will_it_save_the_rhino.

234 **The real tragedy here:** Jason Goldman. "Can Trophy Hunting Actually Help Conservation?" *Conservation Magazine,* January 15, 2014. http://conservationmagazine .org/2014/01/can-trophy-hunting-reconciled-conservation/.

235 **Conversely, it sounded like a good idea:** Taylor Hill. "Airline Takes On Big Game Hunters to Protect Rhinos, Lions, and Elephants." *Take Part,* April 30, 2015. http:// www.takepart.com/article/2015/04/30/south-africa-airline-bans-hunting -trophies.

236 **When Blue Bell Creamery:** Jesse Newman. "Ice Cream Recall Sends Chill Through Food Industry." *Wall Street Journal,* August 2, 2015. http://www.wsj.com/articles/ice -cream-recall-sends-chill-through-food-industry-1438437781.

239 **By adjusting the angle:** Adam Davidson. "High on the Hog." *The New York Times Magazine,* February 2, 2014.

241 **Dumped into Lake Michigan:** Kevin Borgia. "What If the Great Chicago Fire of

1871 Never Happened?" *WBEZ Curious City*. October 8, 2014. http://interactive
.wbez.org/curiouscity/chicagofire/.

242 **Their pleas were all for naught:** "People & Events: The Great Fire of 1871." Collateral to the movie *Chicago: City of the Century*. http://www.pbs.org/wgbh/amex
/chicago/peopleevents/e_fire.html.

245 **It is amusing to realize:** Theodore Roosevelt. "Wild Man and Wild Beast in Africa." *National Geographic*, January 1911.

BIBLIOGRAPHY

Deron Acemoglu and James Robinson. *Why Nations Fail: The Origins of Power, Prosperity, and Poverty.* New York: Crown Business, 2012.

Liaquat Ahamed. *Lords of Finance: The Bankers Who Broke the World.* New York: Penguin Press, 2009.

Daniel Alpert. *The Age of Oversupply: Overcoming the Greatest Challenge to the Global Economy.* New York: Portfolio/Penguin, 2013.

Peter Annin. *The Great Lakes Water Wars.* Washington, DC: Island Press, 2006.

Lawrence Anthony with Graham Spence. *The Last Rhinos: My Battle to Save One of the World's Greatest Creatures.* New York: St Martin's Griffin, 2012.

Daniel Ariely. *Predictably Irrational: The Hidden Forces That Shape Our Decisions* (revised and expanded edition). New York: Harper Perennial 2010 (2008).

Peter Atwater. *Moods and Markets: A New Way to Invest in Good Times and in Bad.* Upper Saddle River, NJ: FT Press, 2013.

Max H. Bazerman. *The Power of Noticing: What the Best Leaders See.* New York: Simon & Schuster, 2014.

Max H. Bazerman and Michael D. Watkins. *Predictable Surprises: The Disasters You Should Have Seen Coming and How to Prevent Them.* Boston: Harvard Business School Press, 2004.

Peter Bernstein. *Against the Gods: The Remarkable Story of Risk.* Hoboken: John Wiley & Sons, 1998 (1996).

Thor Bjorgolfsson with Andrew Cave. *Billions to Bust—and Back.* London: Profile Books, 2014.

Paul Blustein. *And the Money Kept Rolling In (and Out): The World Bank, Wall Street, the IMF, and the Bankrupting of Argentina.* New York: PublicAffairs, 2005.

Ori Brafman and Rom Brafman. *Sway: The Irresistible Pull of Irrational Behavior.* New York: Crown Business, 2008.

Rachel Carson. *Silent Spring.* 1962. Reprint edition New York: Houghton Mifflin, 2002.

Christopher Chabris and Daniel Simons. *The Invisible Gorilla: How Our Intuitions Deceive Us.* New York: Broadway Paperbacks, 2009.

Philip Coogan. *Paper Promises: Debt, Money, and the New World Order.* New York: PublicAffairs, 2012.

Stephen R. Covey. *7 Habits of Highly Effective People: Powerful Lessons in Personal Change.* New York: Free Press, 2004 (1989).

Jared Diamond. *Collapse: How Societies Choose to Succeed or Fail.* New York: Viking, 2005.

Charles Duhigg. *The Power of Habit: Why We Do What We Do in Life and Business.* New York: Random House, 2012.

Peter Firestein. *Crisis of Character: Building Corporate Reputation in the Age of Skepticism.* New York: Sterling Publishing, 2009.

Justin Fox. *The Myth of the Rational Market: A History of Risk, Reward, and Delusion on Wall Street.* New York: HarperBusiness, 2011 (HarperCollins 2009).

Francis Fukuyama. *Blindside: How to Anticipate Forcing Events and Wild Cards in Global Politics.* Washington, DC: Brookings Institution Press, 2007.

Atul Gawande. *The Checklist Manifesto: How to Get Things Right.* New York: Picador, 2009.

Bill George. *7 Lessons for Leading in Crisis.* San Francisco: Jossey-Bass, 2009.

Martin Gilman. *No Precedent, No Plan: Inside Russia's 1998 Default.* Cambridge, MA: MIT Press, 2010.

Malcolm Gladwell. *Blink: The Power of Thinking Without Thinking.* New York: Little, Brown, 2007.

Al Gore. *An Inconvenient Truth: The Planetary Emergency of Global Warming and What We Can Do About It.* New York: Rodale, 2006.

Paul Hawken. *The Ecology of Commerce: A Declaration of Sustainability.* 1993. Revised edition. New York: HarperBusiness, 2010.

Chip Heath and Dan Heath. *Switch: How to Change Things When Change is Hard.* New York: Crown Business, 2010.

Ronald Heifetz and Marty Linsky. *Leadership on the Line: Staying Alive Through the Dangers of Leading.* Cambridge, MA: Harvard Business Press, 2009.

Herodotus. *The Histories.* Translated by Robin Waterfield, with an introduction by Carolyn DeWald. New York: Oxford University Press, 1998.

Noreena Hertz. *Eyes Wide Open: How to Make Smart Choices in a Confusing World.* New York: HarperBusiness, 2013.

Matthew L. Higgins, ed. *Advances in Economic Forecasting.* Kalamazoo: W.E. Upjohn Institute for Employment Research, 2011.

Eugene Ionesco. *Rhinoceros and Other Plays.* Translated by Derek Prouse. New York: Grove Press (John Calder Ltd., 1960).

Richard Jackson and Neil Howe. *The Graying of the Great Powers: Demography and Geopolitics in the 21st Century.* Washington, DC: CSIS, 2008.

Daniel Kahneman. *Thinking, Fast and Slow.* New York: Farrar, Straus & Giroux, 2011.

Robert Kegan and Lisa Lahey. *Immunity to Change: How to Overcome It and Unlock the Potential in Yourself and Your Organization.* Cambridge, MA: Harvard Business Review Press, 2009.

Erwann Michel-Kerjann and Paul Slovic, eds. *The Irrational Economist: Making Decisions in a Dangerous World*. New York: PublicAffairs, 2011.

William Kern, ed. *The Economics of Natural and Unnatural Disasters*. Kalamazoo: W.E. Upjohn Institute for Employment Research, 2010.

Charles Kindleberger. *Manias, Panics and Crashes: A History of Financial Crises*. Hoboken: John H. Wiley & Sons, 1996 (1978).

Gary Klein. *Seeing What Others Don't: The Remarkable Ways We Gain Insights*. New York: PublicAffairs, 2013.

Naomi Klein. *The Shock Doctrine: The Rise of Disaster Capitalism*. New York: Henry Holt, 2007.

Alice Korngold. *A Better World, Inc.: How Companies Profit by Solving Global Problems . . . Where Governments Cannot*. New York: Palgrave Macmillan, 2014.

Steven Philip Kramer. *The Other Population Crisis: What Governments Can Do About Falling Birth Rates*. Washington, DC: Woodrow Wilson Center Press, 2014.

Elisabeth Kübler-Ross. *On Death and Dying: What the Dying Have to Teach Doctors, Nurses, Clergy and Their Own Families*. 1969. Reprint, New York: Scribner, 1997.

Howard Kunreuther and Michael Useem. *Learning from Catastrophes: Strategies for Reaction and Response*. Pearson Prentice Hall, 2009.

Scott B. MacDonald and Andrew R. Novo. *When Small Countries Crash*. New Brunswick: Transaction Publishers, 2011.

Harry Markopoulos. *No One Would Listen: A True Financial Thriller*. Hoboken: Wiley, 2010

John Mauldin and Jonathan Tepper. *Code Red: How to Protect Your Savings from the Coming Crisis*. Hoboken: John Wiley & Sons, 2014.

William McDonough and Michael Braungart. *Cradle to Cradle: Remaking the Way We Make Things*. New York: North Point Press, 2002.

Ian Mitroff with Gus Anagnos. *Managing Crises Before They Happen: What Every Executive Needs to Know About Crisis Management*. New York: American Management Association, 2002.

Charles R. Morris. *The Trillion Dollar Meltdown: Easy Money, High Rollers, and the Great Credit Crash*. New York: PublicAffairs, 2008.

Richard Nisbett. *The Geography of Thought: How Asians and Westerners Think Differently . . . and Why*. New York: Free Press, 2004.

Yalman Onaran. *Zombie Banks: How Broken Banks and Debtor Nations Are Crippling the Global Economy*. Bloomberg Press, 2011.

Ronald Orenstein. *Ivory, Horn and Blood: Behind the Elephant and Rhino Poaching Crisis*. Buffalo: Firefly, 2013.

Naomi Oreskes and Michael Conway. *Merchants of Doubt: How a Handful of Scientists Obscured the Truth on Issues from Tobacco Smoke to Global Warming*. New York: Bloomsbury Press, 2010.

Michael Pettis. *The Volatility Machine: Emerging Economies and the Threat of Financial Collapse*. New York: Oxford University Press, 2001.

Eyal Press. *Beautiful Souls: Saying No, Breaking Ranks, and Heeding the Voice of Conscience in Dark Times*. New York: Farrar, Straus & Giroux, 2012.

Steven Rattner. *Overhaul: An Insider's Account of the Obama Administration's*

Emergency Rescue of the Auto Industry. New York: Houghton Mifflin Harcourt, 2010.

Carmen M. Reinhart and Kenneth S. Rogoff. *This Time Is Different: Eight Centuries of Financial Folly.* Princeton: Princeton University Press, 2009.

Judith Rodin. *The Resilience Dividend: Being Strong in a World Where Things Go Wrong.* New York: PublicAffairs, 2014.

Theodore Roosevelt. *African Game Trails. An Account of the African Wanderings of an American Hunter-Naturalist.* New York: C. Scribner's Sons, 1910.

David Ropeik. *How Risky Is It, Really? Why Our Fears Don't Always Match the Facts.* New York: McGraw-Hill, 2010.

Robert M. Sapolsky. *Why Zebras Don't Get Ulcers: The Acclaimed Guide to Stress, Stress-Related Diseases, and Coping,* 3rd ed. New York: St. Martin's Press, 2004 (W. H. Freeman, 1994).

Ira Shapiro. *The Last Great Senate: Courage and Statesmanship in Times of Crisis.* New York: PublicAffairs, 2012.

Tali Sharot, *The Optimism Bias: A Tour of the Irrationally Positive Brain.* New York: Vintage, 2011.

Robert J. Shiller. *Finance and the Good Society.* Princeton: Princeton University Press, 2012.

Denise Shull. *Market Mind Games: A Radical Psychology of Investing, Trading, and Risk.* New York: McGraw Hill, 2012.

Nate Silver. *The Signal and the Noise: Why So Many Predictions Fail—But Some Don't.* New York: Penguin Press, 2012.

Paul Simon. *Tapped Out: The Coming World Crisis in Water and What We Can Do About It.* New York: Welcome Rain Publishers, 1996.

Andrew Ross Sorkin. *Too Big to Fail: The Inside Story of How Wall Street and Washington Fought to Save the Financial System—and Themselves.* New York: Penguin Books, 2011 (2009).

Graham Spence. *The Last Rhinos: My Battle to Save One of the World's Greatest Creatures.* New York: St Martin's Griffin, 2012.

Keith Stanovich. *Rationality and the Reflective Mind.* New York: Oxford University Press, December 2010.

Lawrence Stone. *The Crisis of the Aristocracy, 1558-1641.* Oxford University Press; 20th ed. (December 31, 1967).

Cass Sunstein and Reid Hastie. *Wiser: Getting Beyond Groupthink to Make Groups Smarter.* Cambridge: Harvard Business Review, 2014.

James Surowiecki. *The Wisdom of Crowds: Why the Many Are Smarter Than the Few and How Collective Wisdom Shapes Business, Economies, Societies, and Nations.* New York: Doubleday, 2004.

Nassim Nicholas Taleb. *The Black Swan: The Impact of the Highly Improbable.* New York: Random House, 2010 (2007).

Nassim Nicholas Taleb. *Antifragile: Things That Gain from Disorder.* New York: Random House, 2014 (2012).

Carol Tavris and Elliott Aronson. *Mistakes Were Made (but not by me): Why We Justify Foolish Beliefs, Bad Decisions, and Hurtful Acts.* New York: Harvest, 2007.

Gillian Tett. *Fool's Gold: The Inside Story of JP Morgan and How Wall Street Greed*

Corrupted Its Bold Dream and Created a Financial Catastrophe. New York: Free Press, 2009.

Richard Thaler and Cass Sunstein. *Nudge: Improving Decisions About Health, Wealth and Happiness.* New York: Penguin, 2008.

Donald N. Thompson. *Oracles: How Prediction Markets Turn Employees Into Visionaries.* Cambridge, MA: Harvard Business Review Press, 2012.

Alexis de Tocqueville. *The Old Regime and the Revolution.* Translated by John Bonner. New York: Harper & Brothers, 1856.

John A. Turner. *Longevity Policy: Facing up to Longevity Issues Affecting Social Security, Pensions, and Older Workers.* Kalamazoo: W. E. Upjohn Institute for Employment Research, 2011.

Ezra F. Vogel. *Deng Xiaoping and the Transformation of China.* Cambridge, MA: The Belknap Press of Harvard University Press, 2011.

Clive and Anton Walker. *The Rhino Keepers: Struggle for Survival.* Johannesburg: Jacana, 2012.

Karl Weber, ed. *Last Call at the Oasis: The Global Water Crisis and Where We Go from Here.* New York: PublicAffairs. 2012.

Edie Weiner and Arnold Brown. *FutureThink: How to Think Clearly in a Time of Change.* New York: Pearson Prentice Hall, 2006.

Eyal Weizman. *The Least of All Possible Evils: Humanitarian Violence from Arendt to Gaza.* Brooklyn: Verso, 2011.

Weiying Zhang. *The Logic of the Market: An Insider's View of Chinese Economic Reform.* Washington, DC: Cato Institute, 2014.

RHINO RESOURCES

For readers who wish to learn more about the ongoing fight to save the rhinoceros, I highly recommend the following websites:

The International Rhino Foundation
www.rhinos.org

Rhino Resource Center
www.rhinoresourcecenter.com/

Save the Rhino International
www.savetherhino.org

WWF
www.worldwildlife.org/species/rhino

INDEX